DON ASLETT'S PET SPOT REMOVAL

PET SPOT REMOVAL KIT

Keep the following handy in a plastic cleaning caddy for pet "accident" patrol:

- ☑ **Plastic scraper**
- ☑ **Small squeegee and dustpan**
- ☑ **Small plastic bags**
- ☑ **Spray bottle of bacteria/enzyme digester**
- ☑ **Bubble-up cleaner**
- ☑ **Chemical deodorizer/cleaner**
- ☑ **Odor neutralizer such as X-O**
- ☑ **Terry cleaning cloths and a roll of paper towels**

GENERAL RULES FOR PET STAIN PATROL

Do it NOW! Clean it up as soon as you see it, while it's fresh; chances of preventing stain and damage are far better.

Remove all you can. Blot up all the liquid and scrape up all the solids. (On carpet, put some cleaning cloths over the spot and step on them.) Be careful not to spread the stain.

Test first! Test any chemical in a hidden area of carpet or upholstery to make sure it won't damage or discolor the surface.

Never use ammonia to clean pet stains out of carpeting or upholstery—it smells like urine, and will trigger more peeing in the wrong place.

Blot and brush! When you're done with your stain removal steps on carpet or upholstery, put a thick pad of clean cotton toweling over the spot, weigh it down with something heavy like several books, and leave it there for a while to "wick up" any remaining moisture. Brush or fluff up carpet or fabric pile after blotting.

Don't expect miracles on old stains.

WHAT TO DO

FRESH URINE

On hard surfaces, blot up fresh urine with paper towels, and then spray and wipe the area with all-purpose or deodorizer cleaner. On carpet, gently blot up all you can with paper towels, being careful not to spread the urine. Next, put a clean terrycloth towel on the spot and apply pressure with your heel to absorb all the remaining liquid. Turn the towel over and press several times until you're not getting any more urine out; switch to a fresh towel if you need to and keep going. After blotting, apply a bacteria/enzyme digester according to label directions. To reach urine that has seeped down into the carpet fibers and backing, let the solution saturate down as far as the urine went. Be sure to leave the solution in the carpet for as long as the label says. In dry climates, you may have to cover the spot with a piece of plastic wrap or a damp towel to keep it from drying out too soon. If there's still a visible spot on the carpet after it dries, follow up with a water rinse or a carpet stain remover. Repeat the enzyme treatment if the odor isn't all gone.

OLD URINE STAINS

Bacteria/enzyme digester is the best for old urine stains on carpet or upholstery; follow directions. It may be necessary to treat the area(s) more than once. Secret: Pour some clean water on old stains and then blot it back up before applying enzyme digester to reduce the amount of urine matter the enzymes have to deal with. Do this more than once if the spot is really urine-saturated. "Bubble-up" cleaners used according to directions can also be effective on old urine stains. Oxygen cleaners are good when the stain from old urine is more prominent than the odor. Test first before using oxygen cleaners on nylon carpeting.

PET POOP

Fresh pet feces on hard surfaces can be removed with a squeegee and dustpan, or your hand slipped into a small plastic bag. Wash the spot with all-purpose cleaner or chemical deodorizer/cleaner. On carpet or upholstery, use bacteria/enzyme cleaner or a bubble-up cleaner according to directions after removing all you can of the deposit. Old, dry feces on hard or soft surfaces should be scraped off with a plastic scraper before applying any cleaning solution.

VOMIT

Act quickly because the acids and dye (from pet foods) can cause permanent damage. Scrape and blot up all you can, and then flush the spot with water. In carpet or upholstery, this means sponge water on liberally and then blot it back out. Then apply bacteria/enzyme digester according to instructions.

Pet Clean-Up Made Easy
2nd Edition

Tackle Any Pet Mess, Any Time,
in a Snap—from Stains and Smells
to Fleas and Furballs

Don Aslett
America's #1 Cleaning Expert

Adams Media
Avon, Massachusetts

OTHER DON ASLETT BOOKS

Clutter's Last Stand, 2nd Edition

Do I Dust or Vacuum First?, 2nd Edition

The Office Clutter Cure, 2nd Edition

Is There Life After Housework?, 2nd Edition

DONE! How to Accomplish Twice as Much in Half the Time!

Published by
Adams Media, an F+W Publications Company
57 Littlefield Street, Avon, MA 02322. U.S.A.

ISBN: 0-7394-5685-7

This publication is designed to provide accurate and authoritative information with regard to the subject matter covered. It is sold with the understanding that the publisher is not engaged in rendering legal, accounting, or other professional advice. If legal advice or other expert assistance is required, the services of a competent professional person should be sought.

—From a *Declaration of Principles* jointly adopted by a
Committee of the American Bar Association and a
Committee of Publishers and Associations

Many of the designations used by manufacturers and sellers to distinguish their products are claimed as trademarks. Where those designations appear in this book and Adams Media was aware of a trademark claim, the designations have been printed with initial capital letters.

Interior cartoon illustrations by jimhunt.us
Interior technical illustrations by Michelle Dorenkamp
Interior layout by Electronic Publishing Service, Inc. (TN)

Printed in the U.S.A.

Acknowledgments

This book would not have been possible without the help of a number of top professionals in a variety of fields. These people demonstrated over and over that expert knowledge and deep concern for the safety and welfare of animals will overcome even self-interest, commercial rivalry, and the chronic lack of time in the modern world.

Mickey Niego, Companion Animal Services counselor of the New York City ASPCA and professional dog trainer, brought us ingenious and down-to-earth answers to a great many of our pet paradoxes.

Gwen Bohnenkamp, of the Animal Behavior Department of the San Francisco SPCA, and **Ian Dunbar** of the Center for Applied Animal Behavior, provided unusually readable and helpful pamphlets on a variety of pet problems.

Shirlee Kalstone, professional groomer and author, added important inside knowledge to the sections on bathing and grooming.

Nicki Meyer, "America's pet crate expert."

Dr. Jan Bicks, animal nutritionist and author.

Boris Tatistcheff of Gem State Pest Control.

Mark Browning, who helped us compile the technical information herein.

Robert Betty, the artist who brought all our pet dilemmas to life in the first edition.

Laura Simons, Nancy Everson, and **Larry Andrews**

Fancy Publications (*Cat Fancy, Dog Fancy,* and *Bird Talk,* especially **Kathy Thornton**) provided a wealth of very-much-to-the-point wisdom.

Cats magazine

Dr. Larry C. Mitchell of the Utah Veterinary Medical Association Lay Education Committee

Dr. Peggy Harrer of Community Animal Hospital, Pocatello, and **Dr. Christine Teets** of Animal Medical Center, Idaho Falls

Dr. Marjorie L. Smith and **Dr. Edna Guibor** of Smith-Sager Publications

The Humane Society of the United States (especially **Barbara Cassidy**)

The Bide-A-Wee Home Association (especially **Debbie Feliziani**)

Save Our Strays (especially **Bea Sellers**)

The Closter Animal Welfare Society of Closter, New Jersey (especially **Joan Keating**)

The American Kennel Club (especially **John Mandeville** and the American Kennel Club *Gazette*)

The Purdue University Veterinary Medical Library (especially **Gretchen Stephens**)

Cornell University College of Agriculture and Life Science

The University of Idaho Cooperative Extension Service

The American Veterinary Medical Association

The California Veterinary Medical Association

Animal Care & Welfare, Inc. (SPCA) of Pittsburgh, Pennsylvania

The Pet Information Bureau

The Pet Industry Joint Advisory Council

The Pets Are Wonderful Council

Associated Humane Societies, Inc.

Friends of Animals, Inc.

The American Humane Association

The Association of Specialists in Cleaning and Restoration

Consolidated Chemical Company (especially **Marvin Klein** and **Warren Weisberg**)

The Bramton Company (especially **Al Irons**)

Franklin Labs (especially **Lowell Grauberger** and **Dr. John Schnackel**)

Nilodor, Inc. (especially **Les Mitson** and **Hal Kehoe**)

Gaines Professional Services

The Alpo Pet Center

The Carnation Company

The Ralston Purina Company

Procter & Gamble

The Ryter Corporation (especially **Barb Nelson**)

Farnam Pet Products

The excellent books on pet care and training by **Matthew Margolis and Mordecai Siegal, Roger Caras, Dr. Michael Fox, Sara Stein**, and **Robert Allen** and **William Westbrook**, among many others

Contents

x   Introduction

1   **Chapter 1**
Pet Cleaning 101: Important Tools and Cleaning
Techniques for All Kinds of Pet Clean-Up
Chores

28   **Chapter 2**
Good, Clean Living–with Pets: Preventative
Measures to Keep Your Home Mess-Free
and Ease Your Allergies

64   **Chapter 3**
Housetraining and Litter Boxes: The #1
Solutions to the #1 Pet Cleaning Problem

106   **Chapter 4**
In Case of Accident: Pointers for Cleaning
Up Pet Messes

121   **Chapter 5**
Hairy Animal Tales: Shedding, Bathing, and
Flea Control

163   **Chapter 6**
       Pets Do the Darndest Things: Solutions to
       Jumping, Chewing, Scratching, Scavenging,
       Tracking in Messes, and Traveling

215   **Chapter 7**
       Beyond Barks and Meows: Caring and
       Cleaning for the Small Pet Set

236   **Epilogue**
       Are Pets Worth Cleaning Up After?

239   A Word of Thanks

241   Index

NOTE: For the sake of simplicity and ease of reading, when the sex of the animal is not relevant to the issue being discussed, pets are referred to in these pages with the pronouns "he" and "him."

Introduction

On the farm in Idaho where I grew up, we had a lot of animals, all of the outside variety. This is how I came to love and appreciate animals, and it wasn't until I left the farm and became a professional cleaner—and married and had six children—that I discovered the very different world of animals kept as pets in homes. I suddenly realized that urban and suburban animal owners were faced with problems we simply didn't have in a rural setting. People and their pets live so closely together in today's smaller homes, apartments, and condos that some of the most puzzling and discouraging housework jobs have to do with pets. And in fifty years of professional cleaning, I've seen firsthand how many people are frustrated because they love their animals but don't know how to deal with the cleaning problems they bring.

In the houses, apartments, offices, and public buildings I cleaned, and in the radio and TV appearances I made, people kept asking hard and pressing questions about pet food mess, litter, shedding, spraying, pet stains, and, of course, *odor*. In letters, calls, and in person, the pleas were the same: How do we make pet clean-up easier and more effective? Pet cleaning was clearly a neglected area.

When I set about finding the answers to all the tough questions pet owners asked, I found that the knowledge was scattered and contradictory or simply outdated old wives' tales. So I sought out and combined the knowledge of professional cleaners and scientists, pet doctors, pet products manufacturers, individual pet owners, pet organizations, and publications (books and magazines, popular and technical)—and put it all together in a way that pet owners young and old could understand and use.

For this new second edition, I did all of the above and more, sifting through the universe of new pet products and aids for the most truly useful, incorporating new training methods that are more pet-friendly than ever, seeking new and better answers to stubborn pet clean-up problems, and drawing on the experience and advice of diverse experts in the field to enhance my own expertise.

You will find, at last, some real help in these pages—how to clean up the mess better and faster, and also how to *prevent* it from ever happening in the first place.

There is no pet that doesn't make some kind of ripple or dent in "House Beautiful"—there's just no such animal. Anywhere there's life, action, and enjoyment, there's going to be some mess, and that's certainly true of pets. But pets also add a certain adventure to life, a feeling of anticipation, of "what's going to happen next?" You can always count on them to make houselife more exciting than the weekly dusting of the piano.

There's no question about it, animals kept inside will mean some extra work and will call for some extra precautions. But if you go about it right—as I explain in this book—it won't be a major or endless undertaking. And it's well worth it, because in the blacktop and concrete world of today, we *need* pets around us more than ever before.

Owning pets doesn't have to be a hassle or force us to abandon our standards of cleanliness and order. We can live happily and harmoniously with our pets if we just apply a little imagination, a little common sense, and a little expert knowledge about proper procedures and equipment. That's the reason for this book—and what you'll find here.

Don Aslett
America's #1 Cleaning Expert

Chapter 1

Pet Cleaning 101: Important Tools and Cleaning Techniques for All Kinds of Pet Clean-Up Chores

No Pets or Children Allowed . . .

Signs like this bother me, because they make public the assumption that a dirty, damaged home is synonymous with pet or child occupancy. We don't need to demand the banishment of furry friends or little humans simply because they require some extra cleaning measures and precautions. They may call for a few minor adjustments in our surroundings and lifestyle, but nothing worth having in life is entirely free and easy. But you can make it as easy as possible, and this updated, second edition of *Pet Clean-Up Made Easy* will guide you through the *what, when, how,* and *why* of pet cleaning.

The three most important ingredients of success in real estate, in order, are: location, location, location. And believe it or not, it's about the same for the happy and healthy ownership of pets: *a place, a place, a place.*

A Place in Our Lives, Homes, and Budgets

This means time, to play with our pets and to exercise them; to train them; to love, groom, and clean up after them. Pets aren't an afterthought that can fit in anywhere—we have to give them the space and liberty to live and move.

Pet owners in this country spend more than $30 billion each year on their pets—for food, vet bills, vaccinations, licenses, accessories. It doesn't have to cost a lot of money to own a pet, but some things are a lot more important than others—such as the right kind of pet food and shelter, and the right kind of cleaning supplies.

When we take pet ownership upon ourselves, we accept the responsibility of keeping our animals safe and clean and well cared for, of providing them with the conditions conducive to a happy and healthy life. And if we give them the facilities they need, and the proper training and encouragement, most pets will do a lot to help keep *themselves* clean and neat.

if You Leave, You Grieve

Timing and tools are the main differences between "pet cleaning" and plain old housecleaning.

You can't let pet mess go until it's convenient, because if you leave it, the mess will spread, stain, smell, attract pests, and encourage repeat offenses.

Spills and "accidents" rarely stain if cleaned up while the mess is still fresh and moist or new. But give them a chance to lie there, and you'll often have permanent damage to fabrics and finishes and furnishings.

Also, odors penetrate deeper and grow more offensive the longer they're left to sit. Germs multiply and many disease spores and parasite eggs reach the infective stage after the mess has been left a while. Clean it up sooner and it's a lot safer.

Four Simple Steps to Most Pet Cleaning

Food slops and spills, sticky pawprints, many a smear or streak might appear stubborn and here to stay. **But softening the mark or material is basically all you need to do to bring it back to its original, entirely removable, liquid state.** What the smudge consists of will determine the solution you need to work with: Grease, oil, or tar call for solvent or spot remover, but all-purpose cleaning solution is fine for most other things.

These basic principles apply to almost every cleanable, hard-surface item. (The exceptions are soft porous materials like fabric, leather, and unfinished wood—cleaning these is tougher.) Pet stuff with a smooth, hard surface always means faster and easier cleaning.

1. **Remove what you can.** Before you clean or wash anything, remember, just as it makes sense to sweep a floor before you mop it, it takes only a second to remove the bulk of the dirt—scrape it off, brush it off, or knock it off—first. This is one of the most important principles of cleaning, yet we so often fail to follow it. If the material has dried into a thick, hard crust, scrape off what you can with a plastic scraper before wetting the spot. Be careful here. You're only trying to dislodge the bulk of the deposit before you move on to . . .

2. **Spray or dampen the article liberally with the cleaning solution.** All-purpose cleaning solution, or liquid dish detergent and water, will do fine for most general-purpose pet cleaning.

3. **Let it soak.** Give the solution a few minutes to work, depending on how tough a job you're tackling. This will give the "surfactant" in the cleaner time to pull the dirt and grease from the surface and suspend them in the cleaning solution. Pro cleaners call this "emulsifying the enemy"! This approach works 90 percent of the time. Once the smudge is softened, you can just wipe it off. Thoroughly waterproof things such as rubber bones or plastic food dishes can be soaked overnight in cleaning solution. Then those tough deposits will wipe right off with little effort.

4. **Wipe or rinse it off.** No matter how good something looks after you've removed, dampened, and soaked, there's still a residue of soap and dissolved goo on there (as well as chemical traces from your cleaning solution that could harm pets if they come in contact with it). Rinsing well with clean water is best—if for some reason that's just not possible, wipe the surface thoroughly with a piece of clean terry toweling dampened in clean water.

Important Tools and Techniques for the Pet Cleaner

In pet cleaning, even more so than in regular cleaning, the right tools and supplies are important to your ability to do a fast and effective job. When it comes to "chemicals," you want something designed and tested to be safe for and around pets. That's why you should use, whenever possible, the products made specifically for pet clean-up. A better selection of these will usually be found in pet stores and pet supply catalogs and Web sites than in supermarkets or discount stores. The personnel will also be better equipped to answer questions you may have.

Also, use products specifically made for the particular kind of animal you have if they will be used on or near the animal. Never use cat shampoo on dogs, dog flea spray on cats, and so forth. All of these things are specially formulated for a specific animal's skin, coat,

> Make it a point to *read* that fine print on the label.

and chemical tolerances. Certain chemicals kill cats but don't harm dogs, for example. Even the age of the pet involved can make a difference. Manufacturers print detailed instructions and warnings on the label that explain how the product should be used. Make it a point to *read* that fine print on the label.

Professional-quality tools and supplies, though available in pet-supply and janitorial-supply stores and specialty mail order catalogs, aren't easy to come by in every part of the country. So, many of the following items—some of the most widely useful ones for pet purposes—can be ordered from the Cleaning Center: PO Box 700-Pet, Pocatello ID 83204. Or e-mail me through my Web site at *www.aslett.com* and I'll send you a catalog.

Squeegee and Floor Squeegee

The squeegee is the undiscovered pet cleaning tool that cleans all kinds of spills and messes—liquid, solid, or unpleasantly in between—off all kinds of surfaces, swiftly and sanitarily. And a squeegee is the professional way to clean windows—and the outsides of fishtanks—quickly and without leaving streaks. Ettore is a good professional-quality brand; use the 6-inch size for general pet clean-up and the 10-inch size (or larger) for windows.

The squeegee's rubber blade will sweep up wet or mushy messes on carpet, concrete, or couches in seconds, leaving only a light film to be wiped up or otherwise dealt with. You can use a floor squeegee, which has a larger blade and a long handle, after cleaning to swiftly remove the rinse water from the area.

The rubber and metal of a good squeegee are chemically inert, so they're resistant to the acids, alkalis, and protein compounds so often involved in pet cleaning. Pet messes won't penetrate or be absorbed by the blade, nor can they hurt it in any way.

Dustpan

A dustpan has 101 uses, especially in pet clean-up jobs. It's the perfect companion to your all-purpose 6-inch squeegee, for getting up pet messes fast. **You want a dustpan that really fits flush to the floor, is easy to wash and rinse, and won't rust.** An industrial-strength molded rubber or plastic pan has a good deep well and a keen edge.

Use your dustpan and squeegee to clean up:

- Food spills—the rubber blade slicks up both liquid and lumps in a second, and can even whisk up cat chow on hard floors
- Feces—let your dustpan and the squeegee do the dirty work of cleaning droppings off hard floors, rugs, or street surfaces
- Vomit and hairballs—get the bulk of it up and off hard flooring or carpet fast to prevent staining, bleaching, and smell penetration
- A variety of other unpleasant pet problems—broken glass, mud, and even unidentifiable messes brought in by pets

A squeegee and dustpan can be washed and rinsed off in seconds, much easier than cleaning rags or brushes. Just slosh a dirty squeegee in a bucket of soapy water, or sponge or hose it off.

Plastic Scraper

An inexpensive plastic scraper can be a big help with the "remove" stage of pet cleaning. You can remove dried deposits of all kinds with this quickly, without scratching the surface they are stuck to.

Professional-Quality Plastic Broom

If you're using a broom with conventional "corn" bristles, the first stroke will move 85 percent of the dust or debris, the next stroke 10 percent of what remains, and a third stroke will get most of the remaining 5 percent. A split-bristle synthetic broom, on the other hand, will move 100 percent in just two strokes. I'm talking about the professional-quality plastic brooms such as the ones made by Rubbermaid and Vileda with an angled head and "split ends."

Brooms like these get in the corners easier, pick up hair better, last much longer, and won't shed like straw brooms. And they're easier to clean when they get soiled or stained.

If you want to sweep the way the pros do, here's a tip: **Most people sweep too slowly; quick, short, downward strokes are the most efficient.**

Dust Mop

There's nothing better for whisking up dust, stray kibble, hair, feathers, and other light-duty pet fallout from any hard-surface floor. Professional dust mop treatment will keep your dust mop "sticky" enough to grab the dirt and dust and hold on to it. (Shake out or vacuum the mophead after you use it; launder it when it gets dirty.)

Nylon-Backed Scrubbing Sponge

A white nylon pad bonded to a sponge, such as the one made by 3M, for scrubbing off hard-to-remove soil safely. The white nylon won't scratch household surfaces the way the more abrasive green or blue nylon pads often will.

Professional All-Purpose Scrub Brush

For cleaning cages and litter pans, and any place in pet cleaning where real scrubbing is called for. The design of this brush keeps your hands out of cleaning solutions and eliminates skinned knuckles, and the all-nylon bristles, bristle bed, and handle won't crack or be affected by hot water or strong cleaning solutions. It's 100 percent sanitary, rinses fast and dries quickly, and will outlast ordinary brushes.

Pet Rake

This is a hair remover that works! The stiff crimpled nylon bristles of this tool do an amazing job of gathering hair, fur, lint, fuzz, and cobwebs off furniture, bedding, draperies, rugs, car interiors, even clothing. You can use it as is, or mount it on a long handle for better reach. (For other hair removal devices see Chapter 5.)

Professional Upright Vacuum or Canister Vacuum with a "Power Head"

This is one of your best friends when it comes to keeping carpeting and other parts of a pet household clean. Be sure your vacuum has a beater bar or brush or a "power head" (head with a motor-driven revolving brush) that will knock the dirt loose. If it doesn't, then the hair and other light debris will cling, with the help of static electricity, to their original nesting place, regardless of how magnificent your vacuum is, or how strong its suction. *Loosened debris* is the secret of effective vacuuming—you have to get the dirt free of the carpet so it can join the airflow and end up in the bag. The beater bar or brush bounces and vibrates the carpet to free hair, dander, dirt, and fleas; then the brushes sweep all this into the flow of air and up into the vacuum bag.

This is also why you want a vacuum, not a carpet sweeper. Carpet sweepers just whisk off the surface litter. The carpet looks clean because the visible stuff is gone, but there's still dirt and grit down in the fibers that make your carpet wear out faster.

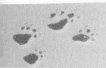 One of the best upright vacuums for home use is the Windsor, a lightweight professional vac with a strong motor and high-efficiency filtration.

If you have a pet allergy sufferer in your home, or an extraordinary amount of pet hair, you might want a specialty vac—see page 128 in Chapter 5.

Wet-Dry Vacuum

The beauty of a wet-dry vacuum is that it can suck in both dry debris and all kinds of liquids at the quick and simple change of a filter. This means that urine, upchuck, or liquid spills can be swooped up, untouched by human hands. For instance, you can use a wet-dry to clean concrete dog runs and other hard waterproof surfaces. It's a much better approach than just "hosing them off," which often leaves concrete surfaces, especially, wet and clammy. Wet the surface with your cleaning solution and scrub with a stiff broom or nylon-bristle brush, then vacuum up the dirty solution. Then rinse and remove every trace of the rinse water with the wet-dry.

You can also use it for disinfecting hard surfaces or carpeting. After cleaning, apply your disinfecting solution (see page 41, Chapter 2), let it sit ten minutes or so, and pick it up with the wet-dry. Then rinse the area and use the wet-dry to pick up the rinse water.

Get a five- or six-gallon model with a rust-resistant metal or plastic tank and a side hose attachment. If a larger diameter hose is available, get it—it will give you much more suction. Be sure to get an upholstery attachment, a small brush head, a squeegee head, a floor tool, and a crevice tool. You can get good five-gallon wet-drys for $100 or less, and a deluxe stainless steel professional model for about $300.

A Hand Vacuum

This vac is great for "wisp cleaning." You can pick up a few stray blades of grass or straw, burrs, feathers, crumbs, or bits of gravel or dropped litter without dragging out a full-size vacuum or dustpan and broom. **In a pet household, you want a mini-vac with a beater on it,** to beat the dirt out of the carpet just like the bigger vacuums do. This will help it to do a good job even on that true test of pet cleaning—hair removal. The stiff bristles on the beater brush stand up the nap and loosen and pull the hair out.

Hand vacs are available in both cordless and corded models; the ones you plug in are less convenient but generally have more suction power.

Professional Mats

Mats are a #1 priority in pet cleaning. Pets aren't likely to wipe their feet, so you have to put something there to do it for them. The right kind of mats outside and inside of your doors is like having a full-time pet janitor-in-waiting. They'll collect and concentrate pet debris for easy cleaning, knock off dirt, and absorb moisture before it gets tracked into the house. A 3' x 5' mat both inside and outside each door assures enough steps on the matting to do a good job of pulling off grit and loose litter. Use mats of nylon or olefin carpeting on vinyl or rubber backing inside your house; for outside, AstroTurf mats are best.

Matting is also a great thing to install in other high pet use areas. Its soft nap provides a tempting place for a pet to lie down, and the matting will pull burrs, loose hairs, and dirt off the pet, onto a surface that is easily cleaned. Nylon or olefin mats with rubber or vinyl backing are soft, warm, and absorbent, and they're also easily cleaned and disinfected. Mats are also portable and can be moved anywhere you need them—it's much easier to clean something that's movable, like a mat, than something that's permanently fixed. And mats are inexpensive enough to have extras and rotate their use. Use mats:

- As a cleaning-off station after your dog comes in from outside (see page 173, Chapter 6)
- On or around clipping or grooming platforms
- Around the litter box (see page 82, Chapter 3)
- Under the food and water dishes
- Inside and outside a pet door (the nylon or olefin type inside, artificial turf type outside), to scrape off most of the trackable stuff
- In front of animal dwellings outdoors (artificial turf type) to keep the inside of the doghouse cleaner
- Inside the doghouse or other animal quarters (a nylon or olefin mat) to provide a soft, warm surface that won't let moisture seep up from below
- As a travel aid (a 2' x 3' nylon or olefin type with rubber backing so it won't leak or rot) in the back of a vehicle or on the floor of a motel room

The Disinfectant That's Safest to Use Around Pets

Chlorhexidine is both the most effective of the commonly available disinfectants *and* the gentlest and least toxic—the most user-friendly for people and pets. It's easy on household surfaces, pet equipment, and living quarters, as well as on human and animal skin. It is sold under several trade names, including Nolvasan, Chlorasan, and Chlorhex. These products are available from veterinarians, feed dealers, livestock suppliers, and the like. Or you can call the manufacturer of Nolvasan (Fort Dodge Animal Health) to find a dealer near you, or even buy it direct. Call 1-800-685-5656. Use Nolvasan to disinfect walls, floors, pet accessories, grooming tools, pet dishes, bedding—you name it. It can even be added to the laundry. (More on disinfectants on page 38, Chapter 2.)

Pet Stain and Odor Removers

The main reason pet stains and odors are so hard to deal with is that these particular messes (urine, feces, vomit, etc.) are largely composed of organic materials that not only have strong odors either initially or as they begin to decay, but also provide excellent fuel for subsequent bacteria and fungal growth, creating a second source of odor and stain.

You may not find all of the products that will do the tough job of removing pet stains and odors on the shelf in the discount store or supermarket. I probably don't need to tell you that pet stains and odors are one of the biggest challenges in home cleaning, and they call for some professional products formulated for this very purpose.

Odor Removers

These are not cleaners; they just remove odor, and the best odor removers do an excellent job of that.

Odor neutralizers chemically convert odor molecules into a new substance that doesn't smell bad. Many odor neutralizers are made from plant extracts, and may include masking fragrances that help out while the neutralizer is doing its job. **Odor neutralizers are usually water soluble and can be sprayed, sponged, or mopped on.** They can be used full strength or added to carpet shampoo, laundry loads, etc. Some odor neutralizers are strongly scented, such as Nilodor's Nilium. Some are less scented, like my favorite, X-O.

A newer form of odor remover is the **odor encapsulator**, such as Petrotech Odor Eliminator by SeaYu Enterprises.

Products like these work by encapsulating the offending molecules and speeding up the natural process of biodegradation.

Chemical Deodorizer/Cleaners

For cleaning pet accidents off nonporous hard surfaces, a chemical deodorizer is the best choice. (Many of these products have a cleaning agent built right into them, so they don't require an additional cleaning step.) You simply spray it on after you clean up the mess and it does the job. For semiporous hard surfaces like flat wall paint, chemical deodorizers are still the best to use, although some products can't be used on plastic, paint, rayon, silk, or noncolorfast fabrics. **It's always best to test any cleaning product you're unfamiliar with on an inconspicuous spot before using it,** to make sure it won't damage or discolor the surface, and always be sure to follow the precautions on the label.

One of my favorite chemical deodorizer/cleaners is X-O Plus, an odor neutralizer plus cleaner. Another good one is Nilosol from the Nilodor Company. (These products are widely available in pet stores and janitorial supply stores.) Nilosol (or its companion product Nilotex, for situations where stain removal is more of an issue than just odor) is safe to use on all colorfast fabrics that won't be damaged by water, and it's gentle enough for upholstery cleaning. Fresh 'N' Clean works well, too, but it leaves behind a perfumey fragrance that you may not care for. Products like these are great for cleaning up accidents on hard floors as well as for deodorizing hard surfaces in pet living areas.

Another set of products I've had success with are those from Robinson Labs: Dog Accident Deodorizer and Pet Stain Remover. You use the deodorizer first to neutralize the odor, and then the stain remover to eliminate any remaining stains.

Odor and Damage—Where is it?
(More Tools and Techniques!)

It isn't always in a single puddle, that's for sure. Often when you find where Fido did it, you don't realize the carpet or corner isn't the whole story. To expand your "where to find it" vocabulary, consider this:

1. Drapes and other fabric surfaces are porous and absorb odors.

2. Heat or air ducts and vents can be part of the problem. The filters of some heating systems can harbor odor, too, because they move malodorous air through the house.

3. The Sheetrock of the walls can absorb and hold accident odor and then release it later.

4. Pet mess moisture can even reach the very structure of the house—such as the wall studs—and stay.

5. The subfloor—generally plywood or pressboard—can allow urine to seep down into it.

6. The carpet tack strip is raw wood and sucks in anything moist.

7. The carpet pad is usually made of materials like urethane or foam rubber that grab and hold odor. Moisture or humidity will activate it forevermore.

8. Even the unfinished back of the baseboard can pick up and hold odor.

9. The carpet gets the bulk of the odor-producing organic substances from pet accidents—in the backing and the nap.

You can see why a drop or two of magic deodorizer won't instantly eliminate a pet odor problem.

As a rule of thumb, the chemical deodorizer/cleaners work well on hard surfaces and may be all you need for your carpet, if you catch the stains quickly. But if you're dealing with old urine stains, or repeated sieges of vomiting, you need different products.

Bacteria/Enzyme Digesters

These strike at the root of the problem and eliminate the very source of the bad odor. Bacteria/enzyme digesters actually feed on the organic compounds that are responsible for the bad odor of materials like urine, feces, vomit, and mildew. The most effective products contain a culture of friendly live bacteria.

When you put a bacteria/enzyme digester solution on an organic stain, the bacteria immediately start producing enzymes, which break down the organic compounds in the stain into substances the bacteria can use for food, just as the enzymes in our stomach break down the foods we eat into things we can digest. If they're kept moist and within the recommended temperature range (above 40° F), the bacteria will continue to eat the offending organic materials, reproduce, produce more enzymes, and eat some more until the odor-causing material is all gone.

You can get products composed of the enzymes alone, but they work only until the enzymes are used up, and require you to rinse away the remains of what the enzymes digested—how are you going to rinse underneath the carpet (where many pet stains penetrate), for example? The products that contain a live bacteria culture, or a bacteria culture plus some enzyme to get them started, are better.

Bacteria/enzyme solutions are safe to use on any surface that can't be damaged by water, but they must be used by themselves; they can't be combined with detergents, deodorants, or other cleaning preparations. You should never use a disinfectant or any other chemical on the spot before applying the bacteria/enzyme solution, because these things can actually kill the beneficial bacteria that destroy the odor.

Nor is enzyme digestion an instant gratification process—when you treat something with a bacteria/enzyme product, it has to be wetted well with the solution and then left to dry naturally, which can take a day or two or even longer. And if it contains no cleaning agent, you may have to follow up a bacteria/enzyme digester with a pet stain remover or spotting chemical such as Nilotex to remove surface stains or water rings. The product Urine Erase (visit *www.reidell.com*, or call 519-285-2083) uses a combination of freshly activated freeze-dried enzymes and an antibacterial completer solution to complete the chemical reaction and prevent any musty odors afterward.

In spite of their drawbacks, bacteria/enzyme products provide one of the best ways to eliminate entrenched odors in carpets and deal with odor on upholstery and other "soft" surfaces, so they definitely have their place. They also work better than the chemical deodorizers on hard porous materials like concrete, because they penetrate the pores of the surface and eat away the organic materials that cause odor. **Be sure to soak the area well with the solution** and get it down to all the cracks and crevices where organic material may be lodged.

A bacteria/enzyme product I've found especially effective is Simple Solution Stain and Odor Remover, by the Bramton Company of Dallas (*www.simplesolution.com*). It can be used on any water-safe surface or material, including carpet, upholstery, drapes, mattresses, clothing, fabrics, tile, terrazzo, wood, metal, plastic, foam rubber, vinyl, concrete, trash containers, and even grass and shrubbery. Added bonuses: It's nontoxic, pleasant smelling, and all natural.

"Bubble Up" Cleaners

Besides the bacteria/enzyme digesters, which are getting better all the time, there are now also other products specially designed for old and stubborn pet stains. These newer pet clean-up products can be lumped together under "bubble up" products, because they involve a kind of bubbling-up action to help remove stains and odors.

The main active ingredient in **oxygen cleaners** is hydrogen peroxide, and they break down stain and odor by an oxygenation process. Oxygen cleaners are usually mixed up from a powder using warm or hot water and then applied to the stain site. A stronger solution (following label directions) may be used for bad or aged stains. The solution is left on for up to a half hour, then blotted out with a terrycloth towel and left to air dry the rest of the way. **When the "stain" component of a pet stain is worse than the odor, the oxy products are a good choice.** Some good oxy products include Tuff-Oxi for Pets (866-269-1953) and Bramton's Oxy Solution Pet Stain and Odor Destroyer. Read label instructions, and test before using oxygen cleaners wholesale—some oxygen cleaners can bleach nylon carpeting or damage finished wood.

One particularly effective bubble-up cleaner is called Get Serious! Pet Stain, Odor, & Pheromone Extractor. As the name indicates, it is designed to remove the pheromones in pet urine as well as the stain and odor for more complete cleaning, and to help prevent pet potty encores in the same spot. Get Serious! is squirted on, brushed in, blotted out well, and then left to dry. If you encounter a particularly stubborn stain, the manufacturer recommends heating the bottle in the microwave and retreating the site with the warmed solution. **Get Serious!** (*www.getseriouproducts.com* or 800-844-7967), used according to directions, can remove many bad and even aged urine stains even better than bacteria/enzyme cleaners can.

All of the bubble-up cleaners can be used on a wide variety of other household stains as well as pet stains. No matter what treatment you use for old, dried urine, if the odor is not completely gone after the area dries well, you may need to retreat.

Plastic Trigger-Spray Bottle

A plastic spray bottle will come in handy when applying bacteria/enzyme or chemical deodorizer solution, and it's great for misting plants, dampening laundry, and scores of other household uses. This type of spray bottle can also serve as a harmless, effective, and inexpensive pet training tool (see page 24). Professional-strength spray bottles are available in 16-, 22-, and 32-ounce sizes.

Carpet Spot Removal Brush

A stain should never be scrubbed, as this can damage the carpet fibers as well as spread the stain. A spotting brush has short, stiff nylon bristles that enable you to pound on a spot with the brush to "agitate" the fibers without spreading the stain. The end of the handle is tapered to a sharp edge so you can use it to scrape up as much of the spot or spill as you can before applying the spotting or stain-removing chemical.

Professional Cleaning Towels

For all those jobs that require wiping and absorbing—and especially for stain removal—this is far better for the purpose than whatever happens to be resting in the ragbag. Made from sturdy terry toweling hemmed on the edges, you can make your own or buy them from a janitorial-supply store, or by mail from the Cleaning Center: PO Box 700-Pet, Pocatello ID 83204. Or e-mail me through my Web site at *www.aslett.com* and I'll send you a catalog.

Absorbent Compound

Sprinkle these highly absorbent clay granules on pet messes like vomit and loose stools and in no time the mess is solid enough to sweep, scoop, or vacuum up. Some compounds deodorize, too, making the cleaning operation faster and more pleasant. (Big D Granular Deodorant, from Big D Industries, is a good brand.) Plain, ordinary "generic" cat litter makes a good absorbent, too.

Stain Repellent

Not only helps to keep your carpet, furniture, upholstery, and fabric pet accessories cleaner in general, but it also helps keep stains and spills from soaking in and possibly doing permanent damage. For more about stain repellents, see page 62.

Area Deodorizers

Remember first that good ventilation is a real plus for pet odor removal, or any odor removal. Circulating air does a lot to keep an area fresh and free of animal odors, so in a heavy pet concentration area, consider a vent to the outside with a fan that will draw the odor out and bring fresh air in. Or open windows on each side of the room for cross-ventilation.

You especially want to get odor out before it can be absorbed by soft materials. A room with lots of upholstery and carpeting will be smellier than a room with a tile floor and wood furniture, because there are more soft surfaces to absorb odor. This is a good reason to put odor-generating litter boxes and the like in a room with a hard floor and hard surface furnishings.

For rooms with persistent odor problems, an ionic air cleaner (such as the Sharper Image Ionic Breeze Air Purifier: *www.sharperimage.com*) can be a real help.

Spraying perfumed aerosol room deodorizers around will mask odors for a short while, but this has little lasting effect. If you want to spray a pet odor problem away, it is far better to use an odor neutralizer spray such as X-O or Nilodor room deodorizer, or an odor encapsulator spray. A few puffs of X-O, for instance, sprayed into the air of a room a couple of times a day will do wonders. You can also spray X-O on cotton balls and tuck them into the air conditioning and heating vents.

Zeolite products are also good for area deodorizing. Zeolite is a negatively charged natural mineral that attracts the positive ions in airborne odors, and absorbs them into its millions of tiny micropores. **Zeolite products have no odor of their own, are nontoxic, and come in granular and powder form.** For room deodorizing, you sprinkle the granules around, leave them a day or so, and then vacuum them up. Since there is no water or solution involved, you can use them on floors such as wood that need moisture kept to a minimum.

Some brand names of Zeolite include Odorzout, Odor Eliminator, and Nature's Miracle. Nature's Miracle offers the product in bags for room deodorizing, and even a wall-mounted unit to hang the bags unobtrusively.

For the home, one of the best solutions to ongoing deodorizing of a pet area is one of the stick-up type deodorants or an oil-based deodorant in a small wick bottle, which can be tucked away in a hidden place and will work for a month or more. These products neutralize pet odors to an extent, and provide a pleasant masking fragrance. Personally, I prefer the scent of the natural oils in products like Nilodor and Big D wicks to the products with strong floral fragrances.

There are also wall-hung battery-powered dispensers available that release a burst of odor neutralizer spray (and, often, fragrance) into a room periodically. Nilodor's Nilotron dispenser is a good one, available in a variety of fragrances.

Carpet Deodorizer

Unfortunately, carpet is a perfect wick to absorb odors, and most ordinary carpet shampoos remove dirt, but not odors. When you're trying to cope with this particular problem, beware of the ads that encourage you to "sprinkle a little Smellzgood carpet deodorizer on the spot where Fido lies, then just vacuum it up for a sweet-smelling dog and carpet." Some of these products can produce contact dermatitis on a dog's sensitive belly skin. If you want to sprinkle something on your carpet to make it smell better, Nilofresh from the Nilodor Company is a corncob-based preparation that's safe to use around pets and is one of the few products that's actually been tested and proven to work well and safely for this purpose. Zeolite compounds can also be sprinkled on the carpet, left for a day or so, and then vacuumed up.

If the situation is beyond a sprinkle-on solution, first vacuum the area with a good beater-bar or beater-brush vacuum. Then apply a bacteria/enzyme product according to label directions. When the bacteria solution has finished working and the area has dried, hand-shampoo the spot with carpet shampoo to which you've added a little water-soluble deodorant such as Nilodor Surface Deodorizer, or use Nilodor Deodorizing Carpet Shampoo. Just dip a nylon scrub brush in the solution and scrub briskly to work up a good lather. Then blot up the suds with a towel or a wet/dry vacuum. While the nap is still wet, brush it first one way and then the other with a dry, stiff brush to get it all fluffed up. Brush the nap all in one direction to finish it off, and let it dry. (For pet accident removal from carpeting, see page 110.)

Deodorizers for Use on Your Pet

Regular bathing and grooming will do a lot to keep pet odor down. There are special shampoos formulated to help control pet body odor, too, such as Nilodor Deodorizing Pet Shampoo.

A lot of pet body odor is hormonal, such as the pungent smell male cats produce. Once you alter the animal, a lot of the musky odor is gone. The same goes for a lot of other animals. Much pet body odor is sexual odor, an attraction odor. To reduce this, you have to spay or neuter the animal.

A healthy cat otherwise should have no offensive odor, either on his body or in his mouth. If he seems to, something is wrong and you should take him to the vet.

Much of the odor associated with our canine companions is the result of the secretions of the tiny oil glands an animal has all over its skin, especially inside the ears and around the genitals and other bare skin areas. For basic, everyday dog odor, there are products designed for spraying directly on a dog's coat and skin to keep him smelling better between baths. Try Robinson Labs' Dog Deodorant and Outright's Pet Odor Eliminator, a bacteria/enzyme deodorizer that can be used right on your pet. These will also work well on the rolled-in-something-awful odors dogs and cats often come home with. There are also Zeolite products made specifically for use on pets, such as Odorzout for Pets, and these have the advantage of avoiding the need to wet down the animal.

If skin odor is very pronounced and hard to control, your cat or dog may be battling a case of dermatitis, which could be an allergic reaction to fleas, for example. Cases like this should be referred to your veterinarian for treatment.

Skunk Odor Remover

When your dog or cat has a close encounter of the worst kind, go to the pet store and get a product designed specifically to counteract skunk odor. Some of the best of these are of the enzyme or bacteria/enzyme digester variety, and can be used without even washing your pet first. A number of good products of this type are available, such as Outright Skunk Odor Eliminator; Skunk Kleen from G. G. Bean, Inc., of Brunswick,

Maine; and Odormute, from the Ryter Corporation. The one I like best is Nature's Miracle Skunk Odor Remover, made by Pets 'N People, Inc. Most of these products will also work well on other pet body odors, and they can be used to remove skunk odor from household surfaces, rooms, and clothes, as well.

When doing skunk clean-up, you need to really soak your pet with the solution (being careful to avoid the eyes and mouth, of course), especially if he is a longhaired animal. And if a skunk hits your pet at close range, it may be necessary to repeat the treatment.

For skunk odor on cats (who can be very resistant to wet cleaning), zeolite compounds can be sprinkled on and then combed off.

Clean with Distraction Action

I'm a professional salesman of cleaning supplies, but I guarantee that a good-quality toy can be a better investment than the best piece of cleaning equipment on the market. Good, strong, carefully chosen toys will entertain and exercise your pet for hours and help divert all that nervous energy—like kids, tired animals sleep!

If you give cats, for example, their own "furniture" with a built-in gym, and all kinds of interesting nooks and hideouts and perches and platforms and textures, they'll spend less time somersaulting off the rockers and excavating your planters. **A stout scratching post is a must in every house with a cat.** The Felix Katnip Tree is one of the best scratching posts available. It has a broad, sturdy base and a solid cedar post covered with tightly woven sisal fiber. Cats prefer a rough, tough surface like this to the carpeting found on many posts, and this post won't crumble or shed particles like cork or log posts do. It's even impregnated with catnip for extra cat appeal.

It would take a whole book to show all the kinds of toys and exercise equipment available for animals; pets love the toys you can make out of ordinary household objects and supplies, too. The bottom line is: What do they really like; what occupies them the most intensely and for the longest time? (If they convert a pair of rubber flip-flops into quintuplets, maybe a sturdy rubber toy is the ticket.) When you figure out what they like, buy it or make it. Just remember that **with toys, quality is important, safety is essential, and rotation is the key** to long-term diversion and entertainment.

More Important Tools for the Pet Cleaner

These devices will give you the edge when training your pet. They either interrupt unwanted behaviors or provide that old famous "negative feedback" on the act you're trying to discourage. Your cat or dog does something you don't want him to do, and something he really dislikes happens when he does it, so he stops doing that thing. It may take five tries, it may take fifty, but after a while he'll get the idea.

From the simplicity of a squirt bottle to the sophisticated electronics of an invisible barrier, the following will give you the assistance you need to produce more "house-friendly" pets.

Squirt Bottle

Thousands of experienced pet owners and trainers agree—this is one of the gentlest and most effective disciplinary measures around. When you catch your pet in the act of misbehaving (chewing furniture, jumping on the table, making long-distance phone calls), simply squirt him with plain water.

The Scat bottle (that's what I call it) is the same type of professional spray bottle used in the cleaning industry. It holds an entire quart and can send a steady stream of water at least twenty feet. If your cat decides to snack on one of your houseplants, give him a squirt from across the room. This is a useful behavior modification tool for dogs, too.

The quickness of your draw is important in this particular type of pet correction—not more than *two seconds* should go by between the forbidden act and your discouraging squirt. When possible, do not let your pet see you take aim. Far better that he think of this as an "environmental" response ("Gee, every time I jump on the table, things get wet in a hurry") rather than a personal attack. Don't spray your cat or dog in the face!

If you have a large dog or one with thick fur, you might want to use a water cannon instead of a spray bottle to get the speed and velocity of water stream needed to get your dog's attention.

Put a few spray bottles in different rooms for when you need them. If the quart size is a little too hefty for you to handle, professional-strength spray bottles are available in 22- and even 16-ounce sizes.

The main drawback of a squirt bottle is that it works only when you're home to use it. And you never want to misuse or overuse the spray bottle technique. Spraying your pet without good reason could bring on behavior problems or cause him to fear and avoid you. And always use only *plain water*.

Adhesives

Tape repellents such as Sticky Paws, a double-sided clear acrylic tape, can be used to make the forbidden area (couch corner, counter) unattractive. Pets, especially cats, hate the feeling of adhesives on their sensitive paws. Sticky Paws is made in regular, extra large size, and a special style for protecting plants. You can find a retailer in your area by calling 903-534-9499, or at the manufacturer's Web site, *www.stickypaws.com*.

"Unwelcome" Mats

Covering or protecting an area you don't want your pet (especially your cat) in or on with plastic sheeting, plastic wrap, aluminum foil, or bubble wrap will help discourage the behavior. Most cats and dogs don't like walking or lying on these. You can also buy rubber or plastic mats such as X-Mat that have hundreds of tiny raised bumps on them. **Used consistently, these can make a cat or dog avoid the spot where the mat was even after it is removed!**

Chemical Repellents

There are a variety of repellants available that can be sprayed or smeared on the area or item you are trying to protect, often made from plant extracts. For outdoor use, pet repellent granules are available as well. Designed to be nontoxic but distasteful to pets, these can be effective but they are not a magical force field. They have to be reapplied usually once a day or sometimes more often, and you need to read the label to be sure the surface you plan to use them on is not a no-no. It's usually a good idea to test them on fabric before applying heavily. Pet repellents include products like Keep Away and B'have, from the Farnum Company (800-452-2404).

See page 185 in Chapter 6 for repellents specifically for chewing; and page 91 in Chapter 3 for repellents made from synthetic pet pheromones that can be quite effective in many situations.

Electronic Repellants (Technology to the Rescue!)

If your cat is jumping on the counters when you aren't home, or the dog is taking goodies out of the garbage pail or taking off with laundry from the basket, consider using an invisible barrier or an "off limits" alarm. These detection devices will emit a startling or unpleasant sound (some of these are ultrasonic so they are heard only by the pet), an electronic impulse, or a noxious odor from either a wall-mounted device or a collar "receiver" worn by the pet. Some, for example, will respond to your pet's body heat or activity near a "forbidden zone," be it your formal living room or the baby's diaper pail in the nursery.

These devices have taken the place of the primitive, and sometimes dangerous, booby traps of yesteryear, like shaker cans, throw chains, and mousetraps. Many of these newer devices do not require you to be present, so your pet does not associate you with the unpleasant outcome or recognize when the "trap" is set.

As an added bonus, many of these twenty-first-century-repellents reset themselves so they are ready for the next intrusion.

One of the best and most pet-friendly for cats is Ssscat, which makes a little beep and then shoots out a harmless puff of pressurized air when its battery-powered motion detector gives it the word. Premier Pet Products at 888-640-8840 can give you the address of a retailer in your area. Spray Barrier (*www.multivet-inter.com*) is a battery-powered device that emits a burst of citronella scent when its motion detector senses an intrusion. These two devices don't have the drawback of some of the sound alarms, which can frighten other nearby pets or wake light sleepers.

Check out pet stores and pet specialty catalogs for the latest in electronic discouragement.

Before using any of these tools, give some thought to which approach or device best suits your pet's personality. A sensitive, nervous, or high-strung pet will respond differently than a bold, confident one. Make sure your approach is pet-friendly rather than adversarial.

Set your pet up for success through consistent, thoughtful training and guidance. It is important to also show your pet what he *is* permitted to chew, where he is permitted to lie down, or what he can scratch on. And when you see him doing the "right" thing, be sure to praise him as quickly and heartily as you would have corrected him had he done wrong.

Chapter 2

Good, Clean Living—with Pets:

Preventative Measures to Keep Your Home Mess-Free and Ease Your Allergies

We've all known people who get overexcited about real or imagined ailments in themselves or others, especially if the disease is unusual or exotic—or from an exotic source, such as pets. As one of this country's top physicians said on a national program I appeared on once, "In the average general family practice, as much as two-thirds of the patients that come groaning and sniffling in for office visits don't need to.

Dear Don,

I want to confess a couple of concerns I have about pet clean-up. I don't think I'm an antigerm fanatic, but animals do seem rather dirty, and the thought of my baby crawling across the floor (where the dog may have walked, rolled, or even dragged his behind) simply makes my hair stand on end.

I never let the dog up on the bed or furniture, and after little Joey's wrapped his crib blanket around our pup, do I need to throw it right in the washer? (For that matter, is it okay to wash pet bedding in the very same machine used for people clothes?) Am I right to get uptight every time I catch the kids sharing their snacks with the cat, or playing with our pets' toys, or letting the dog lick their hands or faces?

And just how germy is the dog bowl? I never want to wash it in the kitchen sink where people food is made; I clean and rinse it outside and throw the dirty water over the fence or down the toilet. Am I being overcautious?

Sincerely,
Annie Septic

They have something that time, rest, or a good bar of soap will eventually cure by itself." Worries about pet diseases can be the same. Though most diseases and parasites are quite particular and usually stick to a single species, there are some diseases that animals can transmit to us—all in all, more than a hundred kinds, although less than thirty are reasonably common.

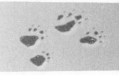

The chances of you catching a disease from your pet—especially if you've had him vaccinated against all the things your vet recommends—are actually quite remote.

Yes, a dog's skin and tongue are literally crawling with bacteria, but then so are ours. Most of these "bugs" are friendly and even useful, and the chances of catching something unpleasant from an animal are far less than the chances of catching it from another person. The odds are definitely in your favor, especially if you follow the basic rules of sanitation, or simple cleanliness, described in the following pages.

The Floor

The floor is the final catchall—for fallout from the sky, air, people, and pets. And floors in a pet home should be kept extra clean. Especially if you have crawling children, for example, who put everything in their mouths. For the three to six months that your child crawls, I'd do "double duty" on the floor.

Keep a spray bottle of disinfectant solution near the damp mop and then every other day quickly spray the floor with it. Let it sit on there for ten minutes and then run the mop over it, and rinse well. This will pick up the dirt and kill any potential disease-causing germs.

When cleaning hard floors in pet areas, use a little bit of water-soluble odor neutralizer such as Nilodor's Surface Deodorizer in your cleaning solution, or use a one-step cleaner and deodorizer such as Nilodor Deodorizing Cleaner from time to time, to keep things smelling sweet.

Walls

The walls in the average home are washed about once a year, though this varies with the lifestyle of the inhabitants

Some Rules for Pet-Safe Cleaning

✓ Keep pets out of the area while you clean.

✓ Follow cleaner, disinfectant, etc., dilution directions carefully— never make the solution stronger than the label says.

✓ Rinse well after cleaning.

✓ Be sure to let the area dry, and ventilate well if necessary, before letting pets back in.

✓ Always store cleaners in a child and pet-safe place.

(smokers and people with woodstoves do have to wash walls more often). With pets, as with kids, you'll probably be spot cleaning more often. You also don't want to let grease build up and stay on walls, because that sticky film will hold hair, dust, dander, and germs. So an overall wall washing every six months or so in areas like the kitchen might be called for.

If you have a pet who sprays, you'll want to wash the lower parts of walls (up to at least 18 inches) and the baseboards, etc., more frequently, and add a water-soluble deodorant such as Nilodor Surface Deodorizer to your cleaning solution. This is a good idea in any room where pet odor might be a problem.

Particular areas of the wall that get a lot of pet body contact—such as the spots where a pet leans against a wall when he beds down—should be disinfected (washed or sprayed with Nolvasan solution that's left on at least ten minutes, and then rinsed well) from time to time.

Alleviating Pet Allergies

At least 10 to 15 percent of people are affected by pet allergies. The percentage rises to 30 percent for those with asthma. **It's not just pet hair that people are allergic to**—the main culprit is a protein found also in pets' saliva, urine, and dander (the tiny flakes of dead skin that we and our pets shed constantly). Just about any animal with fur or feathers can cause an allergic reaction, but that doesn't stop people from having pets. A lot of people are more allergic to cats than to dogs. When a cat cleans itself, it loosens the allergens in its fur, releasing them into the air and leaving them on furniture, clothing, etc. Although some breeds are supposed to cause less of a reaction than others (such as shorthaired poodles, bichon frise dogs, and Siamese cats), they still have fur and they'll cause allergies.

Clean Up!

The best way to reduce the effects of pet allergies is to clean. Allergens cling to and collect in soft furnishings and carpets. Hard surface floors such as vinyl, tile, and hardwood are easier to clean and you can see stray hair or fur more easily than on carpets. Mop water-resistant surfaces frequently, and dust mop rather than sweep. Buy washable throw rugs and clean them frequently. Furnish your house with easy-to-clean drapes, roll shades, wood tables, etc. . . . things that won't collect a lot of dust. Speaking of which, if you have pets, you have to dust more often. Use a damp cloth when dusting to be sure you've collected everything. See also pages 128 in Chapter 5 for more hair removal tools, including a special "hair vacuum."

A modern bagless vacuum with a built-in air filtration system is your best bet to prevent spreading allergens around your house. Use HEPA filters on vacuums with bags. Open the doors and windows in your house for a few hours after cleaning to help clear the air. Some people install air purifiers in their homes. But air conditioners and humidifiers alone won't do the job if they are not cleaned regularly and properly, and they collect mold easily. Change or clean air conditioning and heating system filters often.

Keep your pets out of the bedroom! Don't let them lie on your bed or your pillow. If they do sleep on the bed, wash your linens thoroughly and frequently.

Keep a cleaning routine to rid your house of allergens, and you should find your nose and eyes a lot less red and irritated.

Frequently brushing and cleaning your dog or cat outside can also cut down on the number of allergens that end up in your house. If you're severely allergic, wear a protective face-mask while doing this and change your clothes after you are done. Don't touch your face, especially your eyes, until you have washed your hands. For some pets, a soap and water bath can help, but don't wash them more than needed. Their skin can become dry or residue from soap can make them itchy and this will only cause the release of more allergens into your home.

When Cleaning Isn't Enough

There aren't nonallergenic breeds of dogs or cats just yet, although people are hard at work developing them even as I write this. (The hairless Sphynx breed of cat is hypoallergenic, but it requires more care than other breeds do. And the Labradoodle, a cross between a standard poodle and a Labrador retriever, is supposed to be easy on allergies. The Allerca company of Los Angeles intends to have an allergy-free breed of cat by 2007, via genetic engineering to suppress the protein that causes human allergies.

If you love your dog or cat but don't love the allergies you're getting from him or her, ask your doctor about allergy shots or strong antihistamines.

You can also ask your veterinarian about products like Allerpet, a nontoxic solution applied to your pet's fur once a week. There are separate solutions for dogs, cats, and birds. There are also special shampoos to reduce allergens.

If all else fails, you can always switch to reptiles or fish!

Easy Ways to Control Pet Diseases

Most diseases are spread by coming in direct contact with pet excretions or secretions (or infected surfaces or materials) and then failing to wash your hands. You don't need to be a chemist or professional cleaner to prevent the spread of disease—just be consistent. Simple cleanliness is the best defense.

Always wash your hands after playing with a pet and after cleaning the litter box or cleaning up pet accidents, or doing scooping duty, or cleaning a cage.

Don't touch your mouth, nose, or eyes, and don't eat or prepare food while handling an animal. Also control "extra-close contact" with pets. Yes, this means things like kissing pets and letting them sleep in your bed or lie on your pillow and letting them lick hands and faces. Young children, especially, can catch pet diseases this way, so set clear-cut rules for kids with pets.

Keep pet potty areas cleaned up. Pick up and dispose of pet feces at least daily. **Many pet diseases are spread by contact with the waste of an infected animal,** so if you keep things clean, you'll help avoid those kinds of problems.

Dispose of soiled cat litter promptly, in a sealed bag or container, and keep the litter box away from areas where food is prepared. Outdoors, don't let your cat use the kids' sandbox as a litter box—keep it covered when not in use—because parasites and diseases can be passed on all too easily this way.

Rain dissolves and distributes animal waste, or the waste dries to dust, so it's often no longer visible, but if a child plays in the area, he can be infected when he puts his fingers, toys, etc., in his mouth. **Don't let the children's outdoor play area be one that's regularly littered with dog stools—** and you especially don't want children to run barefoot or play scantily clothed in such areas.

Roundworm eggs or hookworm larvae, for example, can often be found in dog feces, and they can live a long time in the dirt. Worms that infest pets can't usually survive to fulfill their whole lifecycle in the human body, but they can invade humans occasionally and do some damage (to children especially) before they succumb.

Keeping your pet free of fleas will reduce the chances of infection, too. Children can swallow an infected flea and get a tapeworm; fleas spread a number of other diseases, including bubonic plague. See page 148 in Chapter 5 for flea control measures for your pet and his whole environment.

Some diseases that can have serious consequences are spread by ticks, including Lyme disease and Rocky Mountain spotted fever, which is found in areas of the country other than the Rockies now. Apply tick remedies when they seem called for to keep ticks off your pet. Keep your yard mowed and clear of brush to reduce tick habitat. Be careful when removing ticks; avoid touching the tick itself. Using a tissue, tweezers, or rubber gloves, grasp the tick close to the skin and pull straight out (twisting may leave mouth parts in the skin). Try not to puncture or crush the tick during removal. After you've disposed of the tick, disinfect the bite site and wash your hands well.

Keeping the family pets free of worms is one of the most important ways of preventing the spread of disease. Be sure a puppy or kitten has been dewormed before you get him, and have your pet checked regularly for worms. Bring a stool sample with you each time you go to the vet—the test takes only ten minutes! If your pet spends time in areas littered with the feces of other pets or hunts and eats small animals, have him checked at least twice a year. Let the vet prescribe medication if it's needed. **Do-it-yourself dewormers are dangerous and often not fully effective.**

Toxoplasmosis is a tiny single-celled parasite that cats can carry. The disease isn't common, but since the intermediate host for the disease is mice, cats that hunt are more likely to get it. If a cat has this parasite, and the litter box isn't cleaned of feces at least every two days, the spores from the parasite, which are transmitted by air, will develop to the infective stage.

The disease is most dangerous to pregnant women because the parasite settles inside the unborn child, and can result in serious birth defects such as mental retardation. If you're pregnant or if you have any sort of disease that affects your immune system, you should either have someone else clean out the litter box or, if you do it, make sure you do so every day. Or use disposable boxes. For more information on toxoplasmosis, go to *www.cdc.gov* and search for "Toxoplasmosis fact sheet."

Prevention Is the Best Medicine
Avoid problems to begin with by keeping your pet healthy:

1. Feed him a nutritious, balanced diet, and clean his food and water bowls regularly.
2. Keep him clean by regular grooming.
3. Make sure he has a checkup at least once a year, and all the vaccinations your vet recommends.
4. Don't let your pet hunt and eat mice, rabbits, squirrels, or even earthworms. All of these can carry parasites and diseases to your pet, and then possibly to you.
5. Don't let your pet run loose. This is one sure way of picking up diseases from other animals. A fenced yard will keep your dog in and other dogs out.

6. Keep any cage, run, or enclosure your pet spends time in clean and free of accumulated droppings.

7. Make sure your pet's sleeping quarters are clean, dry, and warm (to prevent the chills and drafts that bring on diseases). Remove soiled bedding promptly.

8. Clean your pet's toys and accessories, too, from time to time.

9. Beware of exotic pets: Among the many good reasons not to keep a wild animal as a pet is the fact that a number of diseases can be spread to humans by contact with wild animals, or by wild animals that come in contact with our pets.

10. Clean and apply antiseptic to scratches and superficial cuts on your pet as soon as they appear so infection won't have a chance to start or be spread this way. And if a pet has sores or other skin lesions, keep your own and your children's hands away from them. Don't handle an animal if you have an open wound.

Precautions for Ill Pets

Isolate a sick pet from the other pets in the house. Confine him to a single out-of-the-way area or a quiet room, preferably one with a seamless or well-sealed hard floor and nonabsorbent walls and furniture.

Exchange his regular bedding for disposable bedding such as a cardboard box filled with shredded newspaper, or the commercially available puppy pads. Don't shake a sick pet's blanket in the house, and

remember to dispose of soiled bedding promptly. Minimize your handling of him as much as you can, and wash your hands well after touching him or his food dishes, bedding, wound dressings, etc.

You especially don't want to allow children to handle a sick animal—young children and the elderly are always more susceptible to infection. And no one who has an immunosuppressive disease, is on chemotherapy, or has had an organ transplant should handle a sick animal, because in all of these cases the person involved has a weakened immune system. It's not that they'll necessarily catch what the animal has, but sick animals can easily come down with secondary infections such as strep and staph and we *can* get those diseases.

A Word of Caution about Disinfectants

Like most novices in cleaning, in my early days I was sure that the stronger a solution was, the better it must work. On one of my first professional cleaning jobs, the straight commercial ammonia I was using in the stuffy little sewing room was hard to take and I stumbled out occasionally for a breath of fresh air. When I was finished and was getting ready to leave, my customer came running out, screaming, "My bird is dead, my bird is dead!" And it was. It's a terrible feeling to know you've harmed a helpless animal because of carelessness, and believe it or not, it's common. In our efforts to clean and care for our pets, we often unknowingly harm them.

The idea of "disinfecting" seizes us almost like a crusade or holy war. We'll apply a disinfectant, by gosh, and really zap any little undesirables that might be invading our premises. But even doctors and veterinarians will testify that good, thorough *cleaning* of pet areas and articles will go a long way toward keeping pets and people healthy and free of disease. As one head of Hospital Infection Control put it, "elbow grease is one of the best disinfectants." How well and regularly you clean is more important than precisely what you use, even when it comes to keeping germs at bay.

When and What to Disinfect

Pet areas and objects you should keep good and clean all the time, and disinfect from time to time—especially if you have a number of pets or pets that spend a fair amount of time outdoors—include the following:

- Pet food and water dishes
- The floor and walls near the pet-feeding area
- Your pet's bed
- The concrete or gravel surfaces of dog runs and kennels and backyard "pet potty" areas
- Gutters and drains in dog runs and kennels
- Litter pans and spoons, and the walls and floor around the litter box
- The toilet bowl and seat if the cat uses it, and the tub or shower if the litter box is kept there
- Scooping equipment
- Waste containers used for pet purposes, such as dumping used litter
- Pet cages and crates
- Furniture surfaces or walls or drapes that a pet spends a lot of time lounging against
- Your pet's food bowls, cage or crate, toys, etc., after he's been sick or kept at a boarding kennel (not a few pet diseases are picked up this way)
- Anything a pet with a serious infectious disease used or inhabited, before you bring home a new pet
- The doghouse

What about Bleach as a Disinfectant?

Many vets and kennels use a bleach solution as a general disinfectant—mainly because it's the only thing that's 100 percent effective against the viruses that cause the serious diseases of parvovirus in dogs and panleukopenia in cats. But bleach has a strong odor, can damage many household surfaces, and its disinfecting action is seriously impaired by "organic matter" (urine, feces, dirt, grass, pet hair, etc.). And with all the different cleaners we use in the home today, there's always a danger of someone unknowingly mixing another chemical with bleach, resulting in dangerous or even lethal chemical reactions. So, unless your vet specifically recommends bleach for a particular home cleaning situation, there are better things for the job.

Other Common Disinfectants

Among the most commonly used disinfectants not long ago were the phenolics (made from phenol, or carbolic acid). Phenolics, especially in low concentrations, are generally safe for humans to use and store—many household disinfectants are phenol derivatives—but they can be lethal to cats and some other animals. That is why **most experts recommend not using phenolic disinfectants around pets.** Some products, such as Lysol Spray Disinfectant, contain orthophenylphenol, a synthetic derivative of phenol, which is considered far less toxic to animals than phenol itself. But I would not recommend using any phenol-based disinfectant around small animals, because the potential for harm is certainly there.

The quaternary disinfectants, or "quats," which have an ammonium chloride base, are safer to use around pets than phenolics, and most of them have a general-purpose cleaner added, so the solution cleans as it disinfects. These are widely used today, but quats are skin and eye irritants, and their fumes or mist can damage mucous membranes. They are seriously toxic if ingested. I hesitate to recommend the use of a product of this nature around pets.

This doesn't mean you should rush to the pine-oil products for the purpose, even if they do smell nice and natural. That piney fragrance is their strongest point—they're neither particularly good cleaners nor good disinfectants, and they, too, can be dangerous to pets. (If a pine-oil product solution gets on a pet's footpads, for example, it's ingested when the pet licks its paws.)

The Safest Disinfectant

For situations that do call for a true disinfectant, chlorhexidine, sold under the trade name Nolvasan by Fort Dodge Animal Health of Overland Park, Kansas, is the one I'd use. It does a better job of destroying viruses, fungi, and bacteria than quaternary or phenolic disinfectants, yet is far less likely to sting, burn, or cause skin irritation or reaction than any other disinfectant available. (It's gentle enough that it can be, and is, used in ointments and surgical wound cleansers.) It's much less dangerous if a pet did happen to accidentally ingest a small amount of the solution, and it can even be safely used to disinfect birdcages and small animal cages.

If you have very hard water, don't mix up the solution ahead and store it to use, because the minerals in the water will precipitate out and "tie up" some of the solution's disinfecting power. Mix it right before you use it. If you want to mix some solution for later use in this situation, use distilled or softened water.

Nolvasan is usually available only through vets and pet and livestock supply stores and is used extensively for disinfecting animal hospitals, farm premises, dog kennels, and pet equipment. You can buy it direct from the manufacturer by calling 800-685-5656.

When using Nolvasan for general disinfecting purposes, dilute it to one ounce per gallon of water before using. For disinfection of areas known to be harboring diseases, or for virucidal action, the ratio is usually upped to three ounces to a gallon of water.

Some General Rules for Using Disinfectants

1. Whenever you're performing a major cleaning operation, keep the pets away until you're finished. Never use a disinfectant on the animal itself, and remove food and water dishes, toys, etc., from the area before you apply a disinfectant.

2. Be sure to clean the area or object well first. A solution has to get to the surface of something to be able to disinfect it, and if that surface is covered with dirt and litter, it can't. Besides, the germ-killing powers of most disinfectants are seriously weakened by the presence of "organic matter"—things like hair, excrement, dirt, dander, uneaten food, milk, and many types of bedding materials. So scrape and brush and sweep first, but not so vigorously that you stir up a cloud of dust—that's an excellent way to spread disease germs through the air. It's also important to rinse well after the precleaning.

3. Don't mix a disinfectant with other cleaning products unless the label tells you it's okay to do so—and then, only use the kind specified. Follow the dilution and other directions on the label to the letter; never make the solution stronger than it says.

4. Use disinfectants with care. Many are skin and eye irritants. They can also be absorbed through the skin, so you may want to wear rubber gloves. Avoid spilling or splashing the solution on yourself or in your eyes. Likewise, don't mist a disinfectant solution or apply it in

a very fine spray; when chemicals are sprayed in a fine mist, they can be inhaled easily and may be dangerous to the lungs and bodies of pets and people alike. Avoid aerosols whenever you can, for your own sake as well as your pet's. The mist from an aerosol can is finer and stays airborne longer. (If you must spray, squirt a small amount onto your cleaning cloth, rather than filling the air with spray.)

5. When applying disinfectant, really saturate the surface with the solution. Don't forget the crevices, cracks, and corners. Where would you hide if you were a germ?

6. Leave the solution on the surface for at least ten minutes.

7. Rinse the area thoroughly with clean water to remove the chemicals.

8. To disinfect fabric items, soak them in a bucket or tub of disinfectant solution for at least fifteen minutes before putting them through the usual washing process. Disinfectant can also be added to the final rinse cycle instead.

9. Air out or dry the disinfected articles or areas well before putting them back in use or letting pets back into the area.

10. Store disinfectants in a secure place (preferably a locked place, well out of the reach of children and pets) and don't buy them in too large a quantity at one time.

Sane Storage of Pet Supplies

Pet feeding and care is done daily, so why not set up a special storage area for the pet food and supplies, a handy place that's easy to use and clean and keeps the critters from getting into it? Here are some ideas for a "pet control center"—you may have some good or better ideas for designing your own to fit your unique needs.

Pet Control Center

1. Hooks for leashes, collars, etc. (note: "choke chains" frowned upon now)
2. Scooper, dustpan, broom
3. Dispensers for large and small plastic bags
4. Suspended food hopper/dispenser
5. Suspended food and water dishes
6. Pet placemat to catch spills
7. Visible storage of grooming tools, with sharp tools stored high
8. Pet grooming platform
9. Built-in vacuum with pet grooming head
10. Squeegee
11. Large pullout garbage can or storage bin
12. Vent
13. Heat lamp
14. Extra food storage in plastic containers
15. Spray bottles
16. Paper towels
17. Terry towels
18. Shallow storage for pet medicine, vitamins, oils, etc.
19. Shampoos and conditioners

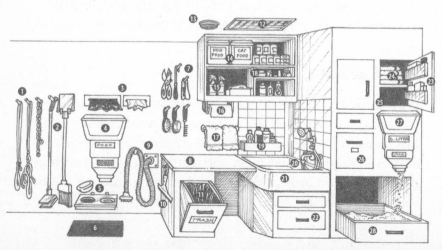

20. Removable spray head

21. Low wash basin with 6-inch lip to hold water in; set up on a 2½-foot cabinet so that you have to bend only slightly to use it (a good place to clean pet dishes and mats, dump dirty mop water, and wash off dirty pets)

22. Miscellaneous storage drawers

23. Flea killers and disinfectants stored up high behind closed doors

24. Pet cleaning cloths

25. Rolled-up mats

26. One file-cabinet size drawer for pet records

27. Suspended hopper to store and dispense cat litter

28. Enclosed pull-out litter box

For the avid pet owner, a pet control center that really provides for every pet activity and cleaning project will concentrate and reduce the cleaning. It'll also solve some tough questions of storage, sanitation, and safety. A control center could take as little room as a big closet; near an outside door is a good place for it.

When you're planning your control center, bear in mind that **shallow storage in which everything is immediately visible is by far the best.** If everything is neat and clean and easy to get to, it's more likely to stay that way. You also want to be sure to store sharp or dangerous or potentially poisonous pet care items where kids and pets can't get to them. Get them up high and even behind a locked door if necessary.

For dry food storage, don't trust the bag it comes in. Set the bag down inside of, or empty it into, a large clean plastic or metal can with a tight-fitting lid. Food stored in open containers or in plastic, paper, cloth, or burlap bags can become infested and it will stale quickly, too. For a strong pest-proof storage container, use a metal or plastic garbage can, or the large metal containers that popcorn and potato chips are sometimes sold in. You can even use the big plastic containers with lids that fast-food stores will often sell you very inexpensively. Pet treats, etc., that come in cardboard boxes can be stored in sealable plastic containers after the box is opened.

Plastic containers are really the best for all kinds of food—no dents, no rust, no noise. A variety of sturdy, airtight, and even stackable pet food containers, such as the Vittles Vault, are available at pet stores and in pet catalogs.

Storing dry or semimoist pet food in a sturdy plastic or metal can eliminates pet food odors, keeps pests and pets from getting in, and keeps the sack from getting wet or breaking open. Cans like these come in handy, too, if you have enough pets to buy pet food or litter in bulk from a wholesale distributor, feed store, or farmers' co-op. You don't want to store anything directly on the floor, even in closed containers—it'll be more susceptible to moisture and pests. Put your containers on sturdy open shelves at least 18 inches off the floor.

Keep a deep metal cup or plastic container inside the can or hanging on a handy hook nearby for scooping; a tall narrow cup can be filled two-thirds full without letting anything spill out.

Don't get more dry food than your pet can use up in about a month—if these foods are stored too long, they lose nutritional value. This is also why you don't want to store pet foods in a hot place; in temperatures higher than normal room temperature, they'll deteriorate quickly. And a damp place will encourage the growth of mold and mildew, as well as posing a rust risk to metal containers.

Clean the containers out every six months and wipe them down with a Nolvasan-and-water solution. Be sure to rinse and dry well before refilling.

Suspend Everything You Can

A sturdy plastic storage and dispensing bin that mounts on the wall, such as the Pour-N-Store by Blitz, will keep pet supplies clean, dry, convenient, and safe from pets and pests.

I think it's the ideal way to store and handle dry pet food, bird-seed, cat litter, and other dry materials such as soap powder and charcoal. If you want to set up the ideal pet feeding situation, and don't want to build an entire control center, suspend the food storage right in the area where the pets are fed. A large plastic dispenser will let the food fall out right into the bowl. This helps prevent mess from pouring or dropping food, and you don't have to dip your hands into dry dog food twice a day. Set the dispenser about chest high so the animals can't get to it and you don't have to bend over or stretch up to reach it.

Maintaining the Feeding Zone

Where do we usually locate the pet dining zone? Right in the heaviest traffic lane where everyone walks over or through—not only disturbing the pet at his meal but tracking stuff around and distributing it. Would you like to be served dinner in the middle of the busiest sidewalk in town? How do you suppose an animal feels being fed in hallways, by doorways, and on porches? Most of us feed them there because it's handy to quickly dump the food in the dish and be done with it. My family fed our cats and dogs by the side of the back door for so many years, I began to spell dog with two o's. It was always a mess.

Put the pet dining in a niche or private area where adults, children, and, for that matter, other pets aren't constantly marching through. Find a place out of the traffic flow and out of drafts. Feed your pets in an area with hard-surface flooring, and choose one feeding place and stick with it. Pets appreciate consistency, and you don't need two or three feedlots to keep clean instead of one. If you have both cats and dogs, however, you might want to feed them at separate times or in different rooms.

If you crate your dog (see page 66, Chapter 3), feeding him in the crate will cut down on feeding mess. And if you allow your dog a bone (an uncooked beef knuckle or "soup bone" only, for safety's sake), you can establish the crate as the only place bones are allowed. In any case, make sure your dog does his bone or treat chewing in one area—don't let him drag these things all over.

Never feed your pet on carpet or on porous surfaces like unsealed concrete or brick. **Where there's food, THERE WILL ALWAYS BE SPILLAGE,** by you and by the pet. Even the most Emily Post pet will slurp, splash, spill, dribble, and spread his food and water all over the area while eating.

Pick a Good Pet Dish

Think of cleaning time and mess potential when you pick a pet dish. Individual dishes for individual pets is a wise and logical move—no pet likes another pet in competition for his food, and it'll save cleaning up "jealousy messes." Cats can share a water bowl with other cats, but not a food bowl.

You want round dishes so there are no corners that an animal can't lick clean, and the heavier and more unbreakable, the better.

Some dishes have tip-proof designs or weighted or nonskid bottoms so they can't be knocked over, slid along the floor, or carried off by an animal. A pet dish should also be tooth-proof; plastic and aluminum, for example, can be chewed. Pets can get dermatitis (sores around the mouth) from some plastic dishes; orange and yellow bowls seem to be the most common culprits. Plastic can also absorb odors and scientists even claim it very gradually dissolves over time, so avoid plastic dishes when possible.

Also avoid two-compartment feeders because, like two-compartment buckets, they can put you into a rubber room! Both sides never need filling at once, and you can't effectively empty one side at one time—the food and water will slop or leak into each other. Get a separate dish for water and put it some distance from the food bowl, so your pets can't drop mouthfuls of half-eaten food into the water dish.

If you have a long-eared dog like a cocker spaniel, you want to get a narrow, steep-sided bowl to keep your pet's ears from becoming messed and matted with food. Likewise, you want a deep dish for a long-nosed pet and a shallow one for pups, cats, and short-nosed dogs. Cats prefer shallow dishes or saucers because they don't like to bump their whiskers on the side of the dish.

There are elevated food dishes for tall pets, too, but be sure such dishes are set in a sturdy stand, or the ease with which they can be knocked over will offset how much easier your pet can reach his food.

There are also dishes set in frames that can be attached to the wall or to the side of the cage. A suspended bowl is much easier to clean up under. And it won't get knocked over. You can also install it at a height that's easier on the dog (he won't have to bend down so far to eat) and easier on you, because you won't have to bend down so far to serve.

Look for a suspended dish with a small ledge around it to catch the dribbles, and also consider putting a splashboard of plastic laminate or vinyl on the wall in back of the dish.

Stainless steel is almost indestructible and is easy to clean in sterilizing hot water; it will never rust or rot. (In very cold climates, however, you wouldn't want to use it outdoors.) Heavyweight ceramic or pottery dishes are the next best, though they can freeze and break if used outdoors in cold weather.

Keep cleanability in mind, too, when selecting pet dishes. Ideally, **pet dishes should be able to be washed in very hot water** or the hottest setting on a dishwasher.

Be Prepared for Spills

Put something under the pet food and water bowls to catch the mess. Ideally, this should be something that is absorbent as well as protective. An old towel under there isn't too bad, but newspapers will just multiply the mess.

A 2' x 3' nylon or olefin rubber-backed mat of the kind available at janitorial-supply stores is a much better idea. Then you can just pick up the mat from time to time and rinse it off or hose it down. The nonslip back will keep the mat in place and discourage your pet from dragging it around to play with it. The Drymate Placemat is another good choice here; it absorbs as well as protects.

You can also use a rubber bath mat (the kind with little suction feet), or a big shallow tray such as a low-sided plastic litter box or a cookie sheet. There are also plastic pet "placemats" available, with a raised lip around the edge. This will eliminate that dusty, grimy, crumby, sticky spot on the floor where the pet dishes are. All the mess and spillage is contained, and after dinner you can simply take the tray or mat to the sink for a quick clean-up. The floor and eating area will stay clean and sanitary.

Self-Feeders

Usually used for dry pet food, self-feeders sound like the best of all possible worlds, and in a few circumstances they can work well for pets, but they do have some disadvantages. The continuous presence of food in an open (or openable) container attracts pests and insects. Pets that continually eat and drink eliminate continually, too. Self-feeding is an especially bad idea for an unhousebroken dog. And many pets *will* gobble their way to overweight in a self-feeding situation.

The automatic waterers, on the other hand, can be a good idea if they're rustproof and designed in such a way that the water can't become stale or freeze. But there are also problems with using an automatic waterer. Too often, people will just forget about a jug-type waterer until they notice it's empty, which could be long after it runs dry. It doesn't take long for water to become stagnant and for bacteria and algae to begin to accumulate; your pet's saliva will also collect on the bottom of the bowl. All of this will make the water taste bad and create a breeding place for germs. The automatic waterers that are constantly refilled with fresh water are better (and may be a good idea for a dog run or the like), but they still have the problem of saliva accumulation in the bowl. And I certainly wouldn't risk having one inside the house—if it got tipped over or somehow stuck open, you'd be left with soaked carpets, flooded rooms, and other expensive damage.

Outdoors, the type that you attach to an outside faucet or garden hose—such as the Farnum Automatic Dog Faucet—so your pet can serve himself presents the fewest cleaning and sanitation problems. The Waterdog even has an electronic sensor to tell it when to turn on!

Keep the Water Clean

It's important to be sure your pet always has fresh water on hand. This doesn't mean leave the water bowl on the floor and top it off from time to time with a little fresh water from the sink. At least once a day, take up the water bowl, wash it out (with soap, not just water!), rinse it well, and refill it with fresh, clean water. **A constant supply of fresh water is essential for any cat or dog**—and only more so for those fed dry food, older pets, and pets kept outside, especially in summer. Cats, especially, are reluctant to drink stale or soiled water. If you use a bowl-type automatic waterer, you need to clean it well, too, and it's a good idea to disinfect it from time to time, especially if it's had an algae, etc., accumulation.

Don't Dodge the Dishes

Contrary to popular belief, pets' licking and the rain won't keep animal dishes clean, any more than people wiping their own dishes out with a crust or napkin will. Even if a pet dish is licked clean, it still has a sticky coating of saliva. Dirty animal dishes entice unwanted crawly intruders and breed bacteria and possibly illness for animals and humans alike.

Wash pet food and water dishes at least every day. And don't be afraid to use the kitchen sink. Animal dishes generally aren't as dirty as ours. Just wash them in a hot dish detergent solution and rinse them like any others.

If you don't want to bowserize your immaculate sink with pet dishes, wash them in the utility sink or in a plastic bucket. If you have enough of them to wash, you can run them through the dishwasher, which, for sanitary reasons, is actually preferable.

Don't forget, dishes that hold dried food need to be cleaned often, too. Don't just keep dropping more kibble in there, never even looking at the bottom of the dish.

To disinfect pet dishes, soak them in Nolvasan solution for five or ten minutes after you've washed and rinsed them, and then rinse them well again before you put them back in service.

Feed the Right Food

What you feed your pet depends on his age and condition, and whether you have a cat or dog or otherwise, but beyond the strict questions of nutrition, which your vet or a good book on the subject can advise you on, there are some KP (kitchen patrol) concerns here, too. Obviously, the softer the food, the messier, because it splashes and drips and runs. Either we can easily clean up any spilled hard food, or our pet will do it for us. And the experts agree that for most purely pet cats and dogs, dry foods are fine.

They're cheaper, less messy, and may keep a pet's teeth cleaner. They can also be stored without refrigeration. Canned pet foods, or a mixture of canned and dry, may be necessary for older or very finicky animals, or for those with certain health problems such as a urinary tract disease, or for those with a problem with the higher carbohydrate content of dry foods. Canned foods are more expensive, messier to handle and clean up after, awkward to store, and tend to have strong odors. Moist foods are somewhere in between dry and canned—they have some of the advantages of each, but many experts think they contain too much sugar to be good for a pet's health.

When feeding raw meat diets, standard precautions regarding the handling of uncooked meat and offal and subsequent clean-up should be observed. Keep storage containers and utensils scrupulously clean, too. Store fresh and raw food correctly and feed it while fresh.

Consider a Specialty Food

Among the thousands of types of commercial dog and cat foods today are many kinds of premium and specialty foods, such as those for pups, older animals, the "couch potato," or the extra-active pet.

"Nutritionally dense" dog and cat foods are of particular interest to the pet cleaner. These cost more, but are carefully designed to provide 100 percent nutrition of better quality in a lesser amount of food. This means less to store, less to spoon out, and less to clean up. A pet eating such food also has smaller and fewer stools, and the stools are firmer and easier to deal with. They'll also be less foul smelling than the droppings of dogs and cats fed the chock-full-of-cereal-filler "supermarket" pet foods. Premium foods also have fewer (or no) added dyes, which can cause permanent stains on carpet and upholstery.

Whatever food you choose, try to stick with it. Frequent changes in diet may produce digestive upset in pets, which means (messy!) diarrhea or vomiting. This is especially true if you are going from a supermarket brand of pet food (more cereal/less meat) to a nutritionally dense brand (more meat/ less cereal) or changing from a single meat/grain formula to a multiple or different meat/grain combination, like chicken, turkey, and/or fish with barley and oats.

For your sake—and for your pet's sake—don't allow him to eat from your table or around the table. Get him in the habit of eating in a certain place at a certain time. If you want to feed him some of your meal, put it in his bowl before or after you serve yourself or save it and mix it in with his regular meal. Just remember that table scraps, which are often greasy, can cause not only diarrhea and vomiting, but also serious problems such as pancreatitis in dogs.

Don't Feed Too Often, or Too Much

The experts agree that adult cats and dogs should be fed only a couple of times a day, and they can get by with just once. (The wild relatives of our pets can go for several days eating only once, staying strong and healthy.) If pets munch and lap all day off and on, their whole life becomes eating and voiding, and yours feeding and cleaning! Nor is it good for a pet's health, over time, to have his system constantly focused on eating and digesting. It's okay to do this with cats as long as the cat in question does not have an obesity problem, and as long as the food is kept fresh.

It's best to establish a strict routine and feed within a certain time frame every day, and remove any uneaten food after about twenty minutes. This will keep food mess from hardening on the plate, keep pests away, and be better for your pet, too. If you are in the midst of a housebreaking program, adhering to a rigid feeding schedule (carefully measured amounts of food at 7 A.M. and 5 P.M., for example) works best.

Apply Some Pet Design to Your Place

The best pet, the best equipment, even the best training, all fall short of the best solution—the simple logical process of building with pets in mind. A few hours and a few dollars spent on this will save you thousands of hours and dollars and a lot of unkind thoughts about your pets.

Prevention is the key. If the mess never happens, you've saved yourself the work. First, apply the following basic maintenance-lowering principles:

Seal or apply stain repellent to all unsealed surfaces, so stains can't get in and stay (see page 61).

Keep animals on hard floors whenever possible. Hard floors are easier to clean, and don't give fleas and their eggs the universe of places to hide that carpet does.

If you have dogs, however, avoid any laminate flooring. Attractive and durable as it is, dogs have a hard time with it—because their nails are always out, they slip and fall on its slick surface.

Select wall coverings and paints that are moisture-proof and scrubbable.

What else can you do to save cleaning time if you have animals in the house? Read on!

Simplify Your Home

Get rid of the excess that complicates the cleaning effort. An animal is bound to disrupt a few things if a house is a maze of trinkets and decorations, so pet-proof the house just as you would kid-proof it:

Put small breakable things high on sturdy shelves.

Minimize loose things such as pillows that can be disarranged.

The fewer things on the floor, the better.

Hang things up out of their reach. Pets, like children, are curious and sometimes bored. They'll experiment with anything that looks interesting, and may make a mess.

Give the Animal His Own Place

Do this so he doesn't make a ruin of yours. Concentrate your pet's living area whenever possible. Keep all his care needs there, or at least together, to save time and storage mess.

Provide entertainment for your pets. If an animal has his own play area and toys, he's more likely to leave yours alone.

Apply Structure Discipline

Anything that will close, spring back, or reseal itself after use is an answer to a pet owner's prayers. Choosing short curtains so the cat can't swing on them is structure discipline. Closed doors are structure discipline. So are the shelves too high to jump for, or stereo speakers mounted where they can't be scratched. If you don't want the animal in an area, structure things so he can't get in.

Build In or Suspend Things

Get things up off the ground whenever you can—shelves, appliances, tables, beds, bookshelves, and other furniture. You'll eliminate cracks that collect hair, and all those cozy little hiding places where your pet likes to take his "kill" and chew on it.

Attached furnishings won't allow a pet to disrupt them. Table lamps, for example, are one of pets' favorite things to knock over. But if you hang lamps from the ceiling or wall-mount them, they don't have to be dusted around, don't offer cords to be chewed, and give you more usable light from fewer fixtures. And they'll never get knocked over again.

You can also build in or suspend such things as dog-houses, pet beds, and playthings; food and water dishes; and shelves for pet supplies. Suspend a little basket on the wall so your pet can stick his head in and get his toys out, and then all his toys can be put back there when he's done. Or go a step further and train him to put his toys back!

Install Surfaces That Endure

Hard, smooth, tough, nonabsorbent surfaces such as plastic laminate (Formica), vinyl, or tile will help a lot in places such as the wall next to the litter box or the pet bed or beside the birdcage. **Plastic laminate is also a good choice** for tabletops, wall units, counters, bureaus, and the legs of furniture in pet territory. Slops and stains will wipe right off— laminate will repel almost anything and hold up to abuse. And it's available in an incredible variety of colors and finishes.

For the most part, glass is a pet-proof material, too, because it only has to be washed. Animals can't scratch it, stain it, or chew on it. A mirror on a door, for example, will pet-proof it as well as serve human grooming purposes. Cats, especially, tend to avoid slick or shiny, smooth surfaces.

If scratching is a concern, choose hardwood for wood-work, windowsills, and wood furnishings, rather than soft-woods that can be easily damaged.

Select Low-Maintenance Fabrics

Choose low-maintenance fabrics for home furnishings such as upholstered furniture, drapes, and bedspreads. Tightly woven, smooth-surfaced fabrics such as chintz are strong and durable and will resist a few little claw marks. And they're less likely to attract and hold hair.

If you have cats, try to tailor your furniture away from "nubby" or highly textured fabrics and wicker or other coarsely woven natural or synthetic fibers. **Anything with a loose or open weave invites cats and dogs to pull at it,** fiddle with it, claw or scratch it. And any filmy, delicate fabric can be shredded in seconds. Slick-surfaced fabrics are much less tempting to a scratcher.

Choose Easy-to-Clean Designs

Look ahead to save yourself trouble and heartache and to make pet accidents easier to deal with if they do happen. Choose upholstered furniture with removable cushions, for example, and flooring that does not have tiny crevices or indentations to harbor germs and traces of pet mess.

Cover It If You Can

Prevent pet damage by covering vulnerable surfaces and furnishings, whenever practical. Make sure you have protective covers on comforters and bed quilts, and even the mattress itself if Kitty has started to think that marking his owner's comfy bed is a neat idea. Get attractive slipcovers or "pet throws" (see Chapter 6) for furniture that pets like to occupy. Put a sturdy, good-looking runner over the top of the coffee table—its handsome grain would *not* be enhanced by claw marks.

Wax to Minimize Pet Mess

The floor in a pet home needs extra protection. Waxing will protect hard-surface floors from spills, stains, grit, sand, and gravel, as well as the usual scuffs, heel marks, and dirt that would otherwise be ground into the surface. Wax or "floor finish" also keeps a floor, especially an unsealed one (see page 62, later in this chapter), from absorbing odors and will even help protect it from scratching.

Even "no-wax" floors need a coat of floor finish or dressing at all times to protect and preserve their bright, glossy surface.

A good professional acrylic finish ("wax") such as Top Gloss from a janitorial-supply store will last a lot longer than anything you buy in the supermarket. Its hard finish is self-polishing, so it doesn't need to be buffed or shined.

The Best Carpeting for Pets

Well, the best carpeting when you have a pet is no carpeting, but we humans do love carpet. So the next-best solution is to select all-synthetic fibers. Wool and cotton are absolute no-no's from a pet mess prevention standpoint; natural fibers absorb everything and that means odors and stains for sure. Nylon, Antron, polyester, and olefin loop pile, especially in "commercial grade" carpeting, are good choices for a carpet in heavy pet use areas. They resist staining, clean up easily, and hold up well under abrasion and wear. The best carpets for holding their color under the assault of stains are those in which the color is added as the synthetic fiber itself is being made—before it's formed into yarn. When the color is built right into the fiber this way, it won't easily fade.

Soil retardant such as Scotchgard Carpet Protector or my own Timesaver Carpet and Fabric Protector can make a big difference in carpet's ability to resist animal abuse. The protective film (such as Teflon) that a retardant puts on the fibers doesn't alter the feel or look of carpet, but it keeps stains and moisture from soaking in. **If you're recarpeting, be sure the carpet has a stain repellent applied at the mill,** or look for the carpets made from the new synthetic materials that simply won't absorb a stain. These go by names like Stainmaster, and even red punch won't penetrate these fibers, so anything from grape juice to urine or blood can be picked right up.

There are also carpets made now with built-in odor resistance, and even built-in enzymes which when activated by moisture in the carpet automatically go to work on the odor. Carpets like these include Mohawk's Forever Fresh and Hollytex Ultimate Performance carpet.

If you have cat and dog accident concerns and are recarpeting, consider installing padding with a moisture barrier, such as Wetlock carpet cushioning by Mohawk. Or in rooms that don't need cushy, deluxe carpeting, have carpet glued down, with no padding beneath it. Then, when accidents do occur, they can't seep down into the padding, creating a very hard-to-remove reservoir of odor and stain. And **underneath the carpet, in pet use areas, concrete is the best surface**—sealed, of course.

If you have cats, or any pet whose hobby is scratching, avoid Berber carpeting or any style with loops, large or small. Otherwise, before long you will have little runs all over it, and perhaps even entire rows of fiber pulled out here and there!

In rooms where pets spend a lot of time, it may be better for you to have area rugs than wall-to-wall carpet. With an area rug, you can simply pick up the rug and apply a pet stain remover or bacteria/enzyme digester (see page 102, Chapter 3) and then machine wash or dry-clean the whole thing to get the smell and spot completely out.

Carpet tiles are another good idea for using in areas where pets live or spend a lot of time. They're available in textures from short loop to shag, they're easy to install (they're laid down exactly like hard floor tiles), and they look just like regular carpet once they're installed. If an animal has an accident, you can just pull up the whole 12″ × 12″ square to clean or replace it, to *completely* eliminate odor.

A textured or multilevel carpet in medium, variegated tones or tweed will hide the most, and a plush carpet with varied hues of the same basic color in it is the next best for hiding dirt and animal hair. Deep shags are the hardest to clean and offer the snuggest home for fleas. Stick to tightly woven dense piles and, of course, synthetics like nylon.

If you match the color of your carpet, drapes, and furnishings to your pet (no, I'm not kidding), those dropped locks will show less.

Camouflage Whenever You Can

Choose colors and fabrics that won't show an occasional hair or crumb. Prints are better than plain solid colors, and lighter is better than darker. Animal hair will advertise itself on dark finishes, especially dark glossy finishes. Natural wood finishes, especially distressed wood, will hide little imperfections better than paint. Match your colors (furniture, drapes, and carpeting) to your animals and mess will show less.

Seal It Out

I've received some blank looks in my cleaning seminars when I advise people to "seal" their floors, concrete, couches, carpets, corners, and fireplace brick. I finally realized that a dramatic demonstration was in order.

Now, when I am discussing sealing for an audience, I hold a piece of clear Plexiglas over the knee of my crisp new suit and pour filthy water over it. Then I ask the audience why my suit isn't getting wet, dirty, and ruined. "Because," they yell back, "there's a piece of plastic protecting it." That's what sealing basically does—it puts a transparent protective coating over a surface, a "membrane" finish that moisture can't penetrate.

I'm sure you can see the value of this where pets are concerned. Urine will soak into an unsealed surface and the odor from the residue will be reactivated every time the area gets damp or wet. Clean-up will now require more chemicals and be five times harder. But if a surface is sealed, when the spray hits, it won't soak in, stain, or be hard to clean off.

On well-sealed surfaces, you can use water-based cleaners and deodorizers to keep the area clean and free of odors. **Sealing costs little and pays big, especially when it comes to ease of cleaning.** And you may be surprised to learn how many different materials and surfaces around your house can be sealed.

Sealing can be done with many substances, most often with a varnishlike coating that's sprayed, brushed, rolled, mopped, or wiped on. Apply a sealer in two or three light coats, letting it dry well in between, rather than one heavy one. And keep an eye on a sealed surface over time to make sure the sealing is still intact. If it begins to chip and wear off, it's time to smooth the surface, if necessary, and to reapply.

Urethane sealers are great for wood and concrete floors. Acrylic (water-based) sealers can be used on concrete, quarry tile, terrazzo, and the like. Semigloss or gloss enamel paint will effectively seal walls or vertical structures such as posts. For brick and stone, a layer of low-luster clear acrylic or masonry sealer will be almost invisible, yet will prevent pet spraying, smoke, and oily hand or pawprints from staining your beautiful masonry surfaces.

Soil retardants such as Scotchgard are the greatest for anything made of fabric, establishing a barrier against dirt and odor penetration. They also make the treated item easier to clean when it does need cleaning, because spills will bead up on the surface rather than soak in. Soil retardants will come off when you wash a fabric item, but you can retreat the surface back into durability easily.

Most newer carpeting comes already treated with a soil retardant such as Scotchgard or Dupont Stainmaster. You can have a soil retardant applied at the mill or factory to large items like upholstered furniture, usually for an minimal charge. You can also get soil retardant at a supermarket or janitorial-supply store to treat furnishings and objects you already own, but be sure they're cleaned well before you apply the retardant.

The spray bottles of soil retardant are great for treating furniture, clothing, and small articles and surfaces like accessories. For carpeting, a Teflon and fluorocarbon soil retardant such as Carpet Guard, Scotchgard Carpet Protector, or Stainshield is what you need. Some of these can be purchased in gallon jugs at a janitorial-supply house and self-applied; others must be applied by a professional carpet cleaner.

Even if your carpet is treated with soil retardant, you still want to work as quickly as possible on urine stains, before the stain seeps, by sheer gravity, past the carpet fibers into the backing and pad.

On carpeting, too, stain retardant must be reapplied after deep cleaning or shampooing.

After they're dry, soil-retardant treated surfaces are perfectly safe for your pets, but make sure you apply the product in a well-ventilated area away from your pets, and don't use the treated article until it dries.

Chapter 3

Housetraining and Litter Boxes:

The #1 Solutions to the #1 Pet Cleaning Problem

> The importance of thorough housebreaking cannot be overemphasized. Everything that makes dogs worthwhile, enjoyable companions is destroyed if they can't be trusted in the house.
>
> —The American Kennel Club

There's no way around it—housetraining can make or break your whole relationship with your pet. More dogs are abandoned for house-soiling problems than for any other reason.

(We'll talk about housebreaking dogs here; the equally important housetraining of cats is covered later in the chapter.)

We have some powerful forces on our side in the housebreaking process. Dogs are easy to train because their natural instincts fit right in with our house environment. **Dogs never want to soil their den where they sleep or eat—** even a four-week-old puppy will stumble away from his box to urinate.

All we're essentially doing in housebreaking is teaching a dog to extend its den to include the entire house.

It's important to understand that housebreaking and paper-training are not the same thing. *Housebreaking* means a dog is never allowed to eliminate inside the house. *Paper-training* means the dog relieves himself inside the house, but only in a specific place that never changes, and on sheets of newspaper. (Dogs can be trained to use a litter box, just like cats, and a box of shredded newspaper or even cat litter is actually a lot cleaner than sheets of newspaper on the floor.) There also are "puppy pads," such as those made by Bramton, which are made of a disposable diaper–like material, with a layer of protective plastic on the bottom. They also incorporate synthetic dog pheromones that actually attract a puppy to using them.

If you have physical disabilities that make it hard to walk your dog, have a puppy that hasn't been immunized yet that you don't want to take out in the street, or some other good reason why you can't housebreak your dog, then paper-training may be the way to go. Otherwise, training your dog to defecate and urinate outside is usually preferable.

Not realizing that paper-training isn't a prelude to housebreaking, but an entirely separate and different training system, many people make the mistake of putting a puppy on newspaper inside the home and encouraging him to eliminate there. Then they try to teach him to go outside, but he continues to mess on the floor because that's how he was first trained.

Don't confuse your dog this way. **Choose one type of toilet training and stick with it.** If you have a puppy that you leave in a crate, playpen, or other confined area while you're gone during the day, you may need to use newspapers simply to protect the floor or absorb any accidents that occur while you're gone. Just don't praise him for using them—save that for when he relieves himself outside, to help eliminate confusion about where you prefer him to go.

The basic ingredients of housebreaking are confining your pet in some manner during the training period; setting up a carefully planned feeding, watering, and walking schedule (and sticking with it so your pet is conditioned to *regularity* of elimination); and giving your pet lots of praise when he does the right thing. Confinement—especially important during the parts of the housebreaking period when no one is home—can be accomplished with a dog crate, a puppy playpen, or a pet gate.

Confining in Cages and Crates

There are lots of good reasons to crate-train your dog. Whenever a dog is feeling stressed, ill, or just tired, he can go to his own little place and enjoy peace and quiet. When he's in his crate, he won't be able to get into trouble (which you'll have to clean up), so he's spared the anxiety and confusion of wrong behavior.

With a crate, a regular elimination routine can be quickly established, greatly reducing the likelihood of accidents. Your pet will have an easier time learning to control his bowels, because a dog does not like to deposit his wastes in the area he considers his den—so he'll usually relieve himself only when you let him out of the crate.

Most people, upon being advised to crate-train their pet, react with doubt and horror—"*What! Put my dog in a CAGE? How cruel! I couldn't do it*—and he'd hate me forever if I tried." But after he's chewed up the coffee table, scratched the walls, and wet on the dining-room floor for the umpteenth time, many of the same people who feel they could never cage their pet see nothing wrong with punishing or abusing him, or giving him up to a pound or a shelter where his chances of finding a new home are slim. Some people will even decide to dump the animal off somewhere to fend for itself—now *that* is cruelty. Actually, because the dog is instinctively a den animal and will very likely seek his own enclosed, protected space—under a bed, desk, shelf, table, etc.—*he* views the crate as a security blanket, a nice private sanctuary of his very own, a "bed with a door." The fact that the door can be shut usually bothers the owner far more than the dog.

Though crates are mostly used for dogs, **a cat that is ill, destructive, or having problems with litter training is a candidate for crating, too.** Because cats don't take to crates as readily as dogs, first try the separate room confinement method. If this doesn't work, then try using a crate.

As animal behaviorist Gwen Bohnenkamp says:

> When introducing your pet to a crate, den, or confinement area, *go slowly.* Make the area a pleasant place to be. Spend time there with your pet. Don't just toss [him] in and walk away. Make it one of the pet's favorite places by giving [him] extra special attention, affection, and treats only when [he] is there. Start out by confining [him] for short periods, and gradually increase the time until you can leave [him] for several hours.

The wire cage type is best for home use because it can be used covered or draped to create a cozy den, or uncovered for more vision and ventilation and to permit the dog to feel like part of the family while confined.

Wire cages are lightweight and fold up for easy storage and portability. Some are slanted on one end to fit in hatchback vehicles and small SUVs.

The better models are made of stainless steel or chrome-plated or epoxy-coated wire with a removable floor pan or tray. The unplated wire cages might cost less and do just as good a job of keeping the pet inside, but they're more susceptible to rust and can discolor the coat of light-colored animals.

Some dogs feel too vulnerable in a wire cage and prefer the security of the more enclosed atmosphere of airline crates. Airline crates restrict a dog's vision more, although the door is usually made of wire and there are wire windows or vents in the sides. Airline crates are usually made of molded plastic, metal, fiberglass, or wood or a combination of these. Fiberglass is frowned upon as a crate material by some pet experts because of the danger posed by splinters if the dog chews on the crate. And the molded plastic crates are definitely susceptible to being chomped on, especially if you have a dog that already has a chewing problem.

Keep in mind that crating is *not* recommended for keeping your dog confined and alone for hours on end while you're away at work, school, or wherever. But if you must make use of the crating technique for at least occasional extended periods, be sure to make up for the dog's time in the crate by giving him lots of exercise and freedom to be with you when you're home. If it's not too far from where you work, go home at lunchtime and take your dog for a short walk to allow him to exercise and relieve himself (if he's a puppy, you probably should give him something to eat, depending upon his housebreaking schedule).

If you have a friendly neighbor nearby who likes dogs, ask or hire him or her to walk your dog for you during the day. Better yet, hire a bonded and insured professional pet walker to do it.

Or you could adjust your full-grown pet's feeding schedule to one meal early in the evening so he'll eliminate before you go to bed, and the urge to go won't be as great during the day while he's crated inside. And when you're leaving a dog in a crate, be sure you leave him with some toys, water in a clip-on dish that can't be spilled, and something to sleep on.

Crate Cleaning

The easiest way to get an empty crate thoroughly clean is to load it into the back of your car—or, if you don't want a mess in your car, into the back of a pickup truck—and **run it down to the do-it-yourself car wash to give it a high-pressure spray cleaning.** If it needs to be sterilized or has a lot of stubborn buildup, you could even take it someplace that has a steam pressure spray (the kind they clean motors with to make them look brand-new). Set the cage down on the floor over the drain and have them shoot it with superhot water that will loosen every bit of dirt and dried doo-doo. The heat will kill the germs and ensure that the weld joints (potential rust spots) dry quickly.

A home pressure washer will do a good job. Or you can simply put the cage out on the driveway, sidewalk, or other hard surface outdoors and hit it with a garden hose, a scrub brush, and some all-purpose cleaning solution or a cleaner like Nilodor Deodorizing Cleaner. Let the cleaning solution sit on there for a few minutes—just don't let it dry—then scrub or wipe the whole crate down, inside and out, with an aggressive brush or nylon pad to dislodge the stuck-on stuff. Then give it another quick shot of solution (after all, the most time-consuming part—getting set up—is already done. It'll take only two minutes to soap and scrub it down again). Now rinse it with the hose, and if you want to disinfect, apply a Nolvasan solution and leave it on there for five minutes. Then rinse well again, and slap the cage with the palm of your hand to shake off all the excess moisture, so it won't dry slowly and rust. If at all possible, put it in the sun to speed up drying.

In between cage cleanings, go over all the wire surfaces every so often with a vacuum dust brush attachment. This may seem unnecessary because you can't see anything on it, but trust me. There *is*, and getting rid of all that dust and clinging dirt and hair will keep things cleaner and more sanitary.

More complete information on crating can be found in *A Pet Owner's Guide to the Dog Crate* by Nicki Meyer. For a copy, send a stamped, self-addressed, business-size envelope and twenty cents to: The Nicki Meyer Educational Effort, Inc., 31 Davis Hill Road, Weston, CT 06883; 203-226-9877.

For an explanation of how to use crates and confinement to correct litter-box problems in cats, as well as other behavior problems in cats and dogs, contact Gwen Bohnenkamp at *www.perfectpaws.com*.

Declare Certain Parts of the House Off-Limits

Even if your pet is completely housetrained, there may still be areas in your home where you'd like to establish his presence as verboten. Places like the nursery, or the room with the Oriental rug, for example—to keep down the amount of shed fur, protect particularly valuable furnishings, or for your pet's own protection.

Designate areas in the house where your animal is allowed and areas where he's not—that way, only those rooms have to be given the extra care animal cleaning requires. (The rooms animals do inhabit will have to be vacuumed more often and deodorized from time to time, and will require a little more miscellaneous cleaning—see Chapter 1.)

Be clear with your pet when designating a specific area as off-limits. If you do not have good verbal control of your dog, have him drag a leash so you can physically stop him from entering "the zone" until he stops making attempts. **Praise him every time he makes the right choice and doesn't enter the off-limits area.**

When you're inside the forbidden room, keep the squirt bottle handy; otherwise, just keep the door closed or use a pet gate (see following section). When you are not around to supervise, you can also use an electronic detection device to set up a perimeter that, if breached, will emit a tone or an odor pets dislike, such as citronella. These work for both dogs and cats. For dogs that are hard to keep in bounds, there are indoor versions of the "invisible fence" systems used outdoors.

Dogs that are not trustworthy regarding house soiling, destructive chewing, scavenging, etc., should be crated or confined to an exercise pen when you are not able to supervise their activities. Cats who possess the same qualities should be confined to a cattery cage so, like the untrained dog, they can't make the wrong move while you are out of the house.

A Pet Gate

Setting up a pet gate will enable you to keep a dog in a particular part of the house without sealing him away behind a closed door. Isolating a dog alone in a room with the door closed can make him feel so cut off from the rest of the family that he freaks out and forgets his housetraining or scratches up the walls or door. Most adult dogs can be trained to respect a gate and not jump over it, and pet gates will keep puppies and perhaps very young kittens from venturing into other rooms. Cats tend to jump over these barriers with ease.

Most gates designed to serve as indoor barriers can be adjusted to fit standard-size doorways. Although child gates can be used, some of these leave enough space for a small pet to squeeze through, or worse, to get its head stuck. And wooden gates can be chewed into dangerous splinters. The metal or hard plastic gates made especially for pets are better since they have smaller openings, yet aren't completely opaque. (Pets like to at least see what's going on, even if they can't join in the action.) A cottage or Dutch door with the top left open can also serve as a pet gate.

Playpens

Young animals, just like young humans, can be kept in a playpen at times or for short periods to keep them out of trouble and confine their messes to one place. This can be a wire exercise pen, a converted human playpen, or a playpen built especially for pets. Playpens are most often used for kittens, puppies, and small adult dogs, but they can be a nice place for a rabbit to frolic in, too.

If you're using a doggie playpen for puppies, you can keep their bed, toys, food, and water right in there with them. They'll play and sleep on one side of the pen, and use the other side to relieve themselves. **A tray on the bottom of the pen will keep the newspapers you lay down from touching the floor, so no odor will be transferred to the floor.** This is a big help in avoiding later housebreaking problems.

Some playpens have a wire grate across the bottom about 1 inch above the floor to allow the droppings and urine to fall through to the newspaper-covered tray below. This keeps the pup's floor cleaner and drier, and prevents him from stepping in his own waste.

Most exercise pens don't have trays in the bottom, so if you use a pen indoors, you'll have to use several small trays or a piece of sealed plywood to cover the floor—or be sure you put the pen on a sealed hard floor.

More Housebreaking How-Tos

Cleaning is actually critical to the success of housetraining. A dog has a natural inclination to go again in places where he, or other dogs, has gone before. So **if you don't clean up promptly and completely after accidents, you're actually cueing him to a repeat performance.** It's also important to remove any old urine or feces odors that may be found in the carpet, floors, or furnishings in your home from previous pets you've had, or even pets someone else had before you moved in. (More on exactly how to do this is in Chapter 4.)

If you paper-train, put a plastic sheet underneath the paper. Or, consider using the commercially available "piddle pads" to prevent urine from seeping through and leaving odor on the floor. Simple Solution Puppy Training Pads have a plastic liner and a chemical attractant to pull puppies to the pad. And, of course, you never want to paper-train a dog on an absorbent surface—only on easy-to-clean surfaces like vinyl or ceramic tile, so any urine or feces that leaks through the paper won't soak into the floor to become a scent marker for the dog to return to later.

Clean your pet's crate or bed or pen promptly if he happens to have a slip there—never let a puppy stay in a soiled bed or crate. Another important principle of housebreaking is not allowing your pet the chance to make mistakes in the first place. Don't give him the opportunity to eliminate indoors without being observed and receiving immediate disapproval. Be alert to the subtle signs of "about to . . ." Generally, when a dog has to relieve himself, he sniffs close to the ground and may whimper or whine, followed by squatting and elimination. With a young puppy, the time between the sniffs and squats might be very short, or he might not give any sign at all. So immediately after the pup wakes up, or right after he's eaten, or after you've been playing with him, you'll have to take him right to where you want him to go. (Don't drop him right outside the back door to do his duty. That's *not* where you want him in the habit of going.) Once he's relieved himself, praise him enthusiastically and he'll come to understand that relieving himself in the right place will make you happy, which is all dogs want their master to be.

Don't expect your pet to be reliably housebroken until he's received four to six months of consistent training and feedback. Puppies younger than four months don't have full control over the muscles involved in elimination until then. And **forget the old wives' tale about rubbing your pet's nose in it to teach him a lesson.** You won't teach him a lesson, but you will frighten and confuse him. (And maybe get him into the exasperating and hard-to-break habit of eating his own stools.) Unless you actually catch your pet in the act, attempts to "correct" housebreaking mistakes don't accomplish much.

There are lots of good books on housebreaking your dog, and the following are a few I especially recommend:

- *How to Housebreak Your Dog in 7 Days*
  by Shirlee Kalstone

- *When Good Dogs Do Bad Things*
  by Mathew Margolis and Mordecai Siegal

- *The Evans Guide for Housetraining Your Dog*
  by Job Michael Evans

- *Good Owners, Great Dogs*
  by Brian Kilcommons and Sarah Wilson

Just remember that the more patience, effort, determination, persistence, and love you put into the few short weeks of housetraining your pet, the faster the training will take effect. And that means less piddle, poop, mess, odor, stain, aggravation, and clean-up.

For Cats

Litter training is essential, but we can't take much credit for it. A cat's natural instinct is to dig a hole in the ground, do its duty in the hole, then cover it up. And the litter box, being the nearest thing to soft earth and the most convenient place to exercise that instinct indoors, is what they'll use—once they know where the box is. You can usually litter train a cat in about twenty seconds—the time it takes to introduce him to the litter box. Sometimes you might have to restrict a cat to a single room for a while to reduce the ground he has to cover to find the box and realize its function, but once he finds it, he'll use it.

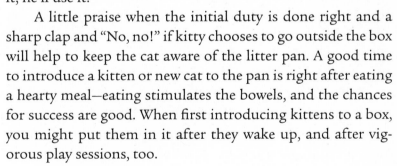

A little praise when the initial duty is done right and a sharp clap and "No, no!" if kitty chooses to go outside the box will help to keep the cat aware of the litter pan. A good time to introduce a kitten or new cat to the pan is right after eating a hearty meal—eating stimulates the bowels, and the chances for success are good. When first introducing kittens to a box, you might put them in it after they wake up, and after vigorous play sessions, too.

The Best Boxes

The litter box is a simple concept, but there must be thousands of choices about how to set it up, where to put it, what litter to use, etc. You can go from totally primitive to Plush Flush (yes, there are boxes now designed to look like colonial cottages or log cabins, and ones with oak trim, cedar shake shingles, and interior wall hangings—and an awesome array of boxes that clean themselves). There are only a few basic principles to bear in mind for odor control and easy box maintenance, so your and your cat's personal opinions are very much to the point here. What you choose to use can make a big difference in how pleasant your pet areas are to spend time in, and how people feel about visiting your house!

> "What's my least favorite chore? Cleaning the kitty box, because it smells bad and looks worse!"

What Kitty Likes . . . Counts

Nope, he isn't necessarily spoiled or finicky. Just like us, our pets feel comfortable with certain things and places over others. Our last cat might have loved and faithfully used a blue plastic litter pan with beet chip litter, but due to some inborn inclination or bad past experience, your new cat may be repulsed by it and refuse to go near it.

An important principle of success when it comes to choosing the type of box and litter to use is finding something your cat really likes. Cats won't do anything they don't want to do, and they especially won't use a potty not of their choosing, so don't get shook if your cat selects a stark open pan over the El Supremo heated toilet chamber.

Plain Open Boxes

Most cats seem to prefer simple boxes. These are also the least expensive. Some important issues to keep in mind here include the size and shape of the box. **A litter box needs to be big enough for cats to turn around in comfortably,** so if you have a big cat, you need a big box. For kittens and aged, ill, or injured cats, you want a box with shorter sides so they can get in and out easily. Make sure the box is heavy enough that it can't be tipped easily, or you will have a big mess on your hands. And if you plan to use clumping litter (see following), make sure the bottom of the box is smooth, without ridges, channels, or indentations. Most open litter boxes are a simple rectangle design, but boxes designed to fit into the corners of a room are available.

Plastic Dishpans and Boxes with Rims

Len Waxman, author of the *First Ever Cat Owner's Guide to Preventing Litter Box Odor the No-Frills Way*, maintains that the best and most perfect cat litter container is a kitchen dishpan. This is the standard 11" × 13" plastic pan with sides that are 6 or even 8 inches high, which will reduce spillage and tracked-out litter. (If you have a kitten, you need a pan with sides no more than 5 to 7 inches high.)

A dishpan has built-in handles and is easy to carry, clean, dump, and replace. Lots of folks get two of these since they're inexpensive. Then, if you're gone for a while and the litter box gets soiled to the point where a cat won't piddle in it, he'll revert to the other and not the floor.

This is too small for a litter box, you say? It's plenty big enough for a cat to turn around in, yet small enough to make it likely that your pet will urinate against the side or in the corner of the pan. The advantage of this will be explained shortly.

Boxes with rims have a wide lip all around the top that leans inward. This type of box is good for unneutered male cats because when the cat sprays, the rim keeps it from spraying out onto the walls and floor. This style of box also does a lot to prevent tracking.

Covered Litter Boxes

Having a covered litter box can help with the spraying problem, too. The cover helps to hide the box and to keep mess down—you can be sure that the litter will stay in the box. And it does keep down odor to a degree—at least *outside* the box.

The trouble is, **covers actually concentrate the odors inside the box,** even to the point that cats may be highly reluctant to use it, especially if you've neglected to clean it (which is more possible with covered boxes—out of sight, out of mind). The lid on covered boxes comes off and you should take it off to clean the litter regularly if you choose this style of box.

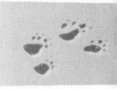

A covered box with a filter to absorb odor does a better job of keeping odor down than a covered box without a filter. The Boodabox, which has a charcoal filter built into the top, is a popular example of this style.

There are a wide variety of covered boxes, and some of these are ingeniously designed and attractive. But none of them fully escapes the big drawback of the covered box, which is that it gets too smelly to be attractive to cats, especially in a multi-cat household.

You can, however, make your own jumbo covered box that your cats will like and use, and it costs a lot less than most of the commercial covered boxes. Get a large plastic Rubbermaid or Sterilite storage container (at least 18-gallon size, but the larger the better). Cut one or two cat-size openings in it at least 5 inches from the bottom, and there it is. Just remove the lid to scoop. (Because the bottom of such boxes usually has channels or indentations, you will want to use a thicker layer of litter in this, to avoid scooping problems with clumping litter.) You can even put a soft mat on top of the plastic lid and cats will enjoy lying on it.

Self-Cleaning Boxes

There are a growing number of these, and although the most elaborate of them are expensive ($200–$300 and up), the best of them can really minimize one of cat owners' least favorite chores.

Some of the best of the fancy electronic models on the market are the Litter Robot (*www.litter-robot.com*) and the Littermaid Mega Advanced Self Cleaning Litter Box (800-548-6243). Units like these have a motion sensor that activates the scooper about ten minutes after kitty has done his thing. It is usually desirable to use one of the better-quality litters (see following), or at least clumping litter, with machines of this type.

If you want to streamline litter-scooping chores, but don't want to spring for the high-end self-cleaning boxes, there are less expensive models that partially automate the chore for $40–$60 or so. Boxes like these include the Omega Paw Self Cleaning Litter Box and Poopsie Cat.

Whatever box you choose, though, remember the first principle of design—keep it simple. If things are too elaborate and complicated, they won't get used. If the box is hard to use, lift, carry, dump, or clean, your pet will delay using it and you'll delay or avoid cleaning it and the result will be odors and anger at the animal.

Creative Concealment

If you had to walk eight miles to the toilet, wouldn't you just go quietly behind a bush?

Pets aren't that different from us, and their elimination drive is just as urgent. When you gotta go, you gotta go, and you don't want to climb, dig, hunt, and wait for a place forever. So you want to be sure the box is handy and available to the cat at any hour of the day or night—and that there are enough boxes, if you have multiple cats.

Like us, cats have some modesty, so they appreciate a little privacy as well as convenience. **Don't put the litter box near the cat's feeding area or in a noisy or heavily trafficked spot.** Many people seem to feel that the laundry room is a great place for a box, but usually it's far too hectic. A place with a little concealment is best. Just make sure the box is set on a hard, nonabsorbent surface such as ceramic tile or seamless vinyl, otherwise any litter box accidents or overshots that occur will ensure "go here again" signals.

Generally, your cat will use the box wherever you put it, but some cats will select their own spot and go there. Remember: What kitty likes counts. Move the litter box to that spot. On the other hand, don't keep switching the location of the litter box, or you may confuse your cat and up the accident ratio.

And if you have a large house, a number of cats, or an older cat who can't get around as easily as he once did, again, be sure to put litter pans in more than one location.

An open box is the cheapest, simplest to service, and most attractive to a cat, but it isn't the sort of thing a guest (or any of us for that matter) cares to gaze upon. The available space in every home differs, of course, but here are a couple of good places to consider when it comes to concealment.

The Bathtub or Shower

What better place to hide the box—you can just pull the shower curtain or shut the shower door. It's close to the toilet, too, for quick disposal of solid wastes. And since the tub has a hard, waterproof surface and a built-in water supply, it's one of the easiest places in the house to clean and disinfect. Bathrooms have built-in fans to dissipate odor, too.

Place a heavy towel in the bottom of the tub or floor of the shower and set the litter box in the middle of it. The toweling should extend at least 4 inches beyond the sides of the box to protect the bottom of the tub or shower and give your pet some traction on the slick tub surface. This will also serve as a little doormat to collect any litter that clings to your cat's paws after a visit to the box. Then when you're servicing the pan, you simply lift the towel up and dump any loose litter back into the pan. You want to be careful to keep litter, especially the clumping type, from going down the drain—it could collect and cause drain blockage.

Cat in the Cupboard

Inside a lower cupboard can be a good place for the litter box, too, if you can train your cat to open the door (and all smart cat owners claim they can). When the cat needs to go, he just paws open the door and uses the box. The advantage of this location is, again, concealment. Just be sure the cupboard has a latch a cat can handle. You can also install a pet door in the cupboard door, if you don't mind sacrificing it. But don't use a kitchen cupboard for this, because a litter box can carry harmful E. coli bacteria, so you don't want it anywhere near where you prepare food. And you'll want to regularly disinfect a cupboard used for this purpose.

The following are some cupboard possibilities:

Place the box in a closet or pantry with the door ajar (if you're in the giddy position of having a closet to spare for the purpose).

Install a cat door. Cathole (*www.cathole.com*) offers an indoor cat door specially made for closets, pantries, and the like.

Put the box in the garage—with a pet door or passageway to it from the house—it's discreet and convenient to the garbage can.

Take out the large bottom drawer of a piece of furniture and replace it with the box, and then string a little curtain across the front.

Put the box on the bottom shelf of built-in floor-to-ceiling shelves, again, with a curtain across the front of the shelf.

You could even construct a square or rectangular bottomless cabinet of sealed, stained plywood, with a cat-size entryway in one side. There are wooden surrounds available from pet specialty catalogs and sites for just this purpose.

Devise your own or purchase one of the attractive "privacy screens" or fabric tent coverings commercially available for a box that has to be in a more conspicuous spot.

Getting Down to the Real Kitty-Gritty

Shredded newspapers, sand, dirt, sawdust, wood shavings, and probably two dozen other things could be used in a pinch, but it costs a dollar less to go first class, especially when it comes to cat litter. Soggy newspaper, for example, inks up an animal's feet and cats don't like standing on it. A lot of things will work, but what works best for you and your cat? There is quite a smorgasbord of litters available today.

Plain old clay commercial cat litter—the "generic" kind—is inexpensive, easy to store, and easy to find at the corner market. If you use a lot of litter, you can buy it in bulk (50-pound bags). Clay litters absorb and hold the liquids and solids of cat waste efficiently, and they do a far better job of minimizing odor than does shredded paper, dirt, or wood shavings. **Look for a brand that isn't excessively dusty, and always pour litter slowly to keep down dust.** The sharp little silicate or clay particles of litter dust aren't good for lungs or allergies, cat or human.

Clumping litter, often also made of clay, has finer particles than ordinary clay litter, less dust, and forms firmer, more distinct clumps when cats urinate in it. This is an important point because it is the urine in litter boxes that causes the worst odor over time. Clumping litter is more expensive than plain clay litter, but if faithfully scooped out, it lasts longer. Be careful—if you spill some litter and it gets wet, or leave a bucket of it out in the rain, you have a sticky mess on your hands.

Crystal litter is one of the newer entries to the litter box scene, made of something similar to silica gel, the little packets of desiccant used in shoeboxes and the like. It, too, is more expensive than plain clay, but it can be used longer, and it is not as heavy to lug around as clay litter. It does an exceptional job of keeping down urine odor but doesn't cover or deodorize cat "Tootsie Rolls" as well as clay litter does. And you need to be careful that pets don't swallow any of it, because it could possibly cause intestinal blockage.

Different brands of crystal litter have different-shaped grains—some are round, some more irregular. Cats like the round grains better but those tiny balls multiply the litter tracking problem big-time! Some of the better brands for superior odor control plus reduced tracking are: Track-Less Litter Pearls, Carefree Kitty Litter Beads, and Fresh Step Crystals Cat Litter.

There are also litters that are a blend of crystal litter and regular clumping litter, to get the superior odor control of crystals while minimizing the disadvantages. You can make your own such blend by mixing a bit of crystal litter into clay or clumping litter.

Alternative litters include litters made from corncobs, corn itself, wood, recycled paper, wheat (super sticky when wet), and who knows what tomorrow. For the most part, these alternative litters are more expensive and often more trackable than the ones you will find in the supermarket, but they are less dusty, lighter, and often more attractive to cats; offer good or superior odor control; and are biodegradable. Some have additional additives like antimicrobials to inhibit the bacteria growth that aggravates odor, or deodorants.

If you can afford these, and don't mind getting out the broom or vacuum perhaps a bit more, go for it!

 A number of alternative litters are advertised as "flushable." Flushing litter is fine in small quantities, but if you have multiple boxes, check with your plumber as to how much of the litter you have in mind your plumbing system can handle.

A litter box filled with *shredded paper* might be needed for several days after a neutering operation, or for a pet other than a cat using a litter box. Don't use magazine paper—most of it is too slick and nonabsorbent. Don't make the strips too wide, and be sure to remove the soiled paper right after each use, or at least daily.

Certain cats won't use some of the best litter, so it might take a bit of experimenting to find out what they like. When you find it, use it.

Filling the Box

How much litter you put in the pan is also important. Too much, and the cat sinks into it; not enough and he can't exercise his "bury my droppings" instinct. One and a half to 2 inches is the perfect depth. In general, underfilling is better than overfilling—it means less kicked-out and wasted litter.

You'll find a variety of plastic litter box liners available, including those with attached drawstrings and some that snap right into a rim specially constructed to hold the liner in place (a worthwhile feature, since liners tend to slip down off the sides). A box liner would seem to be an advantage when box-dumping time rolls around, but they're often clawed through by kitty as he digs, and then urine seeps under the liner and the box smells worse than ever. Also, many cats dislike liners, and will refuse to use a box with one.

Deodorized Litter or Litter Deodorizers

You can either buy a deodorized product or add your own deodorizer to plain litter to extend the time between litter box cleanings. **Some deodorized litters contain chemicals and fragrances that actually repel cats,** forcing them to use some other handy corner of the house.

In a covered box, the scent of the litter deodorizer itself is likely to build up to the point that your pet refuses to go inside. Of the litters made of materials that are supposed to be odor-masking or counteracting in themselves, cedar chip litter is tolerated better by most cats than alfalfa-pellet litter, for example. But cedar litter is so light it not only gets tracked out but sticks to the cat and gets carried all over the house. And a dropped chip, smelling of litter box as it does, can cue a cat to go elsewhere than the box.

It's often easier on the pet and on the pocketbook to buy plain clay litter and add your own deodorizer. A favorite of experienced cat owners in this category is plain old baking soda. Eighty percent of the majority of respondents to one

Cat Fancy survey, for example, indicated that they had better results with baking soda than with chemical treatments of any kind. When you're setting up or changing the box, mix in one part baking soda to three parts litter, and put a layer of soda on the very bottom of the box, too.

If you'd rather use a commercial deodorizer, a bacteria/enzyme type like Simple Solution Cat Litter Odor Remover is probably the best, or a zeolite product like Odorzout.

Arm & Hammer has capitalized on the effectiveness of baking soda for litter deodorizing by creating a whole line of litters enhanced with baking soda, including a clumping litter, a flushable one, and an extra-strength one for multi-cat households.

The Bottom Line of Litter Box Management

Keeping the box clean is the great odor-conquering secret—the precise type of litter you use, exactly where you put the pan, the available ventilation, etc., help some, but *cleaning out the box often* is the bottom line. The more boxes you have in the house, and the more cats using them, the more important this is. Cats like a clean bathroom, too, and their noses are much keener (some scientists say 100 times keener) than ours. Frequent cleaning of litter boxes is the surest way to prevent cat potty accidents.

Litter Box Cleaning

The real experts again go for simplicity. The slotted litter box scoops do a very efficient job of removing feces, but an unslotted metal serving spoon or the like can pick up urine-soaked clumps of litter or loose stools completely, so that nothing falls through the slots to get mixed back down with the clean litter and smell up the box.

For clumping litter, a metal scoop is better than a plastic one, which isn't quite strong enough to detach clumps from the bottom of the pan. If you can't find a metal litter scoop, use an Ecko kitchen scoop. There are special sprays sold to help prevent urine clumps from sticking to the box, but Pam kitchen spray, which is nontoxic and inexpensive, will do fine for this.

The big question is *just how often* should you clean the box? This varies according to the inclinations of the owner and the number and nature of the cats using it and perhaps, too, on where you keep the box. "Pan out" the solid wastes and urine clumps at least daily, and then change the litter completely and wash the container about once a week. You don't have to go wild scrubbing and sterilizing, just do a good general job of cleaning it. Some experts feel that a certain amount of residual ammonia smell in the box helps attract cats to it. The cleaning frequency suggested above is for a one-cat situation; if the box is used by more than one, you're back in the realm of personal appraisal. Some cats are fussy and won't use a "soiled several times" place, so you have no choice but to service it more often or get a mess on your floor. In a multi-cat household, you'll want to change the litter and wash the box at least twice a week to keep down the urine odor.

Remember that cats have much keener noses than we do, so the box might look and smell okay to us but be beyond the pale to our pet. Many "litter box managers" make the mistake of assuming that if they scoop out the solids regularly, they've done all they can to keep odor down between full-scale cleanings. But it's the urine that creates that awful ammonia-like stench too often thought of as the trademark of a cat household. You want to remove the urine, too, daily, the sooner the better.

To do this, tilt the box gently to one side and any urine deposits will stand out as darkened masses of wet litter that stick to the side or bottom of the pan. Slide a spoon or flat scoop carefully under the clump and try to remove it intact if at all possible (corner or side clumps are much easier to remove without breaking than clumps deposited in the middle). If you do break a clump, don't mix it with the remaining clean litter; this is one of the best ways to *guarantee* a smelly box. If the box contains both urine and feces, try to ferret out and remove all the fragile urine clumps first, to avoid broken clumps that will contaminate and smell up the pan. How much odor there is and whether or not your pet uses the box depend more on how regularly you service it than on any other single factor. If it isn't left, it won't smell, and you're much less likely to have "accidents" anywhere in the house. Prompt litter box cleanout also keeps worm eggs and other parasites in the stool from reaching the infective stage.

Take note of any changes in your cat's toilet habits, such as straining, constipation, diarrhea, or blood in the stool. These can be symptoms of a wide variety of illnesses. If they don't clear up soon, consult your veterinarian.

To keep down germs and odor, every week, mop the floor under and around the box with a deodorizing cleaner solution and rinse. And from time to time apply a Nolvasan solution to the area: Leave the solution on for five to ten minutes, then rinse it off with a mop dampened in clean water. Don't forget to wash your hands after handling or changing the litter box.

To keep down the amount of litter tracked around the house, put something around the box to catch and hold what drops off Kitty's paws. There are washable mats made specifically for this, such as the Drymate cat litter box mat (*www.drymate. com*), and even grids with collecting areas beneath them.

Can You Really Toilet Train Your Cat?

You may have heard that cats can be toilet trained, and wondered if this is really possible. What cat toilet training basically does is teach the cat to transfer his litter box talents, in gradual steps, to a higher and rather peculiar litter box. It's that exquisite feline sense of balance and the fact that cats normally excrete in a squatting position that makes this possible.

Toilet training is fine for individual cats, but not every cat will do it. Younger cats learn more quickly than older ones. Some cats may use the seat itself rather than the "hole" we want them to aim for. And if you have four or five cats in the house, the feces may tend to clog up the drain, since cats haven't yet learned to flush. But they can be toilet trained. It's not inhumane, it's not silly, and it's not hard to do. It may be worth a try, especially if you have a spare bathroom, since it eliminates litter box maintenance and saves all that money shelled out for litter, and lugging around clean and dirty litter, too. In 2003, Americans spent $400 million on 1.8 million tons of cat litter! Here are some books that give detailed, illustrated, step-by-step instructions for toilet training Tabby in less than a month:

- *How to Toilet Train Your Cat: The Education of Mango* by Eric Brotman, Ph.D., published by Bird Brain Press

- *How to Toilet Train Your Cat: 21 Days to a Litter-Free Home* by Paul Kunkel and Kimble Pendleton Mead, published by Workman Publishing

If you think you might need a cat potty seat or kit to help out, check out:

- *The Feline Evolution CatSeat*   www.catseat.com
- *Vo-toy Kitty Whiz*   800-272-0088
- *Cat toilet training kit with booklet*   www.potty-cat.com

One Way to Toilet Train Your Cat

Start by putting the litter box on the toilet (make sure the lid is down), and put the cat up there in the box so he realizes it's been moved from the regular spot. If he doesn't seem to want to use it in this new location, figure out when he ordinarily uses the box (usually after his meal), then put him inside the bathroom and close the door at just that time. After you're pretty sure he's used the box, let him out. If you put fresh litter in the box before letting the cat in, you can be sure of whether he's used it or not. Also, it's a good way to get him to go, because **cats are usually attracted to fresh litter.**

Once he gets used to this, begin putting the box on the toilet with the lid up, so the box is sitting on the toilet seat. To a cat, this shouldn't make any difference.

After a few days of this, take a round or oval disposable aluminum roasting pan (make sure it's sturdy enough or use a few stacked together so that it won't bend and fall into the toilet) or a plastic dishpan that will fit inside the hole in the seat without falling through, and set it inside the seat. Put about ¼ inch of litter inside (preferably a flushable litter such as World's Best Cat Litter, to keep from clogging up pipes), and put the litter-filled pan inside the toilet when it's your cat's regular potty time. This will probably seem a little unusual to your pet, but since there's litter inside he should go for it. (Give him some peace and quiet for this initial transition period.)

By now your cat should start standing on the toilet seat when he goes, hanging his rear over the pan. After you get him used to going this way (hopefully within a few days), cut a small hole about 2 inches in diameter in the middle of the pan, and start decreasing the amount of litter inside. A couple of days later, decrease the litter even more and increase the size of the hole by another inch or two. After a week you should be down to no litter in the pan and a hole large enough so there's really nothing inside for the cat to scratch except water down below. If you've got your pet to this point, you're finished with training.

If you do opt for toilet training, a solid plastic seat is better than a painted wood or padded one because cats may scratch a little after using the toilet, as a reflex. For this same reason, a Formica, glass plate, or other scratch-resistant surface on any wall that is close to the toilet might not be a bad idea. And if kitty does use the toilet, wipe the top and bottom of the seat with Nolvasan solution after you do your regular toilet cleaning. Leave the solution on for five or ten minutes, then wipe it off with a cloth moistened in clean water.

If you've instituted a training program and your cat seems reluctant, don't force him! Retreat to the litter box!

Spraying

Even perfectly housetrained animals will spray. Animals use urine (and for that matter, feces) to communicate with other animals, to leave their scent on places and things to give other animals a variety of different messages. In general, **if a urine stain is on a vertical surface, it's no accident**—it was the intentional urination called spraying in male cats and leg-lifting in male dogs. Male cats and dogs are the most notorious for spraying, but females will sometimes spray, especially when they're in heat or feeling threatened. A sprayer's targets are usually the most conspicuous objects in the room—things like doors, stereo speakers, and furniture, or just below or on windows. If you don't act fast on a spray spot, you'll have permanent stain on absorbent surfaces. And if you don't remove all trace of the odor, your pet will be encouraged to christen the spot again. Spraying poses a safety hazard, too: Pets can spray on and in things (such as wall sockets, electric heaters, or even the Christmas tree) and get a serious shock.

Neutering and Spaying—The #1 Solution for Spraying

The majority of spraying is done by unneutered animals. Having your pet altered will give you an excellent chance of preventing or eliminating spraying. Usually your pet will stop spraying within several weeks after the operation, as soon as the hormones have faded from his system. But don't wait until he's old enough to have firmly established "marking" habits or he'll continue to spray after the neutering. **Neutering isn't quite as effective in eliminating leg-lifting by dogs,** because they're more likely to continue to spray out of pure habit after the hormonal impulse is gone.

Preventing spraying is more difficult in a multi-cat household, even if all the cats in it are altered, because in a multi-cat situation, "identifying territory" becomes more important to the animals involved, even when their sexual reasons for spraying have dimmed. Multi-animal households can also mean more stress on the animals living there, which can mean more spraying.

Recent research seems to suggest that cats and dogs can be safely altered as young as two months old without any negative effects on their health, and with a much better chance of avoiding the development of problem behaviors. But if you want your male pet to have full male body conformation, you'll want to wait till he's at least six months old before neutering. As soon after that as you see any sign of an inclination to leg-lift or go outside the box, he's ready.

If spraying persists even after neutering, consult your vet or animal behaviorist. She may suggest treating your pet with synthetic female hormone or anti-anxiety drugs for a while to alter his behavior.

The spaying and neutering procedures are safe, and unless you have a choice purebred and intend to become a professional breeder, there's no good reason *not* to have it done.

Cats and dogs that are spayed or neutered are healthier, happier, more affectionate, tend to live longer, and don't contribute to the tragedy of pet overpopulation. Any one of these is a good enough reason to alter, but here's a reason most people never think of: It makes it easier to keep your home *clean*!

A few more benefits of spaying and neutering include:

- Your pet will be more trainable, because he's less distracted.
- He'll be more content to stay home (and you won't have to worry about him roaming all over and getting hurt or worse).
- He'll be gentler and less aggressive.
- He'll urinate less frequently and forget his toilet training less frequently.
- He won't try to mount your boss's leg or stick his nose where he shouldn't.
- He'll also be less susceptible to prostate trouble and testicle tumors.

Depending upon where you live and where you go to have it done, spaying and neutering can cost you anywhere from $40 to $50 on up (size, weight, and whether a female is pregnant at the time all figure into the price). Prices in metropolitan areas can be significantly higher.

The following groups offer nationwide referrals to reduced-cost spaying and neutering services. These programs aren't just for those with lower incomes; they're for anyone—rich, poor, or in between:

Spay USA can be reached at their toll-free number, 800-248-SPAY. Complete information is also available on their Web site, *www.spayusa.org*.

Friends of Animals also has a toll-free number, 800-321-PETS. Complete information can be found on their Web site, *www.friendsofanimals.org*.

Your local humane society or animal shelter may also have information on low-cost spaying and neutering.

Solution #2: Training

The Scat bottle, good as it is elsewhere, doesn't seem to work for most owners trying to break their pet of spraying. Your pet can very easily spray and say good day before you even notice. And **if you don't correct a pet immediately (this means within a *half second* of the behavior), it does no good**—even a few seconds later is too late. For this same reason, paper-whacking and similar methods don't work—you simply can't do it fast enough.

You might be able to yell "No" or "Stop" fast enough or clap your hands or honk a small bicycle horn, especially if you keep a sharp eye out for the symptoms of "about to spray"— your cat backing up to something with a raised, twitching tail or a set of short funny little steps, or your dog raising his leg.

You can also try the diversion approach when you see the signs: Toss him a toy, start a lively game with him, pick him up and pet him, or carry him somewhere else.

As animal behaviorist Gwen Bohnenkamp points out:

> You can actually teach a dog not to mark inside. Nothing will entice a male dog to urinate more than the smell or presence of another dog's urine. Using cotton balls, soak up some urine from another dog and save them in the freezer in a plastic bag. Tack a half-dozen of the urine-soaked cotton balls to a post outside and let your dog discover them. As soon as he sniffs and squirts, praise and reward him. Repeat this until you know he understands how delighted you are with his marking outside.

> Then find a safe location indoors and tack one of the cotton balls there. Watch your dog very closely. As soon as he begins to sniff and position himself to lift his leg—but before he actually urinates—shout "No! Bad dog! Outside, outside, outside!" and chase him outdoors. Once outside, he'll find the post where you've previously tacked the cotton balls. When he urinates on them, praise him profusely. In just a few seconds, he's learned that trying to mark indoors makes you angry, but marking outdoors makes you very happy and he gets praised for it. (It's a good idea to have previously taught your dog what the word "outside" means.)

The Bramton Company makes a "Pee Post" and a Potty Training Aid liquid that can also be used to help train a dog to urinate where you want him to.

Confinement to Stop Spraying

Keeping your dog or cat confined also may break him of spraying in the house. Confine the sprayer to a small room with washable surfaces and a hard floor, or to a crate. If he's a cat, put the litter box in the room with him, make sure he uses it, and after he does, praise him, let him out, and watch his every move. If you see the slightest sign of about-to-spray, put him back in and don't let him out until he uses the box. If he's a dog, be sure to take him outside to urinate regularly, and again, never let him out of confinement without a sharp eye on him.

Don't leave a sprayer in the process of retraining home alone unless he's confined, and don't be too quick to decide that he's got the idea. Don't give him the run of the house until he's stopped urinating in the wrong places for several weeks running.

Prevention of Spraying

If you have a cat that sprays, keep the litter box extra clean so your pet has no excuse to avoid it. And don't ever attempt to correct your pet while he's in the litter box—it could make him avoid it entirely.

Be sure to place the litter box well away from walls or absorbent surfaces. Get one of the boxes with a high rim that will keep your cat from spraying out of the box. Or consider a covered box with a charcoal filter. Boxes like Charlie's Box (from Cats Rule, *www.catsrule.com*; 212-473-3023) and the Booda Dome by Aspen Pet Products will help keep urine in the box. Cat-attracting litters like Dr. Elsey's Cat Attract cat litter can also help here.

Since spraying is often repeated in the same places, you can move your pet's food or water dish or bed to that very spot, and keep it there until the spraying ceases in that location, since pets never want to soil where they sleep or eat. (This strategy pits one pet instinct against another.) You can also use repellents such as Sticky Paws, or spray repellents, to make a spray site unattractive.

One very effective kind of spray repellent called Feliway, from the Farnum Company, uses synthetic feline pheromones to help alter behavior. Cats do two kinds of marking: urine spraying, and the spreading of "friendly" pheromones with their faces. They don't do both kinds of marking in the same place. The reassuring feel-good pheromones in Feliway also help calm cats to lessen the stress that often causes spraying. There is even a plug-in device ("diffuser") available from the company that automatically disperses the chemical into the air every so often. There is a similar soothing remedy for dog sprayers called D.A.P., or dog appeasing pheromone.

What else can you do to minimize spraying? **Don't leave things that wouldn't survive a spray session sitting exposed on low shelves or tables,** or right in the middle of the floor. Don't leave clothing draped over couches, chairs, or nightstands or you might have a very unwelcome surprise when you go to gussy up in the morning.

If a favorite spraying spot is on a piece of upholstered furniture, you can attach a matching piece of upholstered fabric over the spot and remove it to clean as necessary.

If the sight of other cats outdoors is causing your cat to spray, draw the drapes or install blinds or shutters. It will reduce spraying indoors if you let your cat outside briefly to exercise the spraying instinct. Don't let unneutered strays hang around your house, especially the windows and doors—this is sure to stimulate your cat's spraying instinct.

If your male dog isn't neutered, don't bring him along while visiting, especially to a home with other pets. His urge to leave his calling card will be nothing less than overwhelming and the visitee will be less than happy with the result.

Clean It Up

Although pets can and will spray almost anything (including strangers' legs, other pets, and food), **most of them will spray in the same area, spot, or place over and over**—so cleaning it can actually be easy, as long as you seal the area.

This simply means applying a finish to the surface that moisture can't penetrate (see page 61, Chapter 2). Then, when the spray hits, it won't soak in, stain, or be hard to clean. Spraying can be quickly and easily cleaned off things and won't damage them if they have a slick protective surface. You might want to seal the basement or garage walls, up to a height of about three or four feet, if a spraying pet spends a lot of time there.

You can locate spray spots on furniture and baseboards, especially, by darkening the room and shining a flashlight on the floor so the light bounces upward. The spray will show as shiny streaks. Better yet, use a black light, as explained on page 113 in Chapter 4, to find all the hidden and unsuspected spots so you can clean them up.

On hard or sealed surfaces:

1. Spray the spot with your spray bottle of deodorizing cleaner or all-purpose cleaner with some surface deodorizer added.
2. Let the solution sit on the surface for ten seconds or so.
3. Wipe it off with a paper towel and throw the towel away.
4. Spray it again quickly and wipe the area off thoroughly with a sponge or damp cloth.
5. As a final touch, you can spray the area with Nolvasan solution and let it dry on there, to inhibit the growth of bacteria.

If a pet has sprayed repeatedly on a hard surface such as a painted wall, it may be hard to remove every trace of the odor. Clean the area well as described above, let it dry well, and apply a coat of stain sealant such as Kilz. When that has dried, repaint the area.

For spray stains on carpeting, upholstery, or other absorbent surfaces, be sure to follow the directions for removal of fresh or old stains on page 110 in Chapter 4. Fresh stains can usually be treated with a chemical deodorizer/cleaner, but aged spray stains, or spray on absorbent surfaces, call for a different approach. Bacteria/enzyme cleaners such as Bramton's Cat Spray & Urine Stain & Odor Remover do a good job, but spraying is a marking behavior, so you're better off using products that contain a pheromone remover as well as stain and odor removers. Products such as Dumb Cat Anti-Marking and Cat Spray Remover, and Get Serious! do an even better job of cleaning up spray spots.

Pet Potty Detail

Well here it is, pet owners, the bottom line, the biggest single pet-cleaning problem. **It's the ultimate reality of animal ownership—the clean-up of the potty.**

I remember the shock I suffered as a boy when I heard that Roy Rogers's beautiful palomino Trigger did it right on the stage in front of 10,000 fans. How could he, a famous and respectable horse, do that to Roy? I finally realized the answer was simple—the horse did it because it was the most natural thing in the world for him to do. And it was equally natural and straightforward for Roy to clean it up.

It's hard to face in a polite society, but animals do have to go . . . so we have to pick up, rake up, mop up, blot up, scoop up, scrape up, and shovel. But on the walk or in the backyard, scoop law or not, we all seem a little reluctant about this particular cleaning duty. The fact is, when it comes to the pet potty detail, the secret isn't technique *or* equipment—it's *attitude*.

You can't prevent the act itself, but you can make pickup and disposal as easy as possible and try to control *where* they do it.

A Super Scooper?

We have quite a few choices when it comes to dog dropping clean-up. The arsenal of available scooping hardware notwithstanding, **the ordinary small plastic bag is a hands-down favorite with experienced scoopers for pickup on the go.** Basic bag technique is as follows: You carry a couple of bags in your purse or pocket (or in the handy little bag dispensers made for leashes), and, after the moment of truth, you pull out a bag and stick your hand in it, grab the pile, and pull the bag over your hand, turning it inside out as you go. Then knot the bag closed and drop in the nearest receptacle.

You don't even have to buy special bags. To quote *Dog Fancy:*

> Perhaps the most practical, get-down-to-business device for scooping litter is the plastic bag that comes on the daily paper. Many dog walkers believe that this long plastic bag is the best follow-up for a messy dog because it doesn't cost a thing (unless you don't subscribe to a newspaper) and in fact disposes of an object that would otherwise clutter some kitchen corner.

You can buy black or otherwise opaque bags—there are even opaque bags that come complete with drawstrings or are shaped like mittens. And there are plastic bags that come complete with their own little disposable scooping frames, such as the DispozAScoop, that are small enough to be carried discreetly while still providing a more remote means of pickup. Petsmart offers a scoop designed to use plastic grocery bags, of which most of us have an inexhaustible number.

If you go for bags alone, carry a paper lunch sack along with your plastic bag supply—so you've got a handy means of carrying *and* concealment along if it turns out to be a distance to the trash container.

Then there are the arm's-length scoopers, which are great for yard clean-up, but often take two hands to operate and are too cumbersome to carry on a walk. **One staple is the long-handled dustpan with matching rake or shovel,** which comes as two separate pieces, or connected in the middle. In metal scoopers, stainless steel is probably the most durable and cleanable, with aluminum the next best.

The butterfly net scoopers are popular because they're lightweight and only take one hand to operate, which makes them more manageable for scooping on the go. They usually consist of a plastic bag suspended at the end of an aluminum frame. Some of the butterfly scoops collapse for ease of carrying, and unfold with a flick of the wrist into a full-length scooper. Some of these also feature water-soluble bags that can be flushed down a toilet, or allow you to use ordinary Ziploc bags from the supermarket.

Scooping equipment should be cleaned and/or disinfected after every use. Use a nylon scrub brush and a good cleaner/deodorizer like Nilodor's Deodorizing Cleaner, or a Nolvasan solution (after first washing and rinsing, to be sure the disinfectant has a chance to be fully effective).

Urine Trouble!

One of the most common complaints I hear from dog owners is lawn damage from urine. Many people get frustrated at the sight of brown, damaged patches spotting an otherwise healthy green lawn. Spray or urine marking by dogs and cats can also kill bushes and shrubs, which eventually succumb to uric acid poisoning.

One easy way to help avoid this is to flood the area with water as soon as the dog urinates. Keep a hose ready when you take Fido outside. The water will dilute the urine and cut down on the damage.

There are also products available to help solve this problem. Lawn Spot Away, for instance, is an enzyme treatment that speeds up the breakdown of pet urine so the grass will regrow sooner. Meanwhile, the spray actually colors the spots green to hide the damage while the grass is regrouping. There are also pills and treats such as Lawn Guard you can give your dog or cat to neutralize their urine so that it won't devastate plants.

Bushes and shrubs (especially small or young ones, which are the most vulnerable) can be surrounded by circles of chicken wire supported by stakes as necessary.

Most dogs tend to urinate in the same spot to mark their territory. To help train your dog, collect his urine in a cup and pour it in the designated area. He'll most likely want to use that spot once he realizes he has "been there before." Make sure the designated area is made of concrete, rocks, or mulch.

You can also set a post in the designated area and tack cotton balls dipped in your pet's urine to it. There is even a commercial product for this purpose, the Pee Post, by Bramton, a small plastic stake impregnated with canine-attracting chemicals (synthetic marking pheromones).

If none of the above work, **you can try chemical repellents, usually available as granules or sprays.** Your pets won't like the taste or smell, and you won't even notice it. Some of them even come in lemon scent! The granules are longer lasting than the sprays, which have to be reapplied often. Be sure to keep children away from them, and don't use these chemicals near any food you're growing though, because they are poisonous. Read all the directions before you use them.

The training strategies just outlined will work for female dogs as well, though you will usually have to employ some extra training and reinforcement with the ladies.

Yard Control

Animals have to go somewhere, so wouldn't it be better to create a place for it than to have the yard and the landscape littered at will?

Set aside a certain part of your yard for the purpose. Make a concrete pad, 3' × 3' or so, depending on the size of your dog. Then you can easily scoop the droppings off the concrete surface and flush it off with a hose. Or cover a similar area with 4 inches of gravel. You can surround the area with bushes or shrubs to screen off the area and to give your pet a little privacy.

Take your pet to the potty area when he needs to go (put some of his droppings there to encourage him to start using it if you need to), and praise him when he does. Pet stores and catalogs have chemicals that will help attract a dog to a "potty post" while you train him, or you can use a Pee Post.

Dogs actually prefer to eliminate in the same spot repeatedly—as long as it's kept clean. (If it *isn't*, they'll refuse to go there.) You want to pick up the droppings in the pet potty area—or the whole yard, if you let your dog go anywhere in the yard—very regularly anyway, preferably daily. It will look better and restore the joy of lawn rolling, plus cut down the chances of transmitting diseases and parasites. You can just scoop up the droppings and dump them down the toilet or in the trash (if your city code allows it), or install a waste digester.

You'll also want to deodorize a cement or gravel pet toilet area with bacteria/enzyme solution at least once a month, and disinfect it periodically.

Whatever you do, don't put dog droppings in an ordinary garden compost pile. Dog and cat droppings don't have the same value as fertilizer as the manure of herbivores does, and they may carry parasites and disease germs to your garden soil, and attract wandering pets or wild animals to the pile.

Install a Waste Digester in Your Backyard

This is sort of like a septic system specifically for dogs. It's a cylindrical or pyramid-shaped container that's buried in the ground; you add a culture of harmless live bacteria to it and they produce enzymes that decompose and liquefy the stools so they can be absorbed into the earth. The only hitch is that when the temperature drops below 40°F, the enzymes slow down or stop functioning. This is one of the reasons the digester is set into the ground, because under the earth it's a constant 55°F, even though in northern climates the top two feet or so of the ground may freeze as hard as rock in the winter. If you install a digester below the frost line, it'll work all winter.

You can also have two digesters and put the droppings in one all winter until the weather warms up in the spring, then gradually transfer them from the full digester to the empty one. An additional advantage is that in warmer weather, **two digesters can actually digest as much as three could if you alternate between them.** The best-known brand of enzyme digester is Lim'nate—a one-pound box is inexpensive and will last a one- or two-dog household about a year. Outright Pet Odor Eliminator is a bacteria/enzyme product that also works very well for the purpose. These digesters can also be used to be sure pet stools don't clog up your septic system if you regularly dump pet waste in the toilet.

Many pet-supply distributors or feed or pet stores have metal or plastic stool digesters available, often complete with a scooper and a starter supply of enzyme. The Doggie Dooley is one of the better-known brands. You can also build your own from 10-inch clay bell tile (if you can still find one at your local plumbing outlet) Or bury a steel drum (*not* one previously used for insecticide or other toxic substances) with a piece of PVC pipe about four inches in diameter set into it, and a PVC cap at the top of the pipe, where it comes out of the ground.

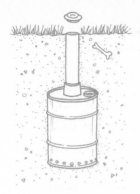

You can also dig a pit or construct an aboveground box that serves the same purpose—the makers of Lim'nate provide the instructions right in the box. Check with your local government officials before building your own, if you have any doubt, to make sure your digester would not violate any local ordinance.

All of these need a secure fly-proof cover. For any of these, you simply scoop the droppings up, drop them into the digester, and add more water and bacteria culture from time to time.

You want to install a digester away from wells and septic tanks, in a spot that has good drainage. Make sure that the digester never dries out; there should always be enough solution in there to keep the stool semimoist. On the other hand, don't add more water than the enzyme directions call for, or more solution than needed to just moisten the droppings, or you'll lower the efficiency of the digester. You also don't want to add strong chemicals to the digester, or you'll kill the bacteria that produce the enzymes.

Teach Your Dog to Eliminate on Command

Training can be an excellent solution to the pet potty detail, too, but like potty training kids, it does take a little time and patience. The purpose of this book isn't to describe training techniques in detail, but *You Can Teach Your Dog to Eliminate on Command* by Dr. Marjorie Smith will teach you every nuance of accomplishing what might sound like the dog walker's impossible dream—getting your pet to go exactly where you want him to. The animal experts agree that the concept is sound and even go so far as to say that it's ridiculously easy to accomplish. You can train any dog six weeks or older to PPC—"piddle and poop on command"—at the sound of a (carefully chosen) trigger word, and the total training time you'll have to spend doing it is less than ten minutes a week.

The technique will ensure that you walk your dog, instead of him walking you. When most people walk their dogs, as soon as the animal eliminates, he's taken home. After a while, the dog probably begins to think, "Hey, if I can hold it in for a while, then she'll have to take me walking all over"—so you end up walking for what seems like forever. After you've taught your dog to eliminate on command, you can see that he relieves himself before the walk begins. Then you take him for his walk (that's his reward for eliminating on your command), and *you're* in control of how long you want the walk to last.

Elimination on command also means that you can assure a prompt "duty" on cold and rainy nights, or when you have to leave soon for somewhere. It also solves the problem of poop pickup in public places. You can see that your pet goes in the area you've set aside as the pet toilet, before you take him out on the town.

For More Scoopable Stools

The scooper's nightmare known as loose stools can have various causes, including a sudden change in diet, a high-fat diet, disease, parasites, or stress and excitement, just to name a few. **Loose stools are a sign that something's amiss;** if they last longer than a few days, take the dog to a veterinarian.

High-quality, nutritionally dense dog food such as Canidae, Innova, or Wellness creates firmer and smaller stools that are easier to pick up and don't leave messy residue when you do. A diet of ⅔ ordinary name-brand dry dog food to ⅓ canned food will also produce eminently scoopable stools.

If you do have to scoop a loose stool, throw some absorbent material on it so it can be picked up more easily. You can use deodorizing absorbent, the stuff you put on the garage floor to absorb grease, cat litter, or even dirt if nothing else is available—anything that will absorb and stiffen the mess so it can be scooped.

You can also use the newspaper technique. Slip a sheet of newspaper under your pet when he squats and try to position the paper so that he does his business in the middle of it, then fold the corners in and slip the paper inside an opaque plastic bag. This way, if there aren't any garbage cans close by, it's easy to carry until you find one. Presto, the mess is up—no runs, no drips, no errors.

Chapter 4

In Case of Accident:

Pointers for Cleaning Up Pet Messes

In fifty years of professional cleaning, my crews have cleaned up everything from skunk spray to smoke and fire damage. But some of the very worst messes we ever face are places where pets have been allowed to piddle and poop all over a house or apartment.

Accidents and odors are the two main reasons people give up their pets, and after my experiences cleaning up abused homes, I can understand the urge to abandon a situation like that. For the most part, though, in this chapter we're not talking about a totally out-of-control situation (caused, incidentally, by the owners, not the pets), we're dealing with the occasional incident. Even the best-trained pet will have an accident from time to time. If we forget to let Fifi out before we go shopping, or fail to keep the litter box clean and appealing, we may force a normally well-behaved pet to seek relief on forbidden ground. And occasionally, an animal may eat something that doesn't quite agree with it, and have a bout of vomiting or diarrhea. These are pure and simple accidents.

A different type of accident is the one where the animal knows a certain behavior is unacceptable, but for emotional reasons, as it were, does it anyway. A new pet or a new baby in the house, a new animal in the neighborhood, or any situation that produces anxiety, for example, may cause a pet to temporarily forget his training. **Many a pet will make messes when frustrated, unhappy, or lonely.** This type of temporary lapse, while certainly not fun for you, can usually be handled with a little reeducation and some patience while you track down the reason for the strange behavior.

In the case of a normally well-behaved animal who has a slip up for reasons he can't control, simply clean up the mess without getting upset at the animal; try to figure out the cause of the problem—and remove it. The same is true of accidents caused by psychological stresses on your pet, although rooting out the problem here and treating it is a little more involved. Many of these types of behavior and their solutions are covered under the individual topics elsewhere in this book. And there are some excellent books on pet psychology and behavior that can help you out further, such as:

- *When Good Dogs Do Bad Things* by Margolis and Siegal
- *The New Better Behavior in Dogs: A Guide to Solving All Your Dog Problems* by William E. Campbell
- *Good Owners, Great Dogs* by Brian Kilcommons
- *Understanding Your Cat* by Dr. Michael Fox
- *The Cat Who Cried for Help: Attitudes, Emotions, and the Psychology of Cats* by Dr. Nicholas Dodman

Amazingly enough, a lot of "accidents" aren't accidents at all but failure of the master to provide his pet with even the most elementary training. Dogs and cats have a natural instinct to not foul their surroundings, and with a little encouragement, they can be taught to be quite tidy in their elimination habits. With proper training, a good diet, and regular health care, your pet's nature calls shouldn't be an ongoing problem for you.

But even the best pet is going to have an accident once in a while, so how do we handle them when they come along?

First of all, don't believe the claims you see or hear about miracle products that just "spray away" pet stains and odor. It just ain't so. There are hundreds of pet stain removers on the market, and none of them work without some effort. If the label says, "Just open the bottle and the chemical does the rest," be suspicious. And bear in mind that no one product can really deal 100 percent with both stain *and* odor. They're two separate problems—and odor is usually harder to get rid of than stain.

Also to be taken with a grain of salt are the "helpful hints" solutions such as vinegar and water, seltzer water, etc. While some of them work to a degree, none of these preparations are nearly as effective as the products manufactured specifically to deal with pet stains and odors.

A Timing Reminder

Before we start here, let me remind you of something I said way back at the beginning of this book. **Spills and accidents rarely stain if cleaned up while the mess is still fresh** and moist or new. But give them a chance to lie there, and you'll often have permanent damage to fabrics and finishes and furnishings.

Also, odors penetrate deeper and grow more offensive the longer they're left. Odors can penetrate some materials, such as foam rubber and plastic, so thoroughly that they are impossible to remove. Germs multiply and many disease spores and parasite eggs reach the infective stage after the mess has been left a while. Clean it up sooner and it's a lot safer.

Cleaning Up Urine

Urine is not a simple substance. It's composed of water, proteins, urea, uric acid, amino acids, ammonia, salts, and other inorganic compounds. Fresh urine is almost acidic, but it becomes alkaline as it ages. **Urine is capable of staining a great many surfaces,** is very hard to remove from fabrics once it dries, and has an offensive odor that only gets worse with time.

If caught while fresh, a urine deposit is fairly easy to remove, and staining can often be prevented. If you catch the spot after it's been there a while, but is still wet, urine can still be dealt with very successfully. But if urine isn't cleaned up within twenty-four to forty-eight hours, it will become very difficult, if not impossible, to remove. The salts and inorganic compounds that remain are not easily dissolved in water, and the acids produced as the urine decomposes often leave a permanent stain.

Cleaning Urine from Hard Surfaces

On a surface that doesn't absorb liquid, such as semigloss or gloss enamel paint, seamless vinyl flooring, or sealed concrete, urine wipes right up with no damage at all. (This should give you a few clues as to the interior decoration of your pet's living quarters.) Just blot the liquid up with paper towels, and then clean the surface with a detergent solution. A solution made with a squirt of liquid dish detergent and water will kill at least 90 percent of the bacteria in fresh urine, and should leave no appreciable odor.

Some surfaces, though "hard," are porous, and will absorb some of the urine. These include flat or matte-finish latex paint, unsealed concrete, and unfinished wood. Vinyl tile can also absorb liquids in the joints between the tiles. In cases like this, where some of the urine has actually been absorbed into the surface, odor can cling and stay, and a chemical deodorizer/cleaner should definitely be used. If the odor problem is serious, you'll want to seal (varnish or polyurethane or repaint) the surface after deodorizing to help seal in any residual odor so your pet can't smell it.

If you're cleaning up after a puppy in the process of being housebroken or an animal who's been breaking housetraining, be sure to spray the spot after you clean it with a chemical deodorizer, to discourage him from smelling it again. The importance of getting rid of *all* of the odor from a pet accident can't be overemphasized. Cats and dogs have a sense of smell that is far keener than ours, and if there's one molecule of urine left, our pets will smell it. And it'll signal them to a repeat performance in that spot. This is also why you should *never* **attempt to clean a urine stain with ammonia or a cleaner containing ammonia.** Ammonia gives off urinelike scent signals that will ensure another pet mess in the very same spot.

Cleaning Urine Out of Carpeting

This is the biggie—the real challenge to pet owner and professional carpet cleaner alike. Urine spots in the carpet tend to soak down through the carpet and into the carpet backing and pad and even the sub-floor beneath, making them very difficult to remove. The quicker you catch a urine stain, the better!

For a fresh urine stain on carpet, gently blot up all you can with paper towels, being careful not to spread the stain or to drive the remaining liquid deeper into the carpet. (If your carpeting is treated with a soil retardant, it'll help keep liquid spills of all kinds from soaking into the fiber, giving you time to blot them up.)

After blotting up all the free liquid, put a clean terrycloth towel or cotton cloth on the spot and apply pressure with your heel to absorb all the remaining liquid. Turn the towel over and press several times until you're not getting any more urine out; switch to a new towel if you need to and keep going. After blotting, apply a bacteria/enzyme digester following the directions on the label. A deodorizer/cleaner may do the job if you catch the stain immediately, but a **bacteria/enzyme digester is really the only way to completely eliminate the organic material deep down in the carpet that causes the odor** from a pet stain in carpeting, especially one that's had a chance to penetrate.

To reach the urine down in the carpet fibers and backing, you have to get the deodorizing chemical or bacteria/enzyme solution down as far as the urine went. Apply to the carpet about 1½ times as much solution as you estimate there was urine, and then work it into the carpet with your shoe or fingers. Make sure you're wearing an old pair of shoes when you do this. It's also a good idea to wear rubber gloves when you work on pet stains with your hands. If it's a big spot or large area, don't try to spray or squirt it on—remove the cap and pour it on.

Then just step on the spot with your shoe and work the solution clear through the back of the carpet and into the pad until it feels squishy underfoot. If you're using a chemical deodorizer, after working the chemical in well, and letting it stay there for as long as the label recommends, use a clean towel to blot as much of the deodorizer as you can, using a towel under your foot and turning it until it comes up dry.

If you're using a bacteria/enzyme product, be sure to leave the solution in the carpet for as long as the label says to before you blot, so it can do its work. In dry climates, you may have to cover the spot with a piece of plastic wrap or a damp towel to keep it from drying out too soon (the beneficial bacteria will die if the spot dries up).

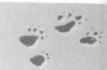

In dealing with any carpet stain, remember to always *blot*, not *scrub*. Scrubbing can damage the carpet fibers and may also spread the stain.

After you've blotted out as much as you can, put a dry towel over the stain and weigh it down with something heavy, like a brick or a couple of books, and it'll continue to absorb moisture for several hours. Then remove the towel and fluff up the carpet fibers to let the carpet finish drying.

If there's still a visible spot on the carpet after it dries, follow up with a water rinse or a carpet stain remover. Repeat the deodorizer or bacteria/enzyme solution if the odor isn't all gone.

Setting a lamp, chair, large potted plant, or some Sticky Paws XL on a "repeat spot" after cleaning and deodorizing may help discourage encores.

Old or Widespread Urine Stains in Carpeting

Even an old, dry urine stain will still have a strong odor, which becomes even more pronounced in wet weather or high humidity. Many a professional cleaner trying to restore a urine-stained carpet has learned this to his dismay. As soon as he puts a little water on the rug, the dormant or "residual" odor roars to life, and the horrified owner cries, "What have you done to my carpet? You're supposed to clean it, and you've made it smell worse than ever!"

Cleaning professionals use a tool called a moisture probe to locate dampness and water damage on floor clean-up jobs. Even if the carpet doesn't feel wet, these probes sense the salts left behind by drying urine and will identify every place the animal has urinated. They can even find ancient dried urine spots such as those left behind by the pet a previous tenant may have had. Probes are battery-powered and give off a beep when they locate an accident site—the bigger the spot, the louder and faster the beeps.

Moisture probes are expensive, so fortunately there is a tool for home cleaners that serves much the same purpose. A number of companies now produce battery-powered ultraviolet ("black") lights. These handy little tools, such as the Stink Free Stink-Finder and Bramton's Spot Spotter, can be used to find all the places—probably more than you realized—where your pet(s) has committed indiscretions such as peeing, spraying, or even vomiting. You do have to do your pet detecting with an ultraviolet light in darkness, which is a bit of a disadvantage, but when you do, all of the assaulted areas will shine forth clearly. Black lights can be used on carpet, upholstery, concrete, tile, Sheetrock, and more. **Once you find those accident sites, mark them with a piece of masking tape so you can find them easily when you come back to deal with them.**

The bacteria/enzyme digester is one of the best removers for an old urine stain. Be sure to pour some clean water on old stains and then blot it back up before starting the digestion process. This will reduce the amount of material that the bacteria and/or enzymes have to deal with. You might even want to do this more than once, if the spot is really urine saturated.

Bear in mind, too, when you're using a bacteria/enzyme product, that the bacteria will release ammonia from the urine as they digest it. If the spot you're dealing with is a multiple accident site, the bacteria may produce so much ammonia that an alkaline atmosphere is created, which will interfere with, or stop, the bacteria's action. So, in cases like this, you need to neutralize the spot after four to six hours with a solution of one cup white vinegar to a gallon of warm water. Rinse the area with this solution and then apply a fresh batch of bacteria/enzyme solution.

The product called Get Serious!—as well as oxygen cleaners—can also be effective on old urine stains. Get Serious!

may do even better than a bacteria/enzyme digester on some stubborn urine stains, and it's designed to prevent re-marking by removing the pheromones in urine, too. Oxygen cleaners are good when the stain from old urine is more prominent than the odor.

If an old urine stain is from cat spray, see also page 96 in Chapter 3.

Worst Case Scenario

If urine damage is extensive and has occurred over a long period of time, it's virtually impossible to eliminate every trace of stain and odor. If you have a carpet in this condition, consider calling in a professional deodorizing technician for an opinion. This isn't just any old cleaning contractor or carpet cleaner, but a professional cleaner well experienced and trained in the specific techniques of urine stain removal.

If the situation is really bad, he'll probably recommend replacing the carpet and pad and sealing the subfloor underneath. If he feels that the carpeting can be saved, it'll involve a process something along these lines:

- Thoroughly cleaning the carpet with hot water and a strong extraction "steam" cleaner
- Lifting the carpet in the affected area and removing the pad underneath; possibly replacing the tack strip if it's badly affected
- Cleaning and disinfecting the subfloor, and sealing it
- Installing a new carpet pad, possibly one that has a polyethylene vapor barrier
- Applying a chemical deodorizer/cleaner or a bacteria/enzyme digester to the carpet back, and pulling it through to the face yarns with the extractor
- Drying and reinstalling the carpet
- Thoroughly cleaning the whole room

If you have a proposal from a deodorizing firm to restore badly urine-damaged carpet that leaves out any of these steps, the work may not completely eliminate the odor problem. And even after all this, some permanent stains may remain.

Obviously, this is a time-consuming and expensive process, and one that would be ill-advised if the value of the carpeting involved doesn't justify it. **In most cases, replacement is the most realistic solution to widespread urine damage.**

The key, of course, is to avoid letting things get to this point. If you make sure your pet is thoroughly housebroken, catch and clean up any accidents as soon as they occur, and seek out and cure the cause of any persistent behavior problems that arise, you can avoid permanent damage to your home and furnishings.

Urine on Wooden Floors

Getting the urine off a wooden floor absolutely as fast as possible is extra important, because any liquid left on wooden flooring, and especially urine, can damage the surface and create a permanent black stain. So use a dry cloth, dry mop, or squeegee and dustpan to get urine off a wooden floor as quickly as possible, then wipe the spot with a cloth dampened with deodorizer/cleaner, or an odor neutralizer, and then a dry clean cloth. Wood floors usually have a protective finish on them, but they also have seams and often tiny holes and cracks that will absorb odor, so you want to apply some kind of odor remover to discourage pets from using that spot again.

If serious urine staining has already occurred, about the only remedy is to sand the area and reapply wood stain (if the floor has had stain applied) and new finish.

Urine Stains on Clothing and Washable Fabrics

Pretreat the stain with a liquid enzyme detergent according to directions, and then launder the item with chlorine bleach (if it's safe for the fabric) or use a color-safe oxygen bleach such as Clorox 2. An alternative method is to soak the garment in a water-and-ammonia solution (¼ cup ammonia to ½ gallon water), if the fabric can handle it (don't use ammonia on wool or silk), and then apply a chemical deodorizer. If you use a bacteria/enzyme digester, limit the prerinse to water only. **And don't dry the article in the dryer till you're sure the stain is gone, because heat will set stains.**

For urine stains in upholstery, remove foam cushions from their fabric covers if possible, and treat the covers just like clothing. If the covering isn't removable, treat over-stuffed furniture just as you would carpeting. To be sure the treatment is effective, you'll have to soak the cushions with bacteria/enzyme solution just as deep as the urine went. Be cautioned, though, that some of the stuffing materials used in upholstered furniture may stain the cover fabric when the upholstery is as thoroughly wet as this.

For urine stains on drapes or curtains, apply a pet spot and stain remover such as Nilotex. Or take the drapes to a dry cleaner, and be sure to explain what and where the stains are.

Cleaning Up Feces

When the dog or cat poops on the floor, it isn't the potential disaster a urine stain can be. On carpet, you can simply pick up reasonably dry, compact feces with your hand slipped inside a plastic bag, or with a dustpan or two pieces of cardboard. Then treat the carpet with the pet stain product of your choice.

Since this type of soil is almost always confined to the surface of the carpet, a chemical deodorizer/cleaner should do the job here. Be sure to remove all the solid waste you can before applying any cleaner or deodorizer—it's a deodorizer, not a miracle worker. An aged, dried-up #2 deposit may have to be soaked and scrubbed gently to get rid of any remaining residue after you've removed the loose material from the surface.

If your pet has diarrhea, or if the stool is combined with urine, the liquids may have soaked down into the carpet, and you'll have to use the more involved procedure described for urine removal. Where you have a stool with considerable liquid content that's soaked into the carpet, use a bacteria/enzyme digester. Any other cleaning method is going to leave some organic matter imbedded in the recesses of the carpet and pad.

Pet foods with heavy dyes (to make the food look nice and meaty—to us, not our pet) will stain carpeting and other home surfaces if your pet has an accident after eating such food. The red dyes are always the worst on carpets. **Dyes in pet food also make it hard to use the stools as an indicator of your pet's general health,** and many dyes are also potential cancer risks. Dye content will be listed on the package, so you should be able to bypass the rations if you're so inclined. (Pinkish stains from pet food dyes on a light-colored carpet may respond to bleaching, but this is a job you should refer to a professional carpet cleaner.)

On hard surfaces like vinyl flooring, #2 clean-up is a simple process no matter how much liquid is involved. Simply blot or pick up the liquid and solid waste and then clean and deodorize in one step with a chemical deodorizer/cleaner. On a hard floor that's been sealed or waxed, simply wiping with a solution of water and dish detergent is usually good enough.

Vomit Clean-Up

Dogs and cats have occasional bouts of vomiting, just as we do, for a variety of reasons. Cats seem more prone to vomiting than dogs are, and the cause can be anything from hairballs in the stomach to overeating to a serious illness. If you find your dog or cat vomiting but he does not show any other signs of illness (fever, diarrhea, sluggishness, blood in the vomit or stool), you may not have to rush him off to the veterinarian. **Often, a pet will just get an upset stomach for one reason or another, he'll throw up, and then he'll feel fine.**

You may be able to identify the cause of the problem when you think about it—motion sickness from traveling, eating grass, eating rodents, parasites, swallowed hair from excessive self-grooming, overeating, a change in diet, or too much fat in the diet.

If you're not sure what caused it, but the animal seems otherwise healthy, try withholding food for twenty-four hours, and the condition will probably take care of itself. If the pet continues to have dry heaves after being off food and water for a time, or if you find blood or worms in the expelled material, you should consult your vet as soon as possible. But no matter what the cause, cleaning up upchuck isn't fun. In addition to being smelly and unsightly, vomit contains gastric juices from the stomach, which are strong acids. These will bleach the color out of many fabrics very quickly, so the first thing to do is to remove as much of the liquid and solid material as possible. Scrape it up with a squeegee and dustpan or a couple of pieces of cardboard, or use an absorbent compound.

Sprinkle the absorbant (usually composed of clay granules) onto the spot, leave it there for a few minutes, and then scoop it back up. The absorbant will absorb the liquid and solidify the mess so it's easier to remove—you can even sweep it up. Absorbants (Big D Granular Deodorant is the name of one good one) usually contain a deodorizer and a pleasant-smelling masking fragrance as well, so all in all, they make the job of vomit clean-up quite a bit more bearable.

As soon as you get up all the loose material you can, flood the spot with water to dilute the remaining gastric acids and prevent bleaching of your carpet, flooring, or upholstery. I recommend you use a bacteria/enzyme digester on the stain, so limit the first rinse to water only. As with urine staining, you'll have to clean the carpet with a spot and stain remover after using a bacteria/enzyme digester, to remove any remaining discoloration.

The problem of red dyes in pet food is more serious here because vomit is more fluid than feces, and the stomach acid in it makes it more likely that the dye will affect the carpet fibers. The best solution to this problem is simply to avoid feeding your pets food that contains red dye.

If a pet has vomited on clothing, treat it as you would a urine stain on clothing (see page 116), after you scrape off all you can.

When it comes to accidents, remember that **prevention is the first line of defense.** Make sure your pet is trained to meet your expectations. Get advice from your veterinarian on proper diet and regular health care. Also be aware that your pet will occasionally have a problem, and be prepared to deal with it. Have the necessary tools and cleaners on hand to deal effectively with accidents and stains and act quickly, and you can avoid permanent damage to your home and furnishings.

Some Pointers for Accident Patrol

Be sure to remove the source first. Whether you're trying to deal with a fresh urine stain or a #2 deposit that's been hidden under the couch for months, do be sure to remove the source of the odor as far as practical, before dousing the area with chemicals and cleaning or deodorizing solutions. (This same rule applies to cleaning the pet feeding or food storage area, pet bedding, etc.)

Be ready ahead. Since swift action is essential, you'll need to have your supplies on hand ahead of time to be prepared to fend off pet stains and odors. The chemical deodorizer/cleaners, bacteria/enzyme digesters, bubble-up cleaners, and odor removers are the most useful and effective for the tough jobs involved in pet stain and odor removal. Buy them now so you'll be ready when the time comes. Stockpile a few clean terrycloth towels or cleaning cloths with your supplies, too.

Keep it together. It helps to keep your pet clean-up supplies all together so you can just grab your clean-up kit and run when a problem strikes. The inexpensive plastic "cleaning caddies" or maid baskets—open, compartmentalized tool-carrying trays with a handle in the middle—are great for this.

Chapter 5

Hairy Animal Tales:

Shedding, Bathing, and Flea Control

Stroking an animal's soft pelt is an entirely pleasant sensation, as long as the hair is still attached to the animal. Once hair is flying loose, you can stroke it with every cleaning tool imaginable and only end up exasperated. Cleaning up animal hair is one of the acid tests of pet patience.

Pets don't merely leave hair lying around, they deposit it over and under every piece of furniture and fixture and room in the home, and they manage to get us moving targets, too. The hair problem is worse than a few loose strands floating around. Fur, hair, and dander (the tiny particles of dead skin that every animal sheds) can cause and aggravate allergies, contribute to indoor pollution, irritate guests (by sticking to their clothes), as well as keep the pet cleaner in perpetual motion. If you have a cat, all that fur, hair, and dander causes furballs, which can result not only in vomiting, but also intestinal blockage and constipation.

Many years ago, shedding was a once or maybe twice a year problem, as our pets would shed their heavy winter coats in the springtime and grow them back in the fall. They needed a heavier coat to protect them from winter cold, and sensibly got rid of it before the heat of summer. They began to shed when given the signal to do so by warmer weather and longer daylight hours. But our **modern indoor lighting, heating, and air conditioning throw the process off and often cause pets to shed constantly.**

Back when I was ten years old and working on our farm, I learned that *diet* can affect a pet's coat. Our black Lab began to look sleek and shiny, and my father said, "That dog looks *too* good—he's been sucking eggs." Sure enough, we began to find empty eggs with a hole punched in them. That egg diet sure slicked Rover up!

Your pet might be shedding excessively simply because he doesn't have enough fatty acid in his diet. To remedy this, there are products made just for the purpose, such as Linatone, by Lambert Kay, and Shed Solution Granules by Farnam.

If you feel your pet is shedding excessively, it might also be caused by a too-tight collar or by stress, such as from being boarded or hospitalized.

Grooming to Control Shedding

By grooming I don't mean cutely coiffed haircuts or colorful claw polish but simply removing the loose hair from your pet before it lands on your furnishings.

We too often think that grooming is only for poodles and Persians, and that ol' Fang, macho creature that he is, would never need or allow such a sissy thing to be done to him. But every dog and cat needs regular brushing and gentle combing, and the longhaired ones will develop real problems if they're not groomed regularly. Though cats do a lot of self-grooming, they pick up a lot of fur on their tongues as they do so. They swallow the hairs, which form into indigestible wads or strings in their stomachs and intestines. These wads can cause vomiting (although vomiting may not get the wad up) and even death.

Grooming will make your pet's coat shinier and his skin healthier, and keep him smelling pleasant. Grooming also gives you the opportunity to check your pet for parasites like ticks and fleas and for cuts and injuries.

Start grooming your pet when he is a pup or kitten, or as soon as you get him. Gradually accustom him to your grooming and handling of every part of his body. Don't wait to groom until your pet gets scroungy looking. Groom at least twice a week during shedding season or if your pet is long-haired or has a very dense coat that's prone to matting.

You'll need some tools to groom properly. Exactly what tools you need will depend on the breed of cat or dog you have, and its hair length and type.

For shorthaired and smooth-coated dogs, use a soft-bristle brush or a grooming glove. This is a mitt with short bristles on one side that slips right over your hand.

For pets with medium-length soft or wiry coats, use a slicker brush, a rectangular-shaped flat-backed brush with short bent-wire teeth set in a rubber base. These come in different sizes and with "firm" or "fine" bristles. On cats use only a soft wire slicker—their skin is more sensitive than dogs'. There is one brand of slicker, the Evolution self-cleaning slicker, whose metal teeth retract into the handle so that all the hair you've collected can be easily removed and discarded. Retracting the fine wire teeth also protects them from bending in between uses.

Use a pin brush on longhaired pets—an oval brush with rows of round tipped metal pins and a long handle. Combs work best on longhaired pets and pets with undercoats. **In general, a comb will remove loose hair better than a brush will.** The Four Paws Ultimate Touch Pet Comb and the Untangler Kitty Kat Comb, with rotating steel teeth, are two good ones. The Hair Buster Cat Comb not only removes loose hair, but has a sleeve to catch it!

The Zoom Groom from the Kong Company (*www.kong company.com*) is a rubbery plastic groomer with long conical teeth that comes in cat and dog models. It does a great job of removing loose hair, massaging as it does so—most pets love it.

Secrets of Good Grooming

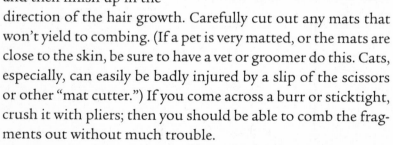

Brush or comb in the direction the hair grows. If your pet has a thick coat, be sure you're getting all the way down to the skin. If there's *lots* of loose hair in the coat, brush "against the grain" first, and then finish up in the direction of the hair growth. Carefully cut out any mats that won't yield to combing. (If a pet is very matted, or the mats are close to the skin, be sure to have a vet or groomer do this. Cats, especially, can easily be badly injured by a slip of the scissors or other "mat cutter.") If you come across a burr or sticktight, crush it with pliers; then you should be able to comb the fragments out without much trouble.

Use your plastic trigger-spray bottle for yet another pet purpose here, to apply antistatic coat conditioner or other liquid products, full-strength or diluted, as you groom.

The grooming area should be a quiet one and your pet shouldn't be distracted by other pets, children, or loud noises. If you can, use a firm surface such as the tabletop or the top of an automatic dryer; there are also special grooming tables widely available.

Especially for small and medium-size animals, a sturdy nonslip surface that brings your pet up to a height that makes it easy to reach every part of him without bending will make you much less likely to skip grooming sessions. Each time you brush or groom the pet, use this same area.

Talking to your pet through the whole process, praising him as you go, and giving him a treat from time to time will usually help him cooperate. If he starts to get uneasy, you can try stopping for a few moments, changing the grooming site, or letting him shift position. If he tries to get away, have someone steady him while you groom.

Longhaired dogs can sometimes send enough hair down the drain to clog the pipes. Make sure your drain has a good metal filtering screen. In extreme cases, consider trimming a heavy-coated dog's coat extra short to reduce shedding fallout.

Wash your hands when you're finished and give the grooming table or area a quick cleaning with Nolvasan solution. Simply spray the surface with the solution and then wipe it off with a damp sponge or paper towel. Wash grooming tools in a mild detergent periodically, as you would a hairbrush.

Stepping up your dog's bathing schedule (such as to once a week during heavy shedding season) will also help head off hair. Bathing will loosen and remove dead hair before it's spread all over the house. If you do bathe a pet as often as this, it's extra-important to use a shampoo that's properly balanced for your pet. Give your pet a good vigorous body massage before you plop him into the tub, to loosen the fur that's about to fall out anyway.

10,000 Miracle Hair Pickup Tools

In teaching cleaning seminars to audiences that include a lot of enthusiastic pet owners, I'm flooded with devices to try. Including hair pickup devices. Some of these do pick up a lot of hair at first, but then usually 50 percent less with each swipe. Foam pickup devices, for example, are less effectual as they age. **The tape or tacky paper roller devices do a pretty good job of pickup.** They even pull embedded hair out of fabric. But they only work well as long as the adhesive is fresh—you have to keep peeling down to a fresh new layer. And while these may be among the best for a limited area like clothing, this can be an expensive way to clean a couch or sitting room. If you are going to use a tape roller on furniture and the like, there are longhandled rollers as large as a paint roller, to make them easier to use on large flat surfaces.

Many people use masking tape for removing hair from furniture and clothes; although it's more universally available, it's almost as expensive as the rollers for use on large areas and more awkward to handle—you waste all the tape that sticks to itself and sticks to you. If you're going to use tape, better yet is wider and stickier plastic packing tape. As for the old housecleaner's trick of rubbing a damp sponge or damp cloth over the surface to be dehaired, this technique is a useful one—as long as the damp cloth is stickier than the surface. If you use a damp cloth on a baseboard, the hair *will* all come off and cling to the rag. But try the same thing on drapes, upholstered furniture, or carpet, and 75 percent of it will roll up into little wads and stay there (even this can be helpful, though, because it makes it much easier than removing those little hair wads with a vacuum).

A damp cloth works on slick surfaces because the water cuts the static electricity that causes the hair to cling. You can also spray a hard surface lightly with water from your spray bottle and then wipe up the hair with a paper towel. There is even a special spray designed to release the static that holds pet hair to surfaces—Fresh 'n Clean Pet Hair Vac Away, by Lambert Kay (*www.lambertkay.com*).

A woman in Eugene, Oregon, gave me one of the few hair pickup tools that has ever impressed me. This "pet rake" (see page 8, Chapter 1) had crimped nylon bristles. I promised to try it on the bed where Snoopy, our thirteen-year-old shameless shedder, spent most of his senior-citizen time. I couldn't believe it—it actually worked! I've bought and used lots of these since then, and everyone who tries them says the same thing. It gets hair (and, for that matter, thread and lint) up quicker and more quietly than a vacuum can. When you sweep it toward you with light strokes, it gets the hair up easily off upholstered furniture, cushions, draperies, stairs, car interiors, bedding, along the edge of the carpet, and under the bed. Use it on edge and it'll even get the hair out of tufting, cording, and seams. These are not easy to find in stores or catalogs, so I've added it to the pro supplies available to my readers by mail (see page 5, Chapter 1).

Hair on the Floor

On soft flooring, vacuum it off. Easier said than done, you say? We've all been in the situation where we made sixteen passes with the vacuum over a clinging, contemptuous strand of hair that completely ignored us and refused to lift up off the floor. Why, we wonder, can that vacuum manage to pick up paper clips, nails, BBs, coins, and even rocks, yet leave feather-light hair lying on the floor, making a fool of us?

The steel balls sucked up so impressively at vacuum demonstrations are just slightly smaller than the vacuum hose. Once in the hose, it's like blowing a dart through a blowgun—there's no way for the air to go around the ball, it has to push (or pull) it along the tube. A hair or thread on the carpet, on the other hand, is hard to dislodge with suction alone. The air current can't get ahold of it, so it just flows fiercely over the surface of the hair, never getting behind it to push it loose.

The vacuum's beater bar or brush is what gives us an even chance with clinging hair. It can root out embedded fur and pull it in. Canister vacs with "power wands" usually have a beater brush in the head. Lots of upright vacuums have beater bars, but they're often not adjusted low enough to be able to reach and grab all the hair and other fine debris. Vacuums have low to high pile settings that determine how low the beater bar will reach—so be sure to read your vacuum's instruction booklet and adjust it accordingly.

The brushes on a beater bar or brush may also be worn down and no longer effective. Check out your beater brushes, and replace them if necessary. Likewise, the belt that turns the beater bar may be stretched or cracked or otherwise worn so that it slips or doesn't turn the beater bar fast enough. Check the belt regularly and replace it when necessary with a new, tight belt.

Professional models of upright vacuums, such as the Windsor XP12, have stronger motors and beater bars and more suction than the ordinary home models do. The Windsor goes from carpet to hard floor without having to make an adjustment or pull out an attachment.

If you have allergies, or if pet hair removal is a major chore in your life, you may want to consider a vacuum made especially for the purpose, such as the Dyson Model DC07 Animal. This bagless vac is expensive ($500 at this writing), but people who have to battle pet hair in a big way day in and day out swear by it. For more information, call 866-693-9766.

A professional dust mop is one of the fastest, easiest, and

"My least favorite household chore is floors, because they are all hardwood, and I have a dog that sheds so much, you'd think I was pulling puppies out from under the couch and chairs! No matter how much I sweep or vacuum, I can never get all the hair."

most effective ways to collect and remove pet hair from every type of hard surface. Most supermarket or discount store dust mops are just dust distributors; what you want is a 12" or 18" professional swivel-head mop from a janitorial supply store. Here are the pro secrets of technique:

1. **Trim:** Your dust mop may have strings around the edges that are a little too long, so they end up scattering hair onto the baseboards. Take a pair of scissors and trim about ½ inch off the strands all around the outside of the mop. This will make the mop less floppy and enable you to control the dust and hair better.

2. **Treat:** Dust mops are most effective when they've been sprayed with dust mop treatment. You can get professional dust mop treatment at the janitorial supply store, or just use a little furniture polish or Endust. Spray the head of the mop generously and let it stand for a while so the oil can distribute itself evenly through the yarn; you might even want to leave the mop overnight before you use it. Now the mop will get a magnetic hold on that hair.

3. **Use:** Push the mop in one long continual stroke in front of you and keep it in constant contact with the floor. Once you start, don't pick up the mop and always keep the same side headed forward—if you lift or reverse the mop head you'll lose some of the dirt. With a swivel-head mop you don't have to lift to get into corners or under and around things—you just swivel the head. Mop the area closest to the baseboard last.

4. **Clean:** A dust mop will collect and hold most of the hair and other loose debris it picks up on the edges and bottom of the mop. To get rid of this stuff, shake the mop outside, or inside a large plastic bag. When the head gets dirty, shake it well and throw it in the washer all by itself. Wash in hot water with a good grease-cutting detergent and

maybe a little bleach, and then tumble it dry like a towel. Don't hang it out to dry or it'll be stiff—it needs to fluff up in the dryer.

5. **Store:** A dust mop should be stored head up and away from the wall. A janitor's closet hook (from a janitorial supply or home improvement store) will keep the mop a little distance from the wall, or you can just slip a sturdy plastic bag over the mop head when it's in storage, to keep oily stains off the wall.

A microfiber mop is another excellent tool for removing hair from hard floors, as is a rubber broom with soft, flexible bristles.

Getting Hair off Furniture

A vacuum with a beater brush is an effective tool for removing hair from furniture. The power wand of a canister vac is good for this (some vacs even have a mini power wand for furniture). Some hand vacs, such as the Electolux Little Lux, also have motor-driven beater brushes, and this is what you want and need for effective hair removal.

You can even vacuum sturdy upholstered seats using an upright vacuum with a beater bar, just as you do the carpet. If you do this regularly, hair won't have a chance to accumulate. Delicate fabrics and loose weaves, however, should *not* be vacuumed in this way.

On a limited area like furniture or drapes, you can also use a tape roller or masking tape. There are also special sponges made for hair removal on surfaces like this. One such is the Pet Sponge, a natural rubber sponge that does a fairly good job and can be washed when necessary and reused. The manufacturer says it does a better job with long hair than short. As for the hair that ends up in places like baseboards, the kickboard underneath the kitchen cabinets, and other places under and beneath that the broom or vacuum always miss, a damp cloth or paper towel will take it right up.

A disposable cloth is really best because it's hard to rinse or wash hair out of a cloth—you often end up just spreading it around onto other surfaces.

Hair on Keyboards

Pet hair is hard on the keyboards of computers, calculators, and the like—it is not uncommon for them to collect so much hair between and eventually under the keys that they cease to function well and have to be replaced. You can help prevent this by covering your keyboard when it is not in use (there are special hard plastic and other covers available for this purpose). Dust keyboards in pet areas regularly with a good feather duster, and turn the machine off and vacuum the keyboard from time to time. There are sets of mini-attachments for vacuums designed for just this purpose.

Hair on Clothes and Blankets

The washing process alone won't necessarily get all the hair off hair-laden fabric, nor will dry cleaning. Hair comes off cotton and polyester fairly well in a washer but sticks tight to a napped or fuzzy material like flannel or wool. **Slick or smooth fabric surfaces repel hair, or at least enable it to be removed more easily.**

Professional launderers say, "We do the same thing you do; we pick pet hair off with our fingers or roll masking tape around our hand and lift it off." Dry cleaners do the same thing. There's no magic cure, but there are a few things that will help.

Shake the article outside, if possible, before you launder it. **Take large items such as blankets down to the Laundromat and use one of the large-capacity washers,** the ones with the bigger and stronger drums. (If you're lucky enough to have one of the new front-loading washers, you can do this right at home.) Then wash the article, being sure not to overfill the machine; you want plenty of water swishing around with what you're washing to rinse away the hair. Use your regular detergent and then add a little Nolvasan to the rinse water for an extra attack on germs and odor. If possible, give the clothes an extra rinse cycle to help float the hair off.

Take the article out when it's done and shake it while it's still damp. Then, put it in the dryer with three or four fabric softener sheets—this will reduce the static electricity that holds the hair to the fabric. You can also use liquid fabric softener, either in the wash or rinse cycle. Putting an article in a dryer set on cool, or in a dryer with a sheet of fabric softener, is another way to help remove animal (or human) hair. Then shake the article again when it comes out of the dryer. Whatever hair is left now will have to be taken off with tape.

Afterward, wipe out the washer and dryer—especially the dryer—with a damp cloth to remove loose hair. Empty the lint traps of both dryer and washer promptly.

A Good Bed . . . Will Lessen Pet Mess

If the pet home base—the bed—is appealing and comfortable, your pet will spend a lot of his sleeping, rolling, and shedding time there instead of on your furniture and carpeting.

Most cats and dogs, as their perennial attraction to human furniture has proven over the years, do prefer "soft" spots, except for very hairy northern breeds of dogs who may actually prefer a cool, hard surface. A padded bed is especially important for older dogs and large, heavy breeds, to prevent sores and calluses. Small dogs and cats often prefer to have the ultrasnug atmosphere of an enclosed or high-sided bed. In general, cats are cubbyholers; dogs are nesters.

Cats can be very individualistic and hard to figure, and they actually prefer a bed above ground level—especially if there are children or other pets in the house. For this reason, a cat perch (usually a wooden or carpeted shelf that can be attached to the windowsill) might please your pet.

The best pet bed is the simplest. It doesn't need carved legs or elaborate headboards for your pet to chew up and scatter all over the house. Two of the simplest pet beds are the soft padded cushions with sturdy fabric covers and the fabric or plastic platforms raised slightly off the floor.

No matter how nice it looks, smells, and feels, make sure the bed is washable—preferably, both the bed fabric covering and any padding or cushioning in it should be machine washable and dryable. At the very least, it should have a washable cover that can be removed like a slipcover. Forget pet beds with foam cores. Even if the covers are removable and washable, the cores can't be machine washed or dried. Pet bed padding with cedar chips included is usually not washable, either. Pet beds made of thick medical-grade fleeces sewn together are completely washable. Earthdog beds are also 100 percent washable; they are sturdy and long lasting, and include designs that fit neatly into corners.

You also want a surface that will hold up to scratching, abrasion, and wear. Good choices here include polycotton, polycotton twill, or polycotton poplin; cotton duck; denim; tight-weave muslin; even oxford cloth or 100 percent medium-weight cotton.

If your pet bed has a wooden or wicker base or enclosure, be sure it's sealed with varnish or polyurethane to make it waterproof and washable. And be sure to buy (or make) an extra cover for your pet's bed so he won't be hovering around homeless on washday.

You *want* the surface of the pet bed to absorb pet body oils and secretions and spills, so **this is one place you should not use stain repellent.** But you don't want the filling to be absorbent, so polystyrene beads are a good choice for a soft, insulated bed. Cedar shavings are much favored as a pet bedding because they're believed to repel fleas and other insects. But it's never been actually proven, and bird dog fanciers insist that constant exposure to cedar and its pungent odor blunts a pet's delicate scenter. Pine wood shavings with a little flea powder added might do just as well, or even better. Foam rubber is *not* recommended, as it absorbs odor and poses a safety hazard if a dog chews through to it.

The Weekly Once-Over

Once a week, shake out the bed and vacuum off the padding. Wipe down any hard surfaces and the floor around and under the bed with a deodorizing cleaner or an all-purpose cleaning solution. To disinfect these areas from time to time, spray or wipe them with a Nolvasan solution, then rinse well. Once in a while, take up grimy toys (if they're washable) and soak them in Nolvasan solution, scrub them, then rinse them off.

Wash the cover of your pet's bed every two weeks or so. Use a lint roller on it first to remove most of the loose hair, and then wash it separately in hot water and detergent, with a capful of deodorizing cleaner added. If you want to disinfect, soak in a Nolvasan solution before washing.

Location

Dogs, especially, like to be in a position to hear and see household activities, so their bed ought to be somewhere right off the main living area of the house. Pick a place that isn't smack in the middle of the traffic patterns, and never put the dog bed or box on or near steps. The room you're likely to confine your pet in while you're away is a good place for the pet bed. In his crate is good if he's crate trained.

Most animals can take cold a lot better than they can take drafts. Never put a bed in a drafty area, or very close to a door. Concrete holds heat and cold—seemingly forever. Eighty percent of the time it's cold, and a thin towel or rag on the floor in the garage or in the dog run isn't very considerate of you. A ¾-inch thick sheet of sealed plywood (with a couple of narrow strips of wood nailed to the underside to keep it off the ground) under your pet's blanket will keep the concrete from passing its cold into your pet's body. This will prolong your pet's life as well as keep him sleeping where you want him to.

For outdoor pet beds in the doghouse, shed, garage, barn, or dog run, it's even more important to have a dry, draft-free spot that's also elevated a few inches above the ground to prevent chill transfer. The "sleeping compartment" should be small enough to help hold in the dog's body heat.

Outdoors, the bedding can be shredded newspapers or clean, dry straw (hay is dusty and may contain weeds to which your pet is allergic). Wood shavings—from a pet supplier, not a sawmill—are even better.

Pets Lying on Furniture

One of the great battles of the pet household between them (the pets) and us (the alleged masters)—and often also between the various human members of the household—is our pets' endless efforts to occupy the furniture.

If you don't want your pet on the furniture, you have to teach him that it's absolutely OUT! The hard part about this is managing to be consistent. You have to teach him this right from the start, from the time he's a pup.

He must understand that it's *never* okay to sit on the furniture—or that it's only okay when we specifically tell him so with a certain command. Our pets suffer a lot from our own vacillation over the question of whether they're allowed on the furniture or not.

If he's an adult animal and has already entrenched his position, rigorous retraining is in order. Lift him off or squirt him with your Scat bottle—all the while uttering a loud and firm *"no"* or *"off"* or *"down."* If your verbal warnings are being ignored, put a leash on the dog and direct him to his clean, fluffy, and inviting dog bed. Bone up on the commands "leave it" and "stay" as well as "come here." If he makes an attempt in your presence, snap the lead and say "off" in a deep and emphatic tone. **Do not use the leash to drag the dog off of your furniture.**

No matter what method you use, you have to stick with it and evict him every time you catch him. Then encourage him to go to *his* bed by making the whole area around the bed clearly his area—an appealing, warm, undrafty place with some toys and maybe a pet mat. Teach him the word "place" or "bed" and train him to understand that *here* is where he goes when he wants to rest, sleep, or just watch the passing parade.

If your pet stays off the furniture while you're there, but you keep coming home to a warm couch, you have to get more ingenious.

The following are some off-putters you can employ:

- Cover the furniture in jeopardy with an old sheet or bedspread to protect it while you're gone, and take it off when you return (the resignation approach).
- Use an electronic detection device to warn the approaching dog that he's heading for trouble if he stays on this course. There are even "Scat Mats" made to give pets a mild shock when and if they plunk themselves down on

a forbidden area, but most pet owners (and people with young children) prefer to use these only as a last resort.

- Apply one of the aerosol pet repellents made for inside use to a rag or towel and drape it over the furniture you want to protect.
- Make the furniture repulsive by cat or dog standards by covering the seat with aluminum foil, or the whole thing with plastic sheeting. (Dogs and cats dislike the feel and sound of foil, and cats hate to lie in plastic.) Or set down an unattractive surface such as an X-Mat.
- Confine him—use a closed door or crate or pet gate to keep him out of the prime-furnishings patch.

If, on the other hand, you feel that your pet is entitled to be up on the furniture, make sure all your upholstered furniture is treated with a stain repellent such as Scotchgard. Or you could designate one piece of furniture—a "sacrificial chair," say—that your pet is allowed on, and buy a sturdy cotton canvas, twill, poly/cotton, or denim slipcover for it. *Surefit.com* has a wide selection of rugged, inexpensive, well-fitting covers. Or cover the chair with an old quilt or an easily washable spread, or make a terrycloth cover for the cushion your pet favors. There are also a wide variety of "pet slipcovers" for furniture in pet stores and catalogs, specially designed to drape over part of the couch or whatever serves as an attractive compromise. **Wash any pet spread or cover regularly.**

And, of course, choose new furnishings accordingly. Rugged fabrics that resist staining and scratching and don't hold hair are the best bet.

Strange Bedfellows

Pets on the bed mean loose hair on and in the bed, stains, and all the other cleaning complications of pets on the furniture. Plus some extra problems: ringworm, ticks, mites, and diseases that our pets may harbor, especially if they're outside animals. Mattresses and beds make excellent homesites for the fleas only too likely to infest our pets. And for those of us allergic to cats or dogs, the bed is the worst possible place we can allow a pet to be.

A pup, kitten, or very small dog could also be injured by midnight rolls and tosses, or they could fall off the bed and get hurt. Cats, being nocturnal animals by nature, have to readapt their schedule to sleep with us. And dogs can be so encouraged by the thought that they get to sleep in this obvious power location—the bed—that they may decide it's their bed, that *they're* top dog and in control, and can even become dangerously aggressive.

Make sure your pet is healthy—disease and parasite-free—before letting him sleep with you. This means a checkup every six months or so to catch pet health problems before they become your health problems.

You can train your pet to stay off the bed, if he's already encroached on it, by any of the training methods described earlier. Give your pet a sense of togetherness and security—without being right up there under the covers with you—by putting his bed in the same room with yours (unless you're allergic to him). There are pet beds for dogs that will give him a little mattress of his own on the floor, complete with mattress cover and orthopedic support.

If you decide to allow your pet on the bed, make sure it has an easily washable spread that camouflages your pet's hair. A printed spread will serve this purpose better than a plain solid color will. **See that your pet stays on top of the spread— not under the covers or on the pillows.** You'll also want to wash the blankets more often (a little Nolvasan added to the rinse water wouldn't hurt). If your pet sleeps with you, it's extra important that you brush him often—even daily.

Bath Time! (Uh-Oh)

Kathy Walter was a student of mine at a college professional cleaning course, and the letter she wrote me could sum it all up.

Dear Don,

My husband was out of town for a few days and I decided to surprise him when he returned with a nice clean dog. With the help of my son, I got the dog (Sam) in the tub and proceeded to lather him up. He was quite taken with the lather and began licking it off. I figured this was fine because at least he stood still and was easy to wash. But he soon tired of the soap bubbles and bounded out of the tub, headed for the back door. Sprinting after him, I slipped on the wet floor, twisting my ankle and hitting my elbow. The dog, of course, had stopped long enough in several spots to shake himself vigorously and dirty suds ran down half the walls in the house. After a lively race in the backyard and a quick roll in the freshly plowed garden, we had the dog back in the house. Naturally, he stopped in the living room to roll his newly acquired mud all over the carpet. We resumed the bath, and within minutes Sam started to gag. (I guess the lather he ate, along with the rousing race in the yard, made him sick to his stomach.) Again he leaped out of the tub and before we could recapture him, he vomited several times in the dining room. We caught him again, cleaned up the mess, and went back to the bath.

The next day the house smelled like a thousand-pound wet dog. All the dog hair we'd washed down the drain had collected in the trap. I called a plumber to clean the trap, and now the drain smelled better, but the carpet was dirty and stinky. As if in answer to my prayers, a vacuum cleaner salesman appeared at the door and offered to clean my carpet if I would listen to a two-hour sales pitch that left me late getting the kids from school, late starting dinner, and totally unprepared for the ten Cub Scouts I'd promised an afternoon of leathercraft.

The next morning Sam had sore paws and began scratching his ear, and as we learned at the vet's, the ear had water in it from the fateful bath. And Sam's sore paws and rear were the result of being on the freshly cleaned carpet before it dried. We left with ointments for both ends of the dog and all four feet.

Now, all of us expert pet bathers reading Kathy's story sigh and say, "Well, no wonder—she did everything wrong," but we know in our hearts that no bathing of pets is without some mess and strain. You could think of pet bathing as making an angel food cake—after quite a bit of work you end up with a fantastic fluffy final result that makes all the mess and effort worth it!

Pets do have to be bathed from time to time, but not as often as we might think. We humans are bath- and shower-crazy. Not long ago, a weekly bath was acceptable; now everyone is in the shower for an hour twice daily. So we tend to think our pets need a frequent bath or washing, too—but not so! Your special pet or situation may be different than the average, but all the experts agree: **If a pet is groomed as often as he should be—he'll rarely need a bath.**

There are healthy, happy, attractive show-quality dogs that have never had a bath—ever! For a hairy creature like a pet, brushing and combing do as good or better a job of removing dirt, dander, excess oil, and even fleas than the immerse-in-water-and-scrub ritual. In general, a dog should be bathed only if he looks dirty; smells bad; gets into something awful; or after he swims in polluted, chlorine-treated, or salt water. There are also some breeds like Airedales and Scotties whose hair holds dirt that can't easily be removed by brushing.

Outdoor dogs should definitely be bathed *less* often because the natural oils in their coats, which bathing removes, help protect them from the weather. If your dog has a BO problem or you're allergic to pet dander, you may want to wash him once a month or so, but the most you should ever wash a dog for any reason is once a week.

If you bathe your pet too often, his skin and fur will dry out. And wet animals are extra susceptible to drafts and chills, so pups under three months should never be bathed, and very old dogs and pups under six months, only when absolutely necessary. Very young and old animals don't have

the resistance to fight the respiratory infections that might follow. You also never want to bathe a sick pet or one near the end of pregnancy.

The same general rules of when to bathe apply to cats, just add the words "or even less often." Neutered cats, especially, tend to have less body odor than dogs, and cats groom themselves more often. And cats make dogs' attitude toward bathing look positively enthusiastic. But longhaired cats, especially, sometimes get into something that really needs to be washed off, or they may need a flea shampoo or a bath for other medicinal reasons.

You might get by with a waterless bath. To clean a pup, an older dog, or a cat, especially, without wetting them, use a dry shampoo to remove the dirt and excess oil in the coat. Powders and spray foams are commercially produced for just this purpose, and some of the best are Vetbasis Foaming Cleanser Waterless Bath, and Veterinarian's Best Dry Clean Waterless Bath.

No-rinse shampoos available, too, and they are usually applied directly from the bottle, worked into a lather, and then toweled off. Pet wipes are made for both dogs and cats now as well, to give you yet another option for cleaning your pet in whole or part without washing him.

You can also use ordinary cornstarch. Simply sprinkle or spray it on, work it into the coat well, leave it on for a few minutes, and then brush your pet vigorously until you get it all back out. This process is best performed outside, if possible, for obvious reasons.

Where Should We Bathe Our Pet?

Few of us have the perfect place to bathe a pet—it usually comes down to a choice between the kitchen sink and the bathtub or shower stall. Either way, there's lots of spilled and splashed water and with the tub, a lot of bending over. If you have stationary tubs in the utility or laundry room, basement, or garage, you can use these, too, but be sure that wherever you bathe your pet is well heated and free of drafts. You can bathe your dog outside, if it's a warm sunny day, but be sure to keep him on a leash throughout the process if you want to be sure the bath ends up a net gain.

In the sink or the tub, a sprayer attachment speeds up the whole process (which pets really appreciate). **A sprayer attachment makes it easier to do a good job of rinsing without panicking a pet,** which a blast from the showerhead proper will surely do.

A rubber bath mat on the bottom of the tub or sink will make your pet a lot happier. From a pet's standpoint, it's bad enough being wet and soapy without having this take place on a slippery, uncertain surface.

A pet tub about waist-high is the ideal arrangement, and fortunately you can buy these now from pet catalogs. There are also tubs a dog can step into easily outdoors that get their water power from a garden hose. Special pet tubs like these usually have nonskid bottoms, sprayers, and leash holders to help keep a dog where you want him through the process.

What Soap or Shampoo Should We Use?

Don't ever think that when it comes to washing an animal, any old soap will do—chemicals are all too easily absorbed through the skin in the act of bathing. Never use dishwashing detergent or any household detergent to shampoo pets, especially kittens or puppies. Cleaners like these can cause serious burns on pets. It's important to use a pet shampoo designed especially for the type of pet you're washing. (Read the label!)

Dog shampoos, for example, can be dangerous or deadly for cats, and people shampoo has the wrong pH for a dog or cat. Human shampoo, which is slightly acid, will give your pet an itchy skin and dry, flyaway hair that breaks easily.

Pet shampoos not only have a somewhat alkaline "proper pH," but many of them are tearless and antistatic, too. There are pet conditioning shampoos; texture shampoos for rough-coated dogs like terriers; shampoos for pets with skin problems such as mange, oily dandruff, or eczema; and shampoos that neutralize and remove pet body odor. There are aloe vera and many other "herbal recipe" pet shampoos. Specially formulated pet shampoos are even available to enhance different coat colors such as black, brown, or bronze; shampoos for white dogs remove yellowish discolorations.

> It's important to use a pet shampoo designed especially for the type of pet you're washing.

If your pet managed to roll in something malodorous, or otherwise has need of serious deodorizing, there are deodorizing shampoos available for both cats and dogs, as well as products that can be used on either, such as Nilodor's Deodorizing Pet Shampoo, and Out! Deodorizing Shampoo for Dogs and Cats.

There are conditioners specially designed for pets, too, that do the same sorts of things the human conditioners do: condition the hair, give it more body, and make it glossier and more manageable. Pet conditioners will also help prevent matting, and if you have a pet allergy problem, you can even apply them and then not rinse them off. This will help keep the tiny skin flakes (dander) from flaking off your pet's body all over the house.

Never use turpentine, paint remover, or other strong solvents to remove tar or paint from an animal's coat. They can burn or irritate your pet's skin, or even poison him. Instead, soak the spot well with vegetable oil and leave it on overnight to allow the oil to penetrate. Then wash the area with pet shampoo and warm water. If that doesn't do it, and the spot isn't right next to the skin, just (very carefully!) cut out the patch of affected hair. It'll grow back soon enough.

Pet Bathing Psychology and How-Tos

First off, remember that if you start getting a pet used to being bathed while he's young, he's much more likely to tolerate or even enjoy the process. A calm, pleasant, but firm manner assures your pet you know what you're doing and that escape is out of the question. Avoid abrupt movements that might alarm an already antsy pet. **Some of the most effective pet bathers keep up a gentle, reassuring patter with their pet throughout the whole process,** pouring on some praise with the water at the most harrowing moments. You may want to recruit a helper to help steady the pet (a cat, especially) through the initial skirmishes.

If your dog is likely to bolt, or is a really stubborn resister, you might want to put him on a leash with a half check or martingale and have someone hold it tight above his head throughout the bath (not so high that he can't breathe, though). If you attach your pet's leash to something to hold him while you bathe him, make sure it's a towel bar, not the hot water faucet.

Right before the bath, make sure your pet has a chance to go outside for a walk or to the litter box. You don't want to have to worry about nature's call in the middle of the bath, and if you have to let a wet pet outside right after a bath, you run the risk of chills and colds as well as rolls in the topsoil.

Brush your pet well to remove loose hair and any snarls, mats, or tangles, or the bath will only worsen them. If you discover that your cat has mats, forget right there and then about bathing him. It will only worsen the matting.

Run a dry cotton ball gently around the inside of your pet's ears to remove debris, and if it seems necessary, gently clean ears with a finger wrapped in a soft cloth moistened with mild soap and water, or a commercial pet ear cleaning preparation. Don't probe deep into the ear with a cotton swab. To keep soap and water out, put cotton balls moistened with mineral oil or Vaseline in your pet's ears. A drop of mineral oil in each eye will help keep shampoo from stinging.

Basic Dog Bathing 101

If you're bathing a big dog, you may as well slip into your swimsuit now and admit that before it's over, you're going to be right in there beside him. Put several inches of lukewarm water in the tub before you start. Then lift your dog gently into the tub. Using a plastic pitcher, wet him down well with lukewarm water, from his neck to his tail. (Save the head for last, to postpone the panic button.)

> Don't rub hard on or twist the dog's hair.

If your pet has fleas, start lathering around the ears and on the head first to keep the fleas from fleeing into his ears, then shampoo back from the neck toward the tail. If he doesn't have a flea problem, working from the tail end forward will scare him a little less.

Work up a good lather with your fingers (the superior tool for the purpose, all the experts agree) and massage your way down to the skin, but don't rub hard on or twist the dog's hair. With longhaired dogs, part the hair of the coat down the middle of the back and keep it parted during the bath to prevent hair breakage and tangling. "*Squeeze* the shampoo through the coat as if you're washing a delicate sweater," professional groomer Shirlee Kalstone says.

Pet bathers are inclined to do a big number on the back, chest, and shoulders, and forget about the tail, the rear end, the underside of the body, and the legs and feet. **Remember that pet BO is strongest on bare skin areas, so don't neglect them.** Feet are best lifted up one at a time to wash. You can usually safely employ the dousing and lathering technique on the neck and up to behind the ears, but the face itself and muzzle are best approached (very cautiously) with a soapy sponge or washcloth.

You may want to repeat the shampooing process, after rinsing, if your pet is longhaired, dense-coated, or very dirty. But resist the temptation to slack off a little on the rinsing. If you don't remove all the soap and shampoo, you'll have a pet with a dull coat and itchy skin. (The old rule of thumb, "Rinse until you think it's all rinsed out, then rinse twice more," is a good one here.) As noted earlier, a hand sprayer can be a big help. To get those last hard-to-reach spots, you can refill the tub with a few inches of clean water and splash it up underneath your pet.

A little vinegar or lemon juice added to the rinse water will cut the soap film, and a little baking soda added to it will make your pet's coat softer, shinier, and more odor-free.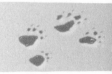

We professionals dry paint rollers by spinning them, and that's exactly how dogs and cats get moisture off themselves. Dogs, especially, are going to shake when they're wet. You're not going to curb or eliminate the shaking instinct, so better they do it in a controlled area than all over the house. In fact, their shaking will get the bulk of the water off a lot more efficiently than our soggy towels can manage. If you're bathing the animal inside, let him shake a few times after you finish rinsing—close the shower curtain or take cover behind a towel and move back and wait; he'll do it. (As soon as the dog is dry, you can grab your squeegee and slick all the droplets off the shower walls in a wink.)

Then dry your pet off with a couple of big, clean towels before you let him loose in the house. Be sure to keep him in a warm, draft-free place for three to four hours, until he's completely dry. Dogs or cats with heavy or double coats may take longer than that to dry fully—you may want to use a hair dryer (set on warm, not hot) to speed the process, or one of the high-speed dryers made specially for pets. If you use a dryer, brush your pet as you dry him, in the direction the hair naturally lays. If it's a warm sunny day, you could let a dog dry off outside—on a leash, or you'll be back to square one before you know it. Don't forget to take the cotton out of your pet's ears when you're done.

After he's dry, brush him well to restore the shine to his coat and remove the hair loosened by the bath. You'll notice by now that for all the struggling he did before and during, he seems prouder than you of the "after."

Cat Bathing 101

Cats in general seem intent on making it clear that they can keep themselves clean, thank you. So a cat bath is best approached as a two-person job. One person holds (restrains, grips, and attempts to soothe) while the other wets, soaps, and rinses. And watch those claws—**a day or two before the bath might be a good time to clip your cat's claws.**

A sink is better than a basin for the purpose—it can't be tipped over in the fray, even if your cat braces his feet against it. A two-compartment sink is better yet, because you can set the cat in one side and fill the other with clean lukewarm water for wetting and rinsing. In cat bathing, faster is always better, and it helps a lot to not have to wait for your pitcher to refill with rinse water. To help keep your cat steady during the bath, try folding a terrycloth towel and putting it in the bottom of the sink, or use an ordinary window screen in the bottom of a larger tub. Either of them will give the cat something to sink his claws into and anchor himself during the bath.

Grip the cat securely by the scruff of the neck and put your other hand under his chest, pointing him (and all those claws) *away* from you. Then set him gently in the empty sink; this will panic him less than an attempt to dunk him in a sink that's already filled with that awful water. Gently pour pitchers of the lukewarm water over him to wet him thoroughly, then apply some shampoo and work up a good lather. If you're using a tangle-removing shampoo, make sure you saturate every tangle with it. **Cat faces, too, are best cleaned with a washcloth.** Be especially sure to rinse a cat well; you can be sure they'll be licking themselves vigorously after a bath. Then wrap Kitty in a big clean towel and dry him off as much as you can before you put him in a warm place to finish drying.

De-Flea Your Life

Fleas often go unseen, but they rarely go unfelt, and a single animal can be infested by 100 or more of the nasty little buggers. Most flea species stick to their own particular host, but if deprived of its usual dinner, a flea will attack other warm-blooded animals, and humans aren't exempt. These tiny bloodsuckers can take big bites, causing skin irritation and even anemia, and a pet can catch tapeworms from a flea if he happens to swallow it.

The only remedy is ridding your life of the tiny rascals. But this isn't a matter of sprinkling a little flea powder on your pet from time to time. It's a full-scale war.

Fleas, just like butterflies, go through four distinct life stages: adult, egg, larvae, and pupa (cocoon stage). Once an infestation gets started, immature stages of fleas (eggs, larvae, and cocoons) can be found in carpets, floor cracks, bedding, furniture, and damp sheltered areas anywhere in the house and yard. So, to get rid of fleas, you have to treat not merely your pet but his whole surroundings, and you have to use measures that will kill the adult fleas *and* the fleas at immature stages. Since no product can yet manage to kill flea pupae, you have to keep treating until all the existing cocoons have hatched and you've destroyed all the future crops of fleas.

A flea elimination campaign is indeed a battle plan—you have a lot of ground to cover. This means: Treat the pet himself (*all* your pets) with a flea control product or thorough flea combing. Treat all the parts of the house your pet frequents, the inside of the car if he goes there, too, and your pet's bedding and roosting places with a spray or fogger, and spray the yard. (Don't let your freshly treated pets back into the house or yard till you've finished treating those areas.) Repeat the process as often as the product labels tell you to.

Then **you have to stay on the alert for reinfestation from animals and areas outside all your treated areas.** You can do this all yourself, or have an exterminator do much or all of it. But thoroughness and tenacity are the name of this game, for sure. You can't do half the steps and neglect the other half, or only attack fleas in fits and starts. The best approach of all is to start flea control before the flea season gets in full swing. In most parts of the United States, that means in the spring, before the weather reaches the 75 to 95 degrees and high humidity fleas like best. By the time you see fleas on your pets, your home and yard are already infested. One female flea lays forty to fifty eggs a day, and in thirty days, ten female fleas can multiply to over a quarter of a million new fleas in various stages of development!

Insecticides

It's easy to be confused by the incredible array of flea products and preparations available, from spot-on treatments and orally administered products to sprays, dusts, dips, shampoos, and foggers. The thing to realize is that when it comes to flea control products, "There's no such thing as a perfect 10."

Before choosing a flea product, take your pet to the vet and have his level of infestation checked out, or take a close look at him yourself. When you part his hair, does it look like crosstown traffic, or do you have to dig to find a flea or two? When you comb him, does the comb quickly fill with black flea "dirt"? Do you get five fleabites on the ankle every time you walk across the rug in your stocking feet? Do you need the extra-strong products dispensed only by vets, or that can be used only by professional exterminators? Fleas, like other insects, become resistant to insecticides over time—your vet will know which are likely to work best in your area at this particular point in time.

Never use dog flea killers on cats, or vice versa—their systems and chemical tolerances are entirely different. Cats are especially sensitive to insecticides, and some products used on dogs can kill cats. **Read the label of any flea product carefully before applying it.** Insecticide application is the *last* place you ever want to consider acting on the popular assumption that more is better—*always* follow directions exactly and don't use more than one kind of chemical flea remedy on your pet at once. Consult a veterinarian before using any kind of flea killer on very young, old, or ill animals, or pets that are pregnant or nursing.

Topical Spot-on Products

These are the newest method of flea control on pets. Most of them are applied to a pet's skin between the shoulder blades or striped down the animal's back. The flea-killing chemical migrates from here to the hair follicles, and continues to be released from the follicles to kill fleas for thirty days or more. These products often also kill ticks, and some of them also prevent flea egg development. Topical spot-ons include products such as Frontline and Advantage. Frontline Plus is a spot-on that will kill adult fleas and keep eggs from hatching as well.

A side benefit of long-lasting flea protection like the spot-ons is that there won't be "flea mess"—little dark and bloody spots—to clean up everywhere your pet sits or lies in the house.

Insect Growth Regulators

Insect growth regulators, or IGRs, can help to prevent a flea infestation because they keep fleas from laying viable eggs and make female fleas sterile. IGRs, which include chemicals like lufenuron, pyriproxyfen, and methoprene, do not kill adult fleas. Used alone or in combination with products that do kill adult fleas, they help break the flea life cycle. Program, for instance, is an IGR (lufenuron) given to dogs as a pill and cats as a liquid mixed with their food once a month. **To effectively break the flea life cycle, every animal in your pet's environment must be treated when using a product like this.**

One quick way to kill all of the adult fleas on a pet is with a pill called Capstar from Novartis Health. Within a short time (usually thirty minutes) after this pill is administered, every flea on your pet will drop off dead.

Sprays

The sprays designed to be used directly on your pet will kill fleas quickly, but the effects of ordinary flea sprays are not long lasting, for the most part. There are some better sprays available now. The same chemical used in the spot-on called

Frontline, fipronil, for instance, is also available in a spray, which will give you a month's worth of flea protection from a spraying. And the IGR pyriproxifen comes in a spray that will kill flea eggs on your pet for 150 days.

Most pet flea sprays are pump sprays, which are a lot less unsettling to a pet than aerosols. You can also **minimize scariness when applying conventional flea sprays by spraying the brush, instead of the pet, or by spraying behind your hand as it moves over your pet's body.** Or spray a towel with the product and then wipe the pet with it. Brush the hair backward and fluff it up as you spray. You don't have to drench the whole pet—concentrate on flea hotspots like the base of the tail, the hind legs, the neck, and the underside. Avoid spraying a pet's face and genitals and try to keep him from licking himself till the spray has a chance to dry.

When applying long-lasting sprays like Frontline, follow the label directions carefully.

When you're handling and applying sprays and other flea killers, wear rubber gloves and clothes that cover your arms and legs, because some insecticides can be absorbed through the skin. Remove and wash your clothes when you're done; don't eat, drink, or smoke after applying such products until you've washed your hands well. Keep all pets (and children) well out of the way when you're applying the remedies, and be sure there's enough ventilation to disperse any fumes—flea killers are poison.

Powders

Powders are messy and time-consuming to apply and somewhat short-lived in their effect, but they're generally safer and more easily tolerated by pets than other means of flea control. Be sure to apply powders in a place where you can vacuum up or hose away the fleas that fall off the animal. Set your pet on an old towel or sheet of newspaper before you start. Apply the powder over your pet's whole body, but don't overdo it, and stay away from the eyes and the inside of the ears. Work it through the hair all the way down to the skin, paying attention to flea havens, including around the outside of the ears, the hindquarters, and the base of the tail. Don't forget the legs and even between the toes.

Leave the powder on for about ten minutes and then brush or comb it out.

A Flea Comb

This nifty tool has thin metal teeth so closely spaced that even our agile and slender friend the flea can't evade them. Flea combs are the best option for older cats, very young kittens, and immune-compromised animals, who can be very sensitive to chemicals. There is also something satisfying about a flea control method that involves no poisonous chemicals, and the process gives you some "bonding time" with your pet. Some of the most highly recommended brands of flea comb include the Fine Idea flea comb for cats, the Four Paws flea comb, and the Lambert-Kay flea combs.

When flea combing, comb your pet thoroughly all over, starting with the head and working back. **Pay special attention to the area around the ears, the neck, and the base of the tail.**

Check your comb after each stroke. If you see a flea struggling on the teeth of the comb, dip the comb quickly into a bowl of water with a bit of liquid dish detergent in it. After you release the flea into the water, wipe the comb clean and dry with a tissue and continue.

Hand-picking fleas is probably the most demanding (it calls for a sharp eye and quick reflexes) and sporting approach—you simply comb your pet till you see a flea and then grab it between thumb and index finger. No matter how hard you grip it there, be assured you haven't killed it, so drop it into a bowl of soapy water. (Or, the most satisfying approach if you aren't using flea powder—into a fishtank so you can watch the thrashing flea be picked neatly off the surface by your favorite goldfish.)

Dips

Dips are another way of killing the fleas and ticks on an animal, especially a heavily infested one, and most dips will provide a good measure of protection for a week or two afterward. **But dips contain strong chemicals, so check with your vet before you use one,** especially on a very young or very old animal.

Despite the name, you don't have to dunk your pet in a dip—you apply it by sponging or pouring it over him after he's been wetted down with water, such as right after a bath. And you don't rinse a dip off; you let it dry right on the coat after squeezing off the excess. A dip is usually mixed up from concentrate; be sure to follow the dilution directions on the package. And since dips are one of the more powerful flea treatments, always be sure to do your dipping in a well-ventilated room.

Use lukewarm water to mix a dip, and when you apply it, stay away from your pet's eyes, mouth, and nose as well as any open sores. Cats are about as fond of dipping as they are of bathing, but if you can manage to dip your cat (better to have the vet or groomer do it), be sure to use a dip specifically for cats.

Flea Shampoos

Milder than dips, flea shampoos will kill the fleas on the pet but they won't keep your pet free of fleas for more than a day or so. Brush your pet well before shampooing to remove loose hair and mats and lather up his neck at the very start to keep fleas from running to his head for cover. Then lather the rest of his body, and do the hindquarters especially well. Leave the lather on as long as the directions say to, to be sure the chemical has time to work. Thorough rinsing is important here, and a spray attachment will be a real help.

Flea Collars

When flea collars—an outgrowth of the famous No Pest Strip, by the way—first came out, we all tended to think that here at last was a simple, neat, clean, effective, one-step way to deal with the problem once and for all. But while flea collars can be a useful aid, they are only an *aid* in controlling fleas and ticks on pets.

Remember, the fleas on the pet himself are only a small part of the story, and a collar only works on those. And there are some limitations and potential problems in how collars accomplish that. Flea collars are usually plastic collars impregnated with an insecticide that's steadily released in small amounts and gradually dispersed over the hair of the pet's whole body. They work more slowly than other forms of flea control—it may take several days after you put a collar on before it really does its thing. The collar (and the greatest force of flea killing) is near a pet's sensitive head, whereas the flea problem is usually worst on the hindquarters and around the tail. And pets can develop allergic or toxic reactions to a flea collar, so you have to watch any pet wearing one closely for redness, sores, or hair loss around the neck, or more serious symptoms such as listlessness or loss of appetite.

Flea collars are more effective on small, shorthaired dogs than on large, shaggy ones, and on shorthaired rather than longhaired cats. It's best to avoid flea collars when possible, since there are better options out there now.

Better than conventional flea collars are the newer ones that dispense IGRs (methoprene or priproxyfen) and thus prevent flea egg hatch for several months. Examples include Ovitrol and Ovitrol Plus Flea Egg Collars, sold through veterinarians, and products like the Fleatrol Flea Egg Collar, sold in pet stores.

If you do use a flea collar, never put it on tight; there should be at least an inch, or two finger-widths of space, between the neck and the collar. A breakaway style is safer, should your pet ever get hung up somewhere. Use only one flea collar at a time on any animal, and never use a flea collar on pups or very young kittens (read the label for the age restrictions), on a sick or nursing pet, or on a pet with no fleas. Never use an Escort flea collar on a Persian cat—they lack the liver enzyme needed to metabolize the chemical used in this collar. Many experts recommend airing out a flea collar for two or three days before putting it on your pet.

Check the expiration date on the box when you buy a collar. (If it has no such date, how shopworn does the package look?) Likewise, **collars are often left on too long, past the point of effectiveness.** Again, check the box—many collars are designed to work for three months or less, though there are some that work for nearly a year.

All in all, collars serve best as a measure of protection against reinfestation from areas and animals outside the bounds of your home-grounds flea-killing campaign.

Perhaps a better way to guard against reinfestation, after you've rid the pet and his quarters of fleas, is to make a practice of treating him each time he comes inside, as Gwen Bohnen-kamp suggests. This is a lot easier than it sounds. All you do is put a blanket in the animal's bed or crate, or in some quiet corner where he likes to idle away the day; liberally sprinkle the blanket with flea powder; and then train your pet to walk straight to his blanket and lie down there for a couple of minutes each time he comes inside. Once a week, wash or vacuum the blanket well and add fresh flea powder. You can also give your pet a flea combing after he's been out in untreated territory.

Treating the Place for Fleas

You can hire an exterminating service to spray inside and out-side the house every few months, or you can do it yourself, using flea-killing sprays, aerosol bombs, or foggers. (Sprays can reach every little crack and corner better than foggers.) A professional exterminator does have the advantage of knowing all of the favorite flea hiding places and of knowing how to get maximum kill.

If you decide to do the spraying yourself, try to choose (your vet can help you here) a spray that's effective on as many stages of the flea life cycle as possible, such as a spray that contains insecticide plus an IGR. You want a spray that is effective, but as safe as possible for the pets you have in your house and the many different kinds of household surfaces you'll have to spray it on. A flea-spraying operation is going to cover a lot of territory: floors, carpets, upholstered furniture and underneath it, drapes, the lower parts of walls, anywhere pets lie or climb, baseboards, edges, cracks, nooks and crannies, and even the insides of closets and underneath furniture cushions and appliances and between the mattress and box spring. If you don't cover all this, the fleas will just jump to the unsprayed places and continue to thrive and multiply. Be sure to clean well—vacuum, sweep, and declutter—before you spray, to get all the debris out of the way of the flea-killing agent.

Don't let any pets back into sprayed areas till they're fully dry and aired out, and be sure to repeat the spraying as often as the label instructs.

Carpet Powders

There are also powders to treat carpeting that use things like specially treated boric acid (sodium polyborate) or silica gel to dry the fleas and their larvae up, or diatomaceous earth to grind holes in fleas' hard outer shells. Products like these, which must be worked down into the carpet fibers and any excess vacuumed up, can really help keep down fleas or deal with an infestation. Examples include Fleabusters and Flea Stoppers Carpet Powder.

Fogging

Because fleas spend most of their time on the ground, fogging is a more practical treatment for problems related to flying insects. A fogger may pump insecticide out over an entire area, but it's hard for a fogger to reach all of the nooks, crannies, and "underneath" places (including beneath the edges of upholstered furniture) where fleas and their larvae hide. A good, thorough spraying is often more effective, and less wasteful, for the purpose.

But if you decide you want to fog your fleas away, **a vet or pet store or pet catalog is the best place to buy a fogger for use around pets.** Be sure to evacuate all pets (including fish and birds) as well as their food and water dishes and toys before fogging. Cover fishtanks well and turn off their filters.

You can't do one room this week and another room next week when fogging, because the fleas will just run from room to room. Put a fogger on each floor or in each room; there are mini-foggers that are just the right size for a single room. Get all pets and people out of there, go to the park or someplace for the day, and fog the whole place. (One good thing to do with the pets is to take them to a professional groomer for an expertly administered dip while you're fogging the fleas out of the premises.) Before you start fogging, declutter as much as possible, vacuum all carpeting and upholstered furniture (and then remove and discard the vacuum bag in the outdoor trash bin), open all the closet doors, and lift the skirts of sofas and the dust ruffles of beds—expose as many possible flea hideouts as you can—so the fog can reach everywhere.

Air out the house well and make sure everything is dry before moving yourself, your family, and your pets back in, and don't be tempted to move anything back in sooner than the label says.

To clear a flea infestation, fogging will have to be repeated as often as the label instructs.

Flea Traps

Fleas, like other insects, are attracted to light (and in this case will jump to it), so flea traps work. If you don't want to use chemicals to battle the flea problem, you can rig a small lamp that's not easy to tip over with a low-wattage bulb (not more than 60 watts) so that it shines all night on a shallow pan or light-colored dish of water set on the floor of a flea-infested room. Be sure to add about a tablespoon of dish detergent to the water in the pan to break the surface tension of the water so the fleas won't be able to crawl out and escape. As an extra safety measure (to keep pets from bumping over the light), it's not a bad idea to secure the lamp at the base to a 2-foot square of plywood or the like.

This method is 100 percent environmentally safe, as well as cheap. Keep the trap in operation in a given area till you don't find any dead fleas in the morning, then move it to another part of the house. But return it to each flea-infested room within three weeks to be sure to catch the next crop of developing fleas. If your house is badly infested, you may want to set up several traps.

A somewhat more sophisticated version of this device, which uses a piece of special sticky paper to catch the fleas, is available from Happy Jack, Inc., of Snow Hill, North Carolina. For more information on this device, call 800-326-5225 or go to *http://happyjackinc.com*.

Don't Forget the Yard . . .

Spraying is usually the most efficient way to treat a large area like a yard.

When you're de-fleaing your house, be sure to remember the backyard, the garage, and the doghouse in your flea-elimination program. Spraying is usually the most efficient way to treat a large area like a yard, and you can use a small power or compressed-air sprayer or a spray attachment on the hose. Or hire an exterminator. Here, again, you want to clean up and declutter before you spray (in this case yard litter, lawn clippings, leaves, dead vegetation in places where pets lie, piles of rotting lumber, and other debris). Use a product specifically for flea killing and concentrate on shaded areas and behind and underneath things. Keep the grass in the yard short and trim, and consider trimming overhanging tree branches to reduce shading.

Yard treatment may not have to be repeated (check the label of the chemical you're using) unless you have a reinfestation. In that case, the whole flea battle campaign will have to be waged over again.

Cleanliness: One of the Best Protections Against Fleas

Cleaning your home and its contents and the grounds around it, as well as the animal itself, will do a great deal to discourage fleas. **Leave no places available or untreated so that the fleas can't comfortably breed and reproduce.** Following are some specific instructions on how to clean to keep those fleas away.

1. Frequent and thorough vacuuming is one of the best ways to reduce the flea population—a good vacuum with a strong, properly adjusted beater bar or power wand will get a lot of the fleas and their larvae right where they live. The top priorities: carpet and upholstered furniture, cracks and corners and crevices, and around baseboards and other woodwork. Don't forget the inside of the car if your pet is a frequent passenger. When you're flea-vacuuming, be sure to use a disposable bag and dispose of it, well sealed in a plastic bag, right after you finish. (Better yet, incinerate it, if burning is allowed in your area.)

2. When you shampoo your carpet, have it steam cleaned by a strong truck-mounted unit. In steam cleaning, the water is heated to 170 degrees and applied under great pressure, which will help kill fleas and their larvae in their prime habitat—carpeting!

3. The pet's bed and anyplace else he beds down are the places you're surest to find developing fleas. Wash your pet's bedding in hot water and strong detergent at least once a week, being sure to rinse well. If he sleeps on disposable bedding,

change it often and discard the old bedding in a sealed bag. Sprinkle some flea powder in your pet's bed every few weeks or include the pet's bed in your spraying campaign if you use a flea spray. Don't forget to also treat any human bedding your pet comes in contact with, as well as furniture, area rugs, etc., he lays on.

4. Eliminate the cracks, crevices, and dark moist corners in your home where fleas and their larvae live. Caulk and fill any small holes or gaps or cracks, any possible places and passages for them to get in from outside. Eliminate all these and you'll be amazed at what you can accomplish with prevention.

5. Use a good flea control product on your pet when you groom and you'll add real help with flea reduction to the other advantages of grooming your pet. Put the combings in a plastic bag with a little flea powder and seal the bag before discarding it. And spray your grooming tools from time to time with a little flea spray to eliminate any fugitives that may be hanging on.

Flea Hideout Hotspot Checklist

Many pet owners spend a lot of time and money trying to control fleas on their pets, yet they do nothing about the pets' environment. Yet once fleas get started, your home and grounds can be full of fleas and their immature stages. So, as soon as fleas are killed on the pet, more jump on. For a flea-control program to be effective, you have to treat both the animal and his whole environment.

These are places fleas hide:

- Attic
- Under edges of throw rugs
- Lower part of draperies
- Beds

- Baseboards
- Walls to a height of about one foot
- Basement
- Carpeting
- Upholstered furniture
- Under furniture cushions and under furniture
- Corners
- Edges of carpet
- Seams and edges of hard floors
- Floor cracks
- Cracks and crevices (and other moist sheltered areas)
- Windowsills
- Pet's bed and bedding
- Other favorite pet napping places indoors
- Vicinity of all entranceways
- Bird or rodent nests
- Shady areas outdoors such as under bushes or trees
- The inside of the car
- Bare dirt or sand
- Crawl space under house
- Porch
- Grass or weeds
- Small holes that lead from outside to inside
- Sandbox or any sandy or graveled area
- The doghouse and around and under it
- Under outbuildings and sheds and in the garage
- Favorite pet napping spots outdoors

Chapter 6

Pets Do the Darndest Things:

Solutions to Jumping, Chewing, Scratching, Scavenging, Tracking in Messes, and Traveling

A pet's determination and agility should never be under-estimated, as an experience I had when I was eight years old taught me. My parents had butchered a prime steer, and selected a gorgeous roast to send to our neighbors. Mom put the roast on a large plate, spread a fresh dishcloth over it, and said, "Now Donny, take this over to Rose and Mel's and leave the cover on so the flies and dust won't get into it."

I knocked at the neighbor's front door, and as I wanted to make the presentation as astounding as possible, I snatched off the dishcloth and held that huge hunk of meat up proudly as Rose opened the door. The second I did this, a big barnyard cat that I hadn't seen stir in weeks sprang thirteen feet and snatched the roast from the plate. He hit the ground with the meat still gripped in his jaws, and Rose and I watched as the six-pound roast was dragged across the gravel and manure of the barnyard, and disappeared into the bushes to be consumed.

Since then, I've never underestimated an animal's ability or desire to jump, be it up cliffs or tables or counters.

Pets Jump to it

If you're going to have a pet, then the physical environment has to be of a strength, quality, and design that can handle it. Small pets usually do less damage than big pets. A Saint Bernard can dent a car if left alone with it in the garage. A big dog needs a big walkway, and a big tail can easily brush objets d'art from the coffee table. **Arranging and decorating your home to fit the size of your pet is much easier than teaching your pet to be small.** Go for sturdy tables and lamps instead of the spindly-legged kind, so bumps and vibrations won't be catastrophes. Eliminate loose and dangling electrical cords, or strategically position them so they won't be tripped over, chewed on, or pulled on to pull something down. Windowsills are naturally attractive because of the warm sunlight and the view of the great outdoors, so don't put things on sills or on the edges of shelves or mantels where they're almost sure to be knocked off.

Design things so that even if a pet does get up and on, he can't do any damage. Tile, marble, and glass sills and table-tops are sleek, cool, and can't be hurt. Plastic laminates, too, are almost pet-proof, and are very easy to clean.

Cats are curious by nature and born climbers, so use a curio cabinet with glass doors to protect your ceramic chicken collection (saves on dusting, too). It's unrealistic to expect a pet to tiptoe around little stands precariously balancing precious bric-a-brac. Pets, like us, can resist everything except temptation. Don't tempt your animal with frilly decorations. Dangling things will drive a playful cat crazy and pets have even more trouble than children understanding, "Don't touch!" Tassels and hanging macramé and heavily fringed curtains are natural playthings to a pet.

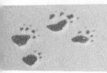

If your houseplants and flower arrangements are in heavy pots or vases (avoid the light little baskets and stork-like plant stands), they'll be less likely to be toppled by a passing or climbing animal.

Holiday ornaments can be a big pet problem. Don't put the ornaments that have been in the family for generations on the lower branches. Instead, put some unbreakables down there and tie them on securely. Tinsel is dangerous for pets, too—they can strangle or choke on it, and it can saw a hole in their intestines.

You can train a pet to not climb—it takes time and patience, but it can be done. Start when it's young and be consistent. The squirt bottle trick is workable here, if you catch him in the act. A good firm "No!" is another convincer. You can also put your pet on a leash, watch him, catch him in the act of going up on something, and then jerk the leash and say *"NO!"*

When you correct a pet for jumping up and get it down off something, take it easy. If your cat's claws are caught in the doily and you pluck him off the end table, whose fault is it when the vase crashes to the floor? Often more damage is done in the correction than in the initial transgression. People and furniture get scratched, and things get broken and spilled when we react violently to our pet's misbehavior.

Restricting the areas of the house the pet is allowed in is an obvious solution. Keep the animal in areas where no climbing can be done, or can't cause any problem if it is.

Tempt your pet away. You can build or buy a pet "swing set" with all kinds of goodies to keep your animal occupied and out of mischief. Place some little rewards on the legal climbing place and have a soft cushy perch at the top. And offer some sturdy active toys as alternatives. If pets, like children, have their own toys to play with, they'll be less likely to tamper with yours. If you have young children and are in the childproofing channel, you're already halfway pet-proofed.

Pets Jumping up on Counters or Tables

This is usually a food-related problem. If your dog or cat is always on the lookout for a tasty morsel or crumb, counters and tabletops are prime targets. **Don't ask for trouble by leaving food lying or defrosting on the counter** or table or in the sink when you're not around. Leaving dirty dishes lying out is almost as bad. Never feed your pet while seated around a table. If your dog is not well trained, remove him from

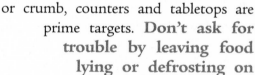

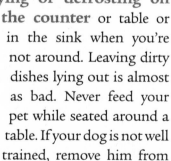

the area rather than risk a "grab and run" scenario. Don't permit your cat to skulk around the dining area, either. Remove him to another room or have your Scat bottle ready and waiting.

Discourage your pet from checking out counters and table-tops with a firm verbal warning. If that is not sufficient, use the squirt bottle, but don't let your pet see you take aim. Once again, when you are unable to supervise the situation, consider detector devices or perimeter alarms, which are equally effective with dogs and cats (see page 26, Chapter 1) and work when you are not around.

Decide on a training program and stick to it. **All family members must act in the same consistent manner if you expect your pet to understand** that jumping up onto counters and tabletops is nonnegotiable. Don't squirt or shoo him away today and find his saucer-slurping cute tomorrow. Harden your heart.

If your pet succeeds in swiping something before your very eyes, don't let him eat it—even if it does mean a totally wasted Cornish hen. (Do you want to *reward* him for his transgression?) But be sensible. If your dog or cat is growling or taking a stance to defend his prize, do not risk serious injury. Regroup, rethink, and restructure your program so this cannot happen again.

Set Ups

The best way to teach your dog to stay off counters and tabletops is to set him up over and over again. Only through frequent supervised exposure to food, clothing, and other objects of attraction on tables, countertops, low shelving, and desks will your dog learn that these areas are off-limits. Don't put unnecessary pressure on yourself and your family to keep an area scrupulously clean and free of tantalizing clutter. This is not realistic; eventually you will slip up and the dog will seize the moment. Time invested in training is worth it in the long run.

The electronic repellents described earlier can be used to discourage cats from counters and tables by sound, a hissing puff of air, or scent. Since cats hate to step on anything sticky, you can also use Sticky Paws or two-sided sticky tape on the counter (you may have to use a lot of it). The "bumpy mats" such as X-Mat can work well here, too.

You can also try a booby trap. Set a piece of cardboard on the counter so it overhangs the edge by 3 or 4 inches, and stack three or more empty soda cans taped shut with a few pennies in them in a pyramid on top of the cardboard. When your pet jumps up on the counter he'll land on the edge of the cardboard, causing the cans to crash down.

You'll probably have to do this setup more than once, and maybe even put the cardboard and cans the whole length of the counter, but after those cans come down a time or two, even the most nonchalant feline will think twice before jumping up there again. You can also set large shallow pans of water on a counter to discourage cats from jumping there, but I don't recommend this unless the whole counter area is due for a thorough cleaning!

Dogs Jumping on People

Any moment now . . . here she comes, through the gate. It's Aunt Elsie in her Sunday best—peach jacket, satin blouse, sheerest hose, flowered hat, and wow, white gloves—go meet her, boy!

A muddied and crumpled Aunt Elsie rings the bell. "Oh, my word, Elsie! I'm so sorry. I thought that dog was tied up out back! Come on in and let's get you cleaned up."

That's the last we'll see of Aunt Elsie for a while. A jumping dog can make a real mess and even be a safety threat, especially to children.

The only way to greet a pet is with all six feet firmly on the ground—your two and his four. Short of teaching your dog to wipe his feet and trim his nails, there's no way to lessen the impact of a jumper, but there are a number of ways to train your pet not to jump. First, you must make the decision to allow jumping or not to allow it. Your entire household must make the decision, because the key to successful training is consistency.

As the pet experts point out, the problem of jumping comes about because the dog was allowed or encouraged to do it as a pup. Remember when you brought home that little ball of fur and nuzzled it to your face and snuggled it under your chin? Well, your pet remembers, too. He's found that warmth and affection center up around your face—that's where your voice, that he's learned to love and obey, comes from, too.

The very least you should do is **tell your guests what to expect before they enter your dog's domain.** Let them choose whether to risk their new suit or not. This courtesy to the jumpee is a basic of pet etiquette. If he chooses not to risk it, then make alternate plans—go out for coffee or excuse yourself and shut Rover in a "safe room."

Any of the following training methods are best practiced over and over in the same way. It may take a month or more to change his behavior, but you must outlast your pet!

1. No one in your household should welcome your dog if he's jumping up on the person. When you come home it excites your dog and encourages him to jump. So instead of making a fuss when you walk in the door, give him only a mild greeting and save the play for a little later. Kneel to bring yourself down to your pet's level when you want to relate to him, instead of encouraging him to come up to yours. Praise and pet him only when all four feet are on the ground. You can also turn your back on a fractious dog that is about to jump up. He is seeking a social interaction; if jumping makes you go away and ignore/shun him, he'll slowly but surely stop hopping around and getting underfoot, the precursors of jumping up.

2. An obedience-trained dog may be told to "Sit-stay," to calm the excitement every time a guest comes to your door. Practice leaving the house and returning, and when you enter, command the dog to sit.

3. Antijump harnesses are made by several companies and work by restraining the hind legs. They keep a dog from jumping over a fence, on furniture, or on people. Once the dog finds out the futility of jumping, the harness can be removed.

4. If your pet's nails are clipped short and filed smooth, there's less chance of injury to your furniture, your skin, and your ninety-dollar dress.

5. Many dogs jump up on people as a simple matter of excess energy. See that such a pet, especially, gets regular vigorous exercise—it'll help calm him down.

Two often-heard suggestions for stopping a jumper are kneeing the dog in the chest as he jumps and stepping on his back toes. These are unwise and cruel methods that could damage your relationship with your pet, not to mention hurt him. Better to invest some time and patience in your animal to discourage the behavior before it occurs, rather than to reprimand or punish your pet when he can't understand why you're doing it.

Bear in mind that shouting or raising your arms often excites a dog into more jumping. And holding things out at arm's length to him is *training* him to jump up. Also, if you allow your pet on the furniture, he's more likely to jump up on people.

Cats Jumping on People

It's too late to inform your guest of your cat's cute habit of jumping up on people after it leaps on his lap and his allergy renders him apoplectic. As the proud owner, you're likely to be more tolerant of your cat snagging your last pair of pantyhose, because you've chosen to keep a pet. But a person who dislikes cats may consider it a minor catastrophe.

Though you will come across an occasional cat who delights in walking right up a person's body to his shoulder or leaping onto a shoulder from a nearby tree, cats don't usually jump up on people and claw them.

In training a cat not to jump on people, you must be persistent. You can try squirting him with your spray bottle or rattling a shake can; many cats also respond to a "Psssst-pssst" vocal reprimand.

Cats may "knead" when they're feeling content. It looks just like someone kneading bread, except that cats use their paws (and legs). Kittens knead when they're nursing and many an adult cat kneads and purrs when he's feeling pleased.

Disciplining a cat for kneading is impractical as well as unfriendly. It's like asking a child not to smile when he's happy. Your cat might turn from kneading to more troublesome habits like chewing. A better solution to kneading is to put a towel between you and the cat. Or give Kitty his own old blanket or pillow to knead and suck to his heart's content.

If you feel the claws coming out in the kneading behavior, you can gently remove the cat from your lap, being careful to disengage your clothing from the claws before pushing him away. Avoid reacting quickly or shoving and panicking the cat, so you won't get scratched or snagged. Keeping your cat's nails trimmed also helps here.

If snagged pantyhose are your pet peeve, there is a solution for this. Several manufacturers make "no-run" pantyhose, including Highland Mills, Inc., of Charlotte, NC (704-375-3333; *www.highlandmills.com*).

Pets Tracking in Dirt and Mud

Out West where I live, it's said that a pro tracker can trace a rabbit's trail over solid rock. Most of us have no trouble at all tracking our pets across our kitchen floors and carpets. The tracker has to call on keen instinct and skill—all we have to do is look!

While our pets are outside exploring, they pick up all manner of debris, which seems to be dislodged only once they're inside the house. It's not just the bits of grit, sand, and gravel that dirty things up inside—pets track in things like mud, salt, tar, poop, grass, burrs, and anything else that can stick to them. And wet feet, once in the house, dry off into dust and dirt particles. So drying off both your and your pet's feet before entering your home is important, winter and summer.

Cut Track-ins at Their Source

We professionals call this "eliminating the watering hole" (or mud hole, in this case). That tracked-in stuff has most likely come from somewhere close by. Let's look at some ways to stop the problem right at the source.

1. Close off underneath things. This means under the house, the porch, stairs, benches, workbenches, planters, etc. Animals in search of shade, privacy, or a cozy den will seek out these places, which are generally bare dirt (because nothing grows there) and strewn with greasy bones and grubbed garbage.

2. Cover up the bare ground in your yard with grass, gravel, or concrete, especially under and around hose spigots or water use areas and right by the entryways. **Traversing bare dirt really lodges trackables in pets' paws.**

3. Seal up outside storage. It's amazing how much stuff we store outside—including the garbage. Our junk is really the most intriguing thing we own, as far as animals are concerned. Lids and covers are cheap and easy to use—though they might keep you from becoming a famous tracker!

4. Clean up. People will at least try to avoid stepping in things, but an animal may track in anything it encounters outside, so the cleanliness of the immediate outdoors will determine the mess indoors. If oil is leaking on the driveway, the dog will track it into the house. If the sidewalk is plastered with mud, soon the entryway will be. If your grounds are cleaned up, your cleaning will be cut down.

5. Rake up. Get a lawn mower that bags the grass so that cut grass isn't lying all over the yard and blown onto sidewalks for people and pets to pick up on their wet feet and drag in.

6. Install professional "knockoff" mats both inside and out-side your doors. Mats are inexpensive, attractive, sound absorbing, and powerful cleaning prevention tools. They also make your entryway safer. The bristly surface of an artificial turf mat will tickle the dirt off a pet's paws, and the magnetic surface of the inside mat will pull the dust off and absorb moisture. A 3′ × 5′ mat both inside and outside each door assures enough steps on the matting to do a good job of pulling off grit and loose litter.

7. Entry training can be another cure for tracking in. You can train a dog to go to a specific spot as soon as he comes in and wait to be toweled off. This training is easy—just have a towel handy, and set a mat in a place close by the pet entryway. Then catch your pet as he comes in and make him stay or sit on the mat. (You might even reward him with a little love or a treat, as long as he does stay.) The longer he stays, even if you don't towel him off, the more he dries off and transfers trackable stuff onto the surface of the mat. You can even design or make a little nook for the purpose by the door the animal enters (in most households the pets make the majority of their entrances and exits from the same door).

Protect!

If you have a pretty good idea where your pet is going to jump or sit as soon as he comes in, cover it (the chair, bed, sofa, whatever) with a pet slipcover or even one of the plastic drop-cloths with an absorbent paper face, such as Neat Sheets.

Take Matters into Your Own Hands

With all the stuff that can be found on the ground today, **it's important to wipe your pet's feet off as soon as he comes in.** Road salt can be toxic to a pet, and if you don't clean it off, he'll do it himself while grooming, possibly ingesting a dangerous amount. Mud, too, is a good medium for bacteria and fungi to flourish in, so it can help transmit diseases to your pet or others in the house.

Professional trainers recommend you start getting an animal used to "handling"—whether a puppy or an adult—as soon as you bring him home. While petting and reassuring him, first touch his head and back (the nonthreatening areas). Then pick up a front foot and put it down just the way you would if you were teaching a dog to "give a paw." Pick up the other front foot for just a minute, and then put it back down. Two hours later play the game again, this time picking up each foot and squeezing it a little, then putting it right back down. At any sign of panic or uneasiness from the animal, stop what you're doing and begin again later. Use treats, toys, anything you can to make it an upbeat experience. You want to get him used to your handling, to rubbing his feet, and to going in between his toes if necessary. Clean all foreign substances from your pet's paws, and check in the long hair many dogs have between their toes for mud, matted hair, and pebbles. Trimming the excess hair around the foot on shaggy breeds will also cut down on tracking in.

You can't really entry train cats, but when you let the cat in, you can scoop him up and put him on a towel on a counter or something and feed him a little goodie and get him purring, then gently take his feet one by one and wipe them with a paper towel or a damp washcloth.

Last, but not least, there are dog boots. After my experience trying to sort and apply boots to six small kids, I'll pass up this possibility. But if footwear for Fifi sounds like the answer to you, I wish you luck and patience.

Mud

If your pet does manage to track in mud, the secret is to wait until it dries. Brush the dry mud loose, then wipe or vacuum it up. Spray some all-purpose cleaner solution on the residue that remains, let it sit for a few seconds, then blot or wipe it up. **Very little soil will penetrate a carpet made of nylon or other synthetic fibers.** Natural fibers like wool are a little more absorbent. Using a soil retardant on the carpet will make spills and stains much easier to deal with.

Tar

Tracked-in tar, too, is simple. Tar and tarlike substances have a solvent base, so water-based cleaners won't touch them. But a solvent-based spot remover such as De-Solv-it, applied to a clean cloth and then blotted carefully on a tar stain, will dissolve and release it even if it's old. Always scrape up as much of the spot as you can before applying the cleaning fluid, and use a white cloth so you'll know whether the fabric is bleeding. Avoid wetting the carpet backing with the solvent, and rinse the area with clean water, and then blot, after removing the stain.

Pet Scratching

Few things come more naturally to cats and dogs and other pets than scratching. Cats, the most frequent offenders, scratch to remove the old layers of nail from their claws, to stretch and exercise themselves, and to leave little messages for their fellow cats (even if there aren't any others in the house) with the scent glands on their front paws. Dogs scratch as part of their bedding down routine; to make nests for imaginary puppies, when they're in heat; and when they want to get in, out, or away. But it costs—in time, money, and lost tempers—if the wrong thing is scratched too often and too deeply.

Since breeding out the instinct and need to scratch is about as likely in the near future as getting us humans to quit it, there are some other measures that can be taken.

Solution #1: A Post

For cats, put up a scratching post. These work by the principle of diversion—they let a pet scratch something that won't be damaged. It's the same principle used on the ranch and farm. Cows, for example, will scratch against and tear up barn siding, fences, and machinery. So the farmer plants a rough post for them to scratch on and they take their itches out on it instead of the other surfaces.

You can buy a scratching post or build your own—you don't have to be a mechanical wizard to do it. Just be sure the post has a large, heavy base to prevent it from tipping over. And make sure it's securely attached to the base—if the cat accidentally knocks the post over while using it, he may never want to use it again. One of the reasons cats like to claw upholstered furniture is that it's heavy and sturdy enough to offer some real resistance. When cats scratch, they are not just sharpening their claws, but toning and strengthening their muscles, and marking. **Bigger and heavier is usually better when it comes to scratching posts.** A larger and better-made post may cost more, but it's still cheaper than reupholstering a $2,000 couch.

You don't want a fluffy-wuffy post. A harsh, scratchy surface like sisal rope is far more attractive to a cat than carpeting of any kind. A cat wants *resistance* when he scratches something, and carpet can't provide it. Besides, a carpeted post may teach him that it's okay to claw carpet. The *backing* of the average carpet, on the other hand, is rough enough to have real claw appeal. Burlap or very highly textured fabric is good, too. Cork, log with bark, and rough-cut wood posts work, but are going to leave crumbs and splinters around.

The post should be at least a foot taller than your cat stretched up on tippy-toe, or at least 30 inches high. But a floor-to-ceiling post will be a lot more stable than a very tall freestanding post. A couple of sturdy cat perches or cozy cat cubbyholes will enhance the appeal of a big, tall post. (Try to find out if the location suits your feline before you start drilling holes or sinking molly bolts.)

Make the post a controlled play center while you're at it. A few safe toys securely attached to or suspended from the post will help intrigue your pet enough to use it.

A company called Felix makes one of the best scratching posts around—a sturdy cedar post wrapped with rugged woven sisal and impregnated with catnip that can be renewed from time to time. Cats go wild over them, and these posts can really take a beating. You can also make or buy a scratching board, rather than a post, if you're pressed for space or think your cat might prefer it. An 18″ × 18″ piece of woven sisal fiber, carpet back-side out, highly textured fabric, or even an old hemp or rope doormat can be attached to the wall beside your pet's bed or to a door or even laid out flat on the floor. A variety of scratchboards made from strips of corrugated cardboard are available, and cats like these, especially the ones set on a slant.

Where to Put the Post?

Near your pet's food and water dishes is a good spot, because cats often stretch and scratch after a good meal. Or try by the pet's bed—cats like to scratch when they wake up, too. Next to, or in front of, whatever he's been scratching would be a prime spot. Then, after he gets used to using the post, you can gradually move the post to where you really want it to be. **Corners are an unobtrusive place for a post, and will help assure that it never falls over.** If you have a large house, more than one post might be a good investment.

Post Persuasion

You can't assume that your cat will instantly recognize the superiority of a post for scratching purposes. You may have to help him out a little here, by spraying the post with catnip spray (available in pet shops) or rubbing and sprinkling catnip on it.

Stand the post on its side to start with, and trail one of his favorite toys across it to acquaint him with that nice scratchy surface. If it's a big post, put a little treat on top, or on one of the higher platforms or perches. When you catch him scratching something else, bring him over to the post and gently rub his paws on it or (I kid you not) demonstrate the right approach by scratching a little yourself. Always praise your cat profusely when he does use the post. You might even try training your cat to scratch the post on command (when you say a certain phrase such as "Kitty, climb") and rewarding him when he obeys.

> Always praise your cat profusely when he does use the post.

Solution #2: Prevent

Make scratching impossible or much less likely by choice of material and design and where and how you place things. Pet-proofing is definitely a big part of the answer here.

When it comes to furniture, wood, metal, glass, or plastic laminate won't have anything like the appeal that upholstered furniture or needlepoint has for a cat. If you must have fabric, go for tightly woven fabrics with a smooth surface. Avoid highly textured fabrics. And bear in mind that leather and vinyl are vulnerable and hard to repair.

The double-sided clear tape mentioned earlier, Sticky Paws for Furniture, is an effective preventive, though you don't want to use it on leather or leave it on indefinitely.

Place or hang scratchable things out of reach whenever you can. Install a hook to hold imperiled drapes and curtains up out of the way when you're not home.

In doors and storm doors, see that the lower portion is solid! Damage prevention is, in fact, the reason so many screen and storm doors are made solid on the lower half. Or cover the whole door with a full-length mirror. A solid sheet of wood or metal or a wooden guard can also be installed over the lower third (depending on the size of your pet) of the screen panels in sliding doors. Replace standard screening in windows and doors with "pet proof" screening. This is a heavier-duty mesh cats and dogs can't claw holes in, or break through and run off (or fall out, if the window or door happens to be in a multiple-story building).

Another form of prevention is to confine your pet, while you're gone, especially, to a room or rooms where scratchables are scarce. You can also make good use of a dog crate for this purpose.

Solution #3: Clip Those Nails

It stands to reason that it will help to trim the sharp ends of your pet's claws or nails, especially if he's an indoor pet who doesn't have a chance to have them worn down by tree bark and rough outside surfaces. Dogs, especially, will develop painful paw problems if their nails grow too long, and cats with long claws tend to scratch more often. You can cut your pet's nails yourself—take a few minutes and ask your vet to show you exactly how to do it—or you can have your vet or groomer do it.

Use clippers or nippers made especially for dogs and cats. We can't even effectively cut human toenails with a clipper made for human fingernails, so we can see that the right tool for the purpose is important. There's a variety of good professional-quality tools available for the purpose from pet shops, livestock supply stores, and pet catalogs. Avoid the guillotine style of clipper because it can split a pet's nails.

Having their nails clipped has never been very popular with pets—this is when many animals act as melodramatic as they're ever likely to get. So, **if at all possible, start training your pet to accept nail clipping from puppy- or kittenhood.** Ease them into it gradually, clipping only one or two nails a day and only a little if necessary, so it's over with before they quite realize what happened. Praise them and give them a little treat now and then as you go along, to further encourage their cooperation. If necessary, enlist a helper to help you steady your pet at least through the initial sessions.

Clipping Cats' Claws

Hold the cat until he's relaxed and comfortable, and then lay him on his back with his feet up. To keep him from wiggling, you can gently hold the scruff of his neck—his reflex will be to relax in this position. Make sure you do not grab too much scruff and that you are not holding too tightly. Or, just have someone else hold the cat for you. Take one paw at a time and press it gently between your thumb and forefinger to extend the claws one by one. **Cut only the thin, clear, hooked end of the nail.** Stay at least ¼ inch away from the quick, which contains nerves and the blood vessels that nourish the nail. There are special bags available that have zippered openings for a cat's legs so you can release one leg at a time to trim it. These do help prevent getting scratched yourself in the process of cutting your cat's nails. But getting him into the device the *second* time may be a lot harder.

Clipping Dogs' Nails

Sit with the dog facing you on a sturdy platform or other secure surface. Pick up one paw at a time gently and cut only the tip or about the first ⅛ inch of the nail—stay away here, too, from the quick that runs about ¾ of the way down the nail. Proceed cautiously on black nails where you can't see the quick; when in doubt, cut less. If you do accidentally cut into the quick, stay calm and reassuring while you apply a styptic pencil or pressure to stop any bleeding. Be especially careful in cutting highly overgrown nails, because the quick extends out farther than in a normal nail. Trim the dewclaws as well—those little claws on the inside of the dog's leg. File the nail smooth after cutting, with a file or emery board, with strokes all in the same direction, from the top of the nail downward.

For dogs, clip when the toenail touches the floor when the dog is standing (and twice a month after that). Cats can be trimmed once or twice a month. If they habitually scratch things other than the post, trim the front nails every week.

Solution #4: Training

Like other pet problem behavior, scratching can be dealt with by the behavior-changing methods outlined on page 185, including Ssscat, Spray Barrier, and Sticky Paws for Furniture. The pheromone spray Feliway will often deter scratching on vertical surfaces.

You can also try the old balloon trick—fastening balloons to the things you don't want him to scratch. After the first few explode in his face, he'll decide he'd much rather go shred toilet paper at the other end of the house. The squirt bottle can work wonders, here, too.

When the behavior you're trying to discourage involves physical damage to things, you are going to pay a certain price during the training period (in this case, a little scarred furniture). You also have to be around enough to do the training and make the correction when the act occurs.

You can cover the object the cat has been scratching with an old sheet, a plastic drop cloth, or even aluminum foil if you can't be there to discipline him every time he tries to sink a claw. You can also cover the imperiled object with netting—cats hate to catch their claws in things. You can even tie a couple of little bells to the netting, and when you hear them ring, rush out and say, "Kitty, climb," and try to maneuver him to the post. This doesn't just tell him he's done something wrong, it tells him what to do that's right. Reward and praise him when he does switch his attention to the post.

For dogs who are prone to scratch doors when their owner leaves the house, you can pretend to be leaving the house, but sneak back and listen at the door after you go out. If you hear scratching, run back in and shout "No!" (and mean it). You can also throw a shake can from outside the door when you hear those little scratches.

Solution #5: Nail Caps

There are soft plastic nail caps available for a cat's claws, called Soft Paws—they even come in a choice of colors! They need to be applied to freshly trimmed claws every four to six weeks. If your cat will let you trim his nails, you may be able to do this yourself. Otherwise it's a job for your vet. These caps are available from some vets and pet catalogs or you can contact the manufacturer, SmartPractice, at 800-522-0800.

Solution #6: "Amputation"

Well, that's what some pet owners call it. A gentler word for it is declawing—the process of surgically removing the claw and the feline equivalent of the finger to the first joint, permanently. The controversy on this subject makes the Democratic and Republican parties look like lovers. There are many who say the claws are there for a reason: to enable the cat to catch his prey and scratch to protect itself (survive!) and climb things to escape. Declawing, according to these folks, is an act right next to killing. They say it handicaps the cat and causes more behavior problems than it solves, and there are even vets who consider the operation inhumane and refuse to do it.

Others say it's the kindest thing you can do for twenty-first-century cats who must live in harmony with humans, as long as you always keep them inside and sincerely intend to keep them as pets for the rest of their lives. I've dehorned cattle to keep them from injuring their keepers and companions, but declawing cats to control scratching does seem like a lot of change to make in a cat and a lot of money to spend to solve just one single behavior problem. If you opt for this operation, have it done before the cat is six months old, if possible—it'll be easier on his psyche and ego. Take the time to find a competent veterinary surgeon—don't be afraid to ask for references from past declawing clients—and depending where you live and who you go to, be prepared to spend anywhere from $50 to over $150 for the operation.

The best compromise I've heard is this: If the only way you're able, or allowed, to keep an animal is to have it declawed (rather than take it to a shelter, where its chances for a new home are slim), and you intend to keep the animal for the rest of your life, then consider having the operation done. If you're thinking of declawing just because it's more convenient, I'd recommend you buy a scratching post instead, trim your pet's nails regularly, and make every effort to train him not to scratch the furniture.

Chewed Up Means Clean Up

. . . And fix up, and eventually fed up! Most cats and dogs are smart enough not to chew tobacco, but everything else tasty or tooth-satisfying is fair game. Pets will chew on plaster, pot holders, walls, door frames, electrical and phone cords, rugs, baseboards, banisters, clothes, children's toys, books, photo albums, pillows, plants, purses, belts, slippers, shoes, socks, luggage, their own beds and dishes, and the legs, arms, and edges of furniture.

The #1 solution for curbing chewing is to provide more tempting alternatives. Pet chew-toys, many of which are impregnated with a pet-attracting scent or flavor, come in all shapes and sizes—bones or balls or rings. They divert, they're enjoyed, and they exercise the chewing instinct harmlessly. They help keep teeth clean and gums healthy, the right kinds are completely safe as well as sterilizable, and they'll last forever. "The right kind" here means sturdy rawhide, hard solid rubber, or rugged nylon bones. There are also nylon bones with a little bit of real bone meal mixed in, and natural bones that have been treated and sterilized to be safe and last longer.

If your pet is teething, provide him with a few ice cubes or frozen damp washcloths to ease his gum soreness and itching. Keep puppies in the chewing stage, especially, well away from household cleaners, chemicals, pesticide containers, medicines, and cigarette butts.

> Chew toys are cheap, when you consider that pets have managed to destroy hundreds and even thousands of dollars' worth of furnishings at a sitting.

A chew toy needs to be the right size for your pet. A small dog won't take on too large a toy, and you don't want your big dog to be able to gnaw up his chewie in nothing flat. You may want to buy different chew toys and see which ones your pet favors before you buy a gross of anything. (You can buy chew toys in bulk through some mail order catalogs, for example, and it will help to keep the price down.) Chew toys are cheap, when you consider that pets have managed to destroy hundreds and even thousands of dollars' worth of furnishings at a sitting. Some training is even called for here, to underline the fact that his toys are what you want your pet to chew on. You can wiggle them around a little, pull them along on a string, or hide them, then praise and reward him for finding them. Or play a few sets of toss-and-fetch with them.

As for real bones, it's somehow a little disappointing to know that they really aren't considered good or safe for our pets. The possible exceptions are big blocky beef shank or "soup" or knucklebones for dogs and cooked chicken necks or backs for cats. Never give a dog or cat chicken, turkey, or pork bones, or any thin or hallow bones. These can splinter and puncture an intestine, or get caught in your pet's throat and choke him.

Repel

Apply something offensive to the thing that you don't want chewed. A few bitter bites and the animal will leave it alone. There are a number of products manufactured for just this purpose only. One that works particularly well, called Bitter Apple, is made from crabapples and comes in a gel or spray. The gel can be used on most all sealed surfaces (it has a petroleum jelly base), but should be reapplied every day until the chewing behavior stops. The spray has an alcohol base and might stain highly polished furniture. In addition, because of its high alcohol content, it evaporates quickly and has to be reapplied more than once a day.

You can mix alum into a paste with water and spread the paste on the thing you want to protect. Hot pepper sauce also comes in handy here; brush it generously on the most recent chew target and then mist it with a little cheap cologne. Your pet will come to associate the smell of the cologne with the hot taste and you can eventually fend him off with cologne alone.

Most chew repellents have to be reapplied regularly, usually once a day, throughout the retraining period to keep an object effectively protected. You can even apply the repellent in front of your pet while saying "Don't touch" (or the discouraging expression of your choice) to make that bad taste a little more educational, when and if they do encounter it.

Catch and Correct

Chewing is one of the harder bad habits to break by on-the-spot correction, since it's actually more likely to occur when you're not there. And it does no good, and even some harm, to correct a pet for chewing after the fact. He'll never be able to connect your 5 P.M. displeasure with the antimacassar he consumed early this morning. As Gwen Bohnenkamp says, "Improper correction is worse than useless. It'll just make your pet anxious, wondering what he did wrong—so he'll chew something else."

But don't let chewing go uncorrected when you do witness it. Say "No" sharply, gently disengage your pet's teeth from the object, and then hand him an acceptable chewie. Or you can say "No" followed by "Go find your toy" and keep it up until he finds one of his chew toys and latches on to it. Be sure to praise him when he does.

You can "set up" a chewing correction session by bringing your pet near forbidden objects, then as he's about to lay tooth to the object, let loose with the "No," "Off" routine. You do have to be careful here to not have directly encouraged or commanded him to chew it.

A variation on this is to leave an expendable sample of a type of thing you never want chewed in a conspicuous spot, liberally doused with one of the chewing repellents mentioned earlier.

Distraction works better than correction with cats, when it comes to problem chewing.

Confine

A dog that chews destructively shouldn't be left unsupervised—he should be wherever you are. When that's not practical, pass him off to another capable family member or put the dog in his crate with a delectable chewie that he gets only when crated. As soon as you are able, release the dog from his crate and have him rejoin you. The crate is a marvelous tool; use it to supervise Bowser when you can't.

When you have to be away from home for several hours, consider confining your pet to a room where what he prefers to chew (wood furniture, carpeting, shoes) is not present. If it's hard to find a room that quite fits that description, confinement in a securely fenced yard may be a good solution. Have a plan "B" for seasonal extremes and bad weather. Once again, leave your dog with a wonderful chewie. Since the dog is outside, this may be time to break out that oversized knucklebone you have in the freezer!

Stimulate

A lot of chewing is the result of boredom and loneliness. Make sure your pet gets plenty of vigorous exercise each day—how much depends on your pet's age, size, and breed. (Check with your vet.) Letting your dog just run loose in the yard, by the way, is only considered "mild" exercise.

Design

You don't want any chew toys for your pet that in any way resemble chewing contraband. **Don't give your animal a pair of sneakers to play with, then wonder why he chewed on your new running shoes.** Old towels or new towels, old gloves or new gloves, scrap wood or fine furniture—they all look the same to a pet.

To help prevent the chewed shoe syndrome, store your shoes out of reach on a wire rack suspended above the bottom of the closet. (It'll also make cleaning the closet floor a snap.)

Prevent

Pets of all kinds seem to have an irresistible attraction to electrical cords and many a pet has been badly burned or killed, and many a fire started, in the process of chewing. Pets also tug on the cords and could bring a lamp or small appliance crashing down. Heavily wrapped cords that are sturdier and at least somewhat safer can be purchased for only a little more money than the cheapies. But try to eliminate dangling cords by using suspended lighting, for example, or attaching cords to baseboards. You can also thread a cord through a curtain rod or piece of garden hose to protect it, or wrap it in aluminum foil. Protect the loose cords you can't do without with hot pepper sauce, alum paste, or Bitter Apple.

If your pet is chewing plaster, he may need a mineral and vitamin supplement (or he may have a case of acid stomach that he's trying to treat with Sheetrock antacid). Consult your vet.

And in case you're wondering, a muzzle isn't a good solution for a pet that chews. A muzzled dog will still want to chew, and the muzzle will only upset him more.

Pets Digging

What dog or cat doesn't like to dig? And what more perfect place than your lawn or garden! But few backyards are improved by pets' enthusiastic excavations. Doggie digging can have more than one cause. **Some breeds just like to dig, and there's not much you can do to "train" it out of them.** Digging can also be a sign of separation anxiety (see page 205), boredom, or pent-up energy.

Avoid punishing your dog when he digs—he may just keep on doing it whenever you're not around. Repellents and low wire-mesh fences can prevent your dog from digging. If you sense he is bored, take him on long walks to release extra energy so that he stops taking it out on your lawn. A fenced-in play area is the best solution. Make sure the area is shaded and that your dog has plenty of water. Give him lots of chew toys and bones so he has things that are okay to chew. Add a sandbox with hidden treats so he can exercise his digging urges. If you're against confining your dog, put him in a dog run so he can run around in a specific area.

Speaking of sandboxes, if you have one for children in your yard, and also have cats that go outside, be sure the sandbox has a cover, and that you keep it on when the kids aren't playing in the box. A sandbox is irresistible to cats looking for a place to "go," and contact with cat stools can spread diseases and parasites. (You can always make Kitty her own sandbox in a different part of the yard, and scoop it every so often.)

Since cats tend to look for loose soil to do their business in, they can also damage seeded beds and new plants. You can build a fence around your garden to keep your dog (and wild animals) out—it's by far the easiest way to minimize dog damage. But no ordinary fence will keep a cat out—only the special fences designed for just this purpose. These usually employ an ordinary fence such as chain link with wire or netting set in at the top at a ninety-degree angle to the main fence. You've seen setups like this at the zoo. If you don't want to go to this trouble and expense, the next best thing you can do is cover newly seeded beds, and beds full of young seedlings, with light wire like chicken wire until the plants are big enough to offer no stretches of nice, loose, empty earth to invite digging.

There are motion-activated water sprayers designed specifically to shoo pets from garden areas, such as the Scarecrow. The sprayer senses heat and movement and will spray your dog or cat (or a child, watch out) with water if it gets too close. Some of these sprayers can protect 1,000 square feet of lawn and will shoot a 35-foot stream of water. Most cats hate water and will learn quickly what to avoid outside. Of course, if your dog loves water . . .

Pets Getting in the Garbage

> The solution is so simple: Don't make the trash accessible.

Careless garbage handling and curious pets are the ingredients for a lot of trouble. Garbage doesn't just get knocked over and climbed on and dug through and spread throughout the house or neighborhood; in that garbage, amidst the savory morsels, are broken glass, cigarette butts, not-quite-empty containers of chemicals and poisons, sharp can lids, tempting but easily splintered chicken bones, and all the rest, possibly dealing you a dead pet or an expensive vet bill. The solution is so simple: Don't make the trash accessible.

If you have a pet that's strong enough to knock the garbage can over and make the lid pop off, mount the can so it can't be knocked over. Use a square can on a wood or metal strip notched to slip under the lip of the can and hold it securely. Or keep your container inside a lower cupboard or behind strong, securely closing doors or doors secured with child safety locks.

The kitchen has the most seductive garbage in the house, so be sure to use a lidded container. **Garbage cans that open when you step on a pedal aren't really safe;** it doesn't take long for a dog to figure out how to use it. Always wrap smelly things in plastic before dropping them in the can, and take the garbage out often, before it has a chance to develop those compelling "aged" odors. Use a small can inside in the kitchen and empty it daily into a larger can outside.

You can train your dog not to get into the garbage. Take half of a tuna fish or peanut butter sandwich and stick it under a few pieces of rolled-up newspaper in the can. Then go sit down and read a magazine. As the smell wafts over to your dog, he'll probably mosey over and put his nose in the garbage. Then you say a loud, firm "No."

Consider using a detection device suited for your particular situation around garbage cans and recycling bins. It will work when you're there and when you're not. It also works with curious kitties. You could also apply Bitter Apple, powdered alum, extra-hot mustard, or hot pepper sauce to the bag (not to any of the food in it).

Reinforce the "no garbage" rule consistently until your pet no longer shows an interest in that area of the kitchen.

Cats can be trained, but it's slightly more difficult. A cat will wait until you're gone and then dig in, so be sure all garbage cans around cats have sturdy lids or covers. Cats don't have the weight some dogs do, so they can't step on pedals and open cans; but if you set your garbage on the counter where the dog can't get to it, the cat still can.

It's even more important, when you have pets, to disinfect and deodorize the garbage can from time to time to keep down germs and odors. To disinfect, fill the container with one ounce of Nolvasan per gallon of water and let it soak for ten to fifteen minutes. Add a squirt of water-soluble deodorizer (like Nilodor Surface Deodorizer) to the disinfectant solution for supereffective odor control. Use a nylon scrubbing sponge, a toilet brush, or other long-handled brush to scrub it out. Rinse it well and sun-dry if possible. I'd let a last squirt or two of Nolvasan solution dry on the can to discourage bacteria growth.

Outside

Store your outside garbage in metal or hard plastic cans with tight-fitting lids. The most durable are heavy-duty molded plastic cans such as Rubbermaid Brutes, available at janitorial-supply stores in 30- or 44-gallon sizes. They'll outlast a metal can many times over, are quieter than metal, and are even available with casters.

The biggest single clean-up problem is that of pets tipping over and spilling the garbage, so **get a can with a heavy, tight-fitting lid that will stay on even if the can tips over.** You can weigh down the lid with a big rock, or bricks, but it's still susceptible to knockover; better are the quick-release locking straps available for the garbage can, or elastic bungee cords with metal hooks on the ends.

Put a sturdy five- or six-foot wire fence or enclosure around the garbage area, with a gate. Or if you don't enclose them, make the cans unable to be tipped over somehow. A lot of mess and spills can be avoided if animals can't tip the cans over. You could use a rope or chain to attach them to the house, a wood deck, a post or pole, a sturdy fence, etc.

If your municipality requires you to put out garbage in disposable bags rather than closed cans, you can try one of the commercial pet repellent sprays on the bags to keep pets away. (And don't put the garbage out the night before.) It's also worth the investment to buy extra-thick or super-strength bags or even double bag your garbage if it has to sit outside until pickup. Nothing attracts rats and mice faster than free food, and you don't want them outside your house feasting and reproducing.

Dragging in Unmentionables

You can't believe—or can you?—the size, variety, and condition of things a pet can bring home. Our dog once dragged in the complete head and hide of a four-point buck from a distant neighbor's farm. Dogs always enjoy a fresh mess out in the open, then bring it home to you when it's rank and fly-infested. And a cat will sit there and expect you to enjoy its proud offering, or will devour a live meal in the middle of the living room. What to do with the pet in such a case is definitely second to what to do with the "whatever."

To get rid of the stuff your pet has dragged in, get a plastic bag and turn it inside out, then put your hand in it and use it like a glove to pick up the mess. Turn the bag right-side out again, tie up the top securely, and throw it away. If you don't even want to touch it through a plastic bag, scoop it into a small box or paper bag with a couple of pieces of cardboard. Then put the whole mess in a plastic trash bag and take it to the trash disposal area immediately. This will seal off odor and reduce the chance of it being dragged off again. **If you're left with a lingering odor, treat the area with bacteria/enzyme solution,** and it may not be a bad idea to apply some Nolvasan solution to the area of a particularly messy pickup. (If you want to disinfect *and* deodorize here, be sure to use the bacteria/enzyme product first and give it time to work before applying any disinfectant.)

Be sure to wash your hands well after drag-in clean-up duty. Rodents and rabbits and the like carry diseases that can be transmitted to humans. (A pregnant woman should recruit someone else to do this particular clean-up chore, or if she has no choice but to do it herself, she should wear rubber gloves to avoid any risk of toxoplasmosis.)

What do you do if your pet brings in a critter that's still alive? *Don't* try to pry the animal away from your pet—your pet may scratch or even bite you to keep from losing his trophy. Try to startle your pet into dropping it (try rattling the car keys or biscuit box, or ringing the doorbell to draw the pet away from his catch). If he does drop it, put him outside or confine him to another room to keep him from snatching up the wounded animal again.

 Make sure your pet is up to date on all rabies and other vaccinations if you plan on letting him outside.

The next step is really a judgment call. You can either try to collect the animal yourself to put back outside or take to a vet, or call someone else (like your city's Animal Control Department) to come take care of it. Try not to pick up a hurt animal with your bare hands, since it might still have the strength to bite you. You also don't want to put a stunned animal inside your car without a cage or carrier to take him to get help, because he can wake up and go berserk while you're trying to drive. And hopefully your pet has already had his rabies vaccination, since many wild animals can pass on the disease.

Other Outdoor Hazards

Other animals can also be hazardous to your pet. Most cats like to, can, and will catch birds, but birds carry diseases, mites, and bugs—and all of the country's kitties doing their best to catch birds is not helping the national bird count, especially of already-threatened and attractive native species. Try to be aware of what your cat is doing while outside. Put a small bell on his collar to make sure the birds hear him coming. There are types of collars you can get that make noise without posing the danger of catching on trees, fences, and such while the cat roams.

Dogs tend to chase anything that comes into their line of vision, so be wary of streets, other dogs, cats, and stray balls from the kids. To protect your pets from the many dangers "out there" (beyond the boundaries of your property), especially the big one—cars, against which no pet can win—**consider pet-proof fencing or the invisible boundary collar systems.** Or build him a big sturdy outdoor play area, complete with a covered top. Discourage stray animals from hanging out in your yard, because even if they don't fight with or bully your pets, they may pass diseases to them.

Prevention

If your dog routinely treasure hunts and brings his prizes home, consider teaching him to "drop it." The easiest way to do this is with two toys or chewies, one that he likes and one that he LOVES! First, give him the less attractive of the two. When he's busy with it, show him the high-value goodie. When he directs his attention to your current offer and releases what he has, say "drop it" and complete the exchange. Repeat this exercise again and again. Soon "drop it" will mean *"upgrade,"* not "give up your treasure."

You can bell a cat to sabotage his hunting, though some cats do learn to time their leaps to account for the bell. If you do put a bell on your cat, make sure it's on a breakaway collar. And fencing can certainly help here. Dogs and cats can't drag large things over a fence, or through it, and if they're kept in a fenced yard, they can't get out to get "it" in the first place.

Pets Chewing Outdoor Greenery

Outdoors, cats and dogs sometimes chew not just grass but also plants and shrubs. This usually does nothing to beautify a yard, and it can also be dangerous to your pet. In addition to the water spray repellent mentioned earlier, there are a variety of other repellents (see page 185) that can be used to keep pets away from specific plants or areas.

There are many types of plants that pets can ingest (especially in a garden) that can be toxic. Some of the more common garden plants that are dangerous to pets include the following:

American bittersweet	Iris
Calla lily bulbs	Lilies
Castor bean	Lily of the valley
Cherry seeds	Mistletoe
Clematis	Mushroom
Cocoa bean shell mulch	Narcissus
Daffodil bulbs	Oleander
Daylily	Onion
Deadly nightshade	Pokeweed
Delphinium	Rhododendron
Eggplant leaves	Rhubarb
English ivy	Tiger lily
Foxglove	Tobacco
Gladiolus	Tomato
Holly	Tulip
Honeysuckle	Wisteria
Hyacinth	Yucca
Hydrangea	

Be sure to find out exactly what is safe and what is not in your garden. If you think your pet has eaten a toxic plant, call a veterinarian or emergency pet clinic immediately (see page 198 for a emergency number that can be used nationwide).

Pets Eating Houseplants

Life is funny. We coax, tempt, and bribe our kids for years to get them to eat their vegetables, and our pet, who has no apparent reason to consume anything green, does so of his own free will—enthusiastically, even. But houseplants actually pose a greater threat of poisoning to cats than household chemicals do; not a few of the exotic species of plants we keep to cheer our interiors are poisonous to animals in whole or in part.

Cats actually do have their reasons for chomping on the caladiums, which range from the desire for a little roughage or green tonic to the need to vomit up a hairball (they somehow know that eating grass or other greenery will bring on the heaves). Here are some ideas to keep your plants intact, give your pet some healthier eating habits, and make it easier on the cleaner.

1. Grow your cat his own pot of greens. There are prepackaged and preplanted kitty grazing gardens available (usually sold as "kitty grass"), or you can just plant a little pot of lawn seed mix, wheat, rye, oat grass, alfalfa, or even parsley.

2. Add some safe greenery to your pet's diet. Cats are carnivores, but some enjoy a chance to eat vegetables and even fruits. Add a little chopped raw or cooked green vegetables to his food. Many cats like corn, and even asparagus!

3. Make your plants inaccessible, which generally means hang them. (If a cat wants to get on the highest, narrowest shelf, he'll do it, and once up there, the cat isn't what falls off.) **Hang plants somewhere that can't be reached by a flying leap,** or from a cat perch a neck-stretch away. For plants too heavy to hang, put chicken wire around the base so the cats can't get to the pot but you can still water it through the wire.

4. Choosing heavy pots for your houseplants will lessen the likelihood of knockdowns. And covering the entire surface

of the exposed soil with decorative rocks or brown needlepoint canvas will discourage "litter box" excavations. Sticky Paws for Plants and Grannick's Bitter Apple also do a good job of keeping pets away from houseplants. You can lay down a protective barrier of aluminum foil in front of your plants, too—cats don't like to walk on it. **Avoid mulches, such as shredded bark, that make great playbait.** Also, try to avoid the most pet-tempting plants such as those with frilly or feathery foliage (house palms, ferns), etc. Check with your fellow cat fanciers as to what plants seem to have a fatal attraction for felines.

5. Train your pet away from your plants with a sharp, loud "No!" and a handclap or the old squirt bottle (you can mist your plants while you're at it, too).

6. A pitched-over houseplant can be vacuumed up after you've scooped up the bulk of the mess with your dustpan and squeegee. If any dirt stains remain after vacuuming, give them a little squirt of all-purpose cleaning solution. Wait a minute or two to let the chemicals work to release the solids from the surface, and then you can blot them up easily.

For extreme cases, remove all your houseplants from sight except one luscious specimen. Coat the bottom of the leaves of that plant with hot pepper sauce and mist or sponge the tops of the leaves with a solution of cheap cologne, diluted to one part cologne to five parts water.

Then make sure your cat notices the rigged plant. Plunk it down in the middle of the floor and call your cat over to it and waggle the branches around a little. After he nibbles on the plant and tastes the pepper, he'll probably sprint for the water dish. And he'll associate the smell of the cologne with the sting of the hot pepper. Move the peppered plant to different locations in the house and freshen up the pepper sauce and cologne from time to time. Soon you only have to mist this plant (or any of your plants) with diluted cologne to keep your pet away from it—he'll think the hot pepper is still there. All the while that you're discouraging him from your plants with the hot pepper technique, encourage him to chew on his own greens.

A variation on this technique is to sprinkle powdered ginger on the tips of the most accessible leaves of your plants, misting the leaves first to help the powder adhere.

Don't use systemic insecticides if you have a houseplant-prone pet. It'll only multiply the poisoning possibilities.

If your cat does manage to consume a plant and is showing signs of intense distress or poisoning, you can call the National Animal Poison Control Center twenty-four hours a day, 365 days a year: 800-548-2423. The charge (which can be charged to a major credit card) is $50 per case, including as many follow-up calls as necessary. Calls can also be charged to a 900 number: 900-443-0000. The center suggests calling the 800 number first, even if you intend to use a credit card, because some consultations may be paid for by the manufacturer of the product involved.

Or, you can rush your pet to the veterinarian or animal hospital along with a sample of the plant he ate.

Some common houseplants (and plant products) poisonous to pets include the following:

Aloe	Caladium
Amaryllis	Calla lily
Asian lily	Cutleaf philodendron
Asparagus fern	Cyclamen
Avocado	Daffodil
Azalea	Dracaena
Bird of paradise	Dumb cane

Easter lily	Lily of the valley
Elephant ears	Mistletoe
Fiddle-leaf philodendron	Mother-in-law plant
Foxglove	Narcissus
Gladiolus	Onion
Heartleaf philodendron	Poinsettia
Holly	Rhubarb
Hyacinth	Swiss cheese plant
Hydrangea	Tiger lily
Iris	Tomato
Jerusalem cherry	Tulip
Kalanchoe	

Pets Drooling All Over

Many of the media broadcasts I do are call-ins, where listeners call and pose their cleaning problems. Rarely have I been stumped entirely, but a pet owner who called KMOX in St. Louis finally did it.

"Mr. Aslett, I have two boxers, and they have a tendency to drool a bit—like by the bucketful. When they shake their heads, they shower the walls, furniture, windows, and any people passing. How do I clean off all those glistening dried droplets?"

I had no idea that dogs could drool enough to cause a cleaning problem. But heavy-duty drooling in pets is a reality, and if you happen to own a boxer, bloodhound, mastiff, bulldog, Saint Bernard, or other breed with a "pendulous lip," it's more than a reality—it's a river! One pet owner offered the profound solution, "Wipe off their jaws frequently," and a frustrated chow owner suggested, "Put a bib on 'em!"

If it weren't for drooling by old Pavlov's pooches, we'd never have known about conditioned responses—the key to a lot of animal and human behavior and training. Preventing conditioned response, in fact, is one way to cure at least some of the drooling. Hunger and anticipation of food is one big reason for drooling, especially when we get in the habit of feeding animals around the table. They start drooling the minute they hear that fork clink on the plate. If you train your pet to keep strictly away from the table (or even out of the room) and all its food stimuli before and in between meals, that alone will eliminate a lot of drooling.

Cats drool, too, often when they're feeling especially happy, such as when they're being petted. If you can't stand your cat kneading and drooling on you, about the only thing you can do is avoid lap-sitting and heavy petting.

If kitty drools constantly, take him to the vet. He may have a dental problem, or there may be something lodged in his mouth.

Abnormal drooling can be caused by a number of other things, too, such as poisoning, a medicine the animal is taking, nervousness, overheating, a respiratory disease, or a gum or tooth problem.

As for clean-up, a solution of all-purpose cleaner in warm water is the best way to remove saliva when fresh. Hardened, dried saliva doesn't come off surfaces instantly or easily, and a strong degreaser may be called for to get the deposits up. Wet the spot down with the cleaning solution and leave it on for a few minutes before you wipe it off. One dog trainer I know has such a drool clean-up problem that she uses a Black & Decker Scumbuster to clean it up: "Drool, like other protein stains, is very hard to remove when dry, and a power tool like this is much better for removing it (my dogs drool so much I often don't discover it all until it's dried and hardened). This little machine gets it all off without removing paint or anything else I don't want it to, and it's much easier than elbow grease."

The enzymes in saliva can react with light, causing the droplets to darken as they dry. If there is staining, blot the area carefully with a hydrogen peroxide–wetted cloth, but be sure to test this first in an inconspicuous area.

If the saliva deposits are on a porous surface such as upholstery or carpeting, you might want to give the area a couple of quick sprays of Nolvasan solution after cleaning and just let it dry there, to prevent bacterial growth.

Pets "Scooting" on the Floor or Carpet

If you catch your cat or dog "scooting" around on the carpet on its rear end, he's not protesting the lack of toilet paper in the litter box. This kind of behavior, while sometimes a sign of worms or loose stools that have soiled the hair, more often than not means anal gland impaction. Dogs and cats both have glands on either side of the anus that excrete a scent when they defecate, as a territorial marking device.

When these glands fail to function properly, they become impacted and uncomfortable, and the animal will scoot its rear end on the floor or ground in an attempt to clear them. It may also lick the rectal area or bite its tail. Anal gland secretions can have a very strong, unpleasant odor, especially when the glands are infected or inflamed.

The vet can squeeze the glands to empty them during your pet's regular visits, and this may be all that's needed. If the glands are infected, treatment with an antibiotic is usually called for, and in cases of chronic impaction, the glands can be surgically removed. **Spayed animals don't have as much of a problem with anal gland impaction,** and cats suffer less from this than do dogs. It's a very common problem with unneutered male dogs.

For the sake of your pet's good health, and that of the human household members (impacted anal glands can harbor strep germs, for example), as well as the cleanliness of your home, don't let an anal gland problem continue untreated. Consult your veterinarian as soon as you notice the problem. And if you do get anal gland secretions on your carpeting, floors, or bedspread, clean and deodorize the spot the same way you would the infamous #2 (see page 116, Chapter 4). This basically means treat the spot with Nilotex, or if it's become an embedded odor problem, with bacteria/enzyme digester.

The Heat is On

Legendary people in powerful leadership positions have been known to destroy cities and pillage entire continents for love, so why should it be different for pets? An unspayed female would much rather listen to what her sex drive has to say, than to you.

A female dog's first heat usually appears when she's between the age of six and twelve months. After that, she'll come into heat twice a year, with each heat period lasting for two to three weeks. During this time, she will begin to discharge a small amount of blood. Blood is one of the harder stains to remove, and she'll be leaving spots of it all over the house, and all over the furniture, if she's allowed to jump up there. The heat period also causes a female dog to urinate much more often than normal. If you leave her home alone all day, she may not be able to hold herself until you return. A female dog, eager to mate but unable to get outside, may also try to escape by scratching at doors and floors. Some females experience a "false pregnancy" and try to build a nest by digging holes in or tearing up pillows, beds, or sofa cushions.

The following are some ideas to keep the mess and damage down (and keep your pet from getting pregnant):

- Have her spayed—the best and healthiest solution of all!

- Confine her to an easy-to-clean area of the house, a securely closed garage or reliably fenced yard, or a crate.

- Keep her inside all day and watch her like a hawk when she goes outside (or walk her only on a short leash, accompanied by a bodyguard).

- Put her in a boarding kennel until her period is over (and shell out beaucoup bucks for it, most likely).

- Cover any furniture you do allow her on with plastic or an old sheet.

- You can give her chlorophyll pills or liquid (available from veterinarians, pet catalogs, and health food stores) every day while she is in heat. Chlorophyll is a great deodorizer, and will mask the male-attracting scent she gives off during her heat cycle. It will help discourage male dogs, but remember, it will not prevent pregnancy!

- You can also use antimating sprays to try to cover up her mating scent, but like brewer's yeast and cedar oil for fleas, nobody can say for sure whether they really work or not—you pay your money and take your chances.

- Buy her a few pairs of doggy sanitary pants or pads to absorb the blood. These can be uncomfortable for your dog because they hold bacteria in close to the body and keep the area moist, often causing chafing or a rash much like a diaper rash. Use them only as a last resort.

- Keep your cleaning arsenal handy—bacteria/enzyme digester and a pet stain remover.

A female cat becomes sexually mature anywhere between six and eight months, and may come into heat two or three times a year after that. Some cats cycle in and out of heat frequently until they are bred. A cat in heat usually won't cause as much mess as a dog because she's smaller and doesn't discharge blood, though she can still cause damage by her frantic rolling, rubbing, and lunging, and by such things as tearing holes in the screen door to get outside and even spraying. And the yowling of a female cat in heat is enough to set your teeth on edge. Once again, the best solution is spaying.

Blood Stains

There are two good things about blood clean-up:

1. Red is easy to see and so we usually catch bloodstains quickly.
2. Fresh blood is a fairly easy stain to remove.

The bad news is that dried bloodstains are one of the tougher things to get out, especially if "set" by heat (as in a clothes dryer).

For fresh stains, always use cold water. Wet a cloth or sponge with cold water and blot the spot; wet and blot, wet and blot. I always prefer using a white cloth for stain removal because you immediately see whether or not the fabric you're treating is colorfast, and whether or not the stain is coming out.

The absolute best blood remover is plain old household ammonia. Make a solution of three tablespoons of ammonia to a gallon of cool water, and, after you've blotted with cold water, blot with the ammonia solution and the stain will come out. Rinse with vinegar to reduce the alkalinity left in the area, and then rinse with water.

If the article or material you're trying to get the stain out of is white and a slight stain is left, you might try rust remover. Bleach it with a 3 to 5 percent solution of hydrogen peroxide as a last resort.

If the bloodstain is old and really set, soak it with a bacteria/enzyme digester. If the stain is on clothing or sheets or the like, you can soak the article in a solution of several tablespoons of enzyme detergent such as Biz or a product like Oxy Clean overnight, then launder in cold water.

For old spots in carpeting, scrape off all of the dried blood and then flood the area with cold water. Pull the water out with a wet/dry vacuum or home carpet extractor. Use rust remover to remove any remaining stain.

Lassie Wants You to Come Home

Pets become very attached to their human families. When you leave, your pet isn't at all sure you'll ever be back. Coping with destructive behavior caused by what the pet experts call "separation anxiety" calls for the same concern and understanding you'd use with a child.

Dogs are descended from animals that live in family groups, or packs, whose members spend three-quarters or more of their time together, so staying all alone is alien to them. In the animal world, if your pack leaves you behind, it's because you're diseased, dying, or unwanted. So your pet thinks he has leprosy and actually you're just going to work.

Dogs that have come from a shelter or had previous owners are more likely to suffer separation anxiety, because they really do know what it is to be abandoned, and they live in constant fear of that happening again.

When a dog gets anxious, he'll nibble on this and chew on that, and anxiety also increases the possibility of accidents in the house. He may also lose his appetite and get depressed.

Punishment is completely off the point here. To reduce destructive behavior brought on by separation anxiety, we have to reduce our pet's anxiety by gradually accustoming him to being alone. There's an excellent pamphlet, *The Dog That Cannot Be Left Alone,* devoted solely to this subject. You can get it from *www.pet-tenders.com/articles.shtml* for $1.50 a page. For more information on separation anxiety, you can also check out *www.greytdogs.com/cooper.html.*

Here's a quick review of the kind of training you have to do:

1. Start with short absences the dog can tolerate; for example, five or ten minutes.
2. Remain calm and quiet as you come and go, no wild or enthusiastic greetings.

3. Repeat until you're sure the animal is not anxious, then gradually increase the length of your absence. If the animal backslides, practice more short absences.

4. Next, practice being gone for different lengths of time so the dog can't anticipate exactly when you'll return. After he's used to you being gone an hour or more, he'll gradually learn to tolerate longer intervals.

The less fuss you make over coming and going, the less anxiety-producing your absences will be. **Don't let your pet bowl you over when you come in.** Greet him quietly, keep excitement to a minimum, and save the play for later. Wild hellos get a dog so keyed up for your return that he may turn to destructive behavior if you're delayed.

A whiney, anxious good-bye from you also signals the dog that something is wrong and leaves him to wonder about it all day. So, if you find yourself saying, "Now, goodbye, sweetheart, be a good dog and don't eat Mommy's shoes—please, please be good," you may be part of the problem. Instead, calmly say, "Goodbye," toss him a toy, and go!

When you're home, have your pet stay alone in a room for at least some small part of the day. A puppy shut in alone for his nap every day, for example, will learn to accept it. It will also help this particular problem if you discourage your pet from being in constant contact with you: always sitting on your lap, sleeping with you, etc. This will help him be less dependent on you.

Confinement

It's a good idea to confine a pet left alone to a certain part of the house, and "pet-proof" the area: Make sure there's nothing he can harm and nothing that can harm him in there.

You want the room to be large enough that he can get some exercise (exactly how big depends on the size of the animal). A vinyl or tile floor is a much better idea than a carpeted one, and be sure to put his bed in the room or some washable rugs or blankets to lie on. If at all possible, go for a sunlit room with a window, and leave it open a crack so he can catch a whiff of what's going on outside. Remove any furniture that can't stand a little chewing or be slept on by your pet. If a dog is paper-trained, put newspapers in one corner of the room, and be sure to leave a clean litter box when confining a cat. You might want to put in some food and water, too—depending on how long he'll have to stay in there. You don't want a room packed with your prize possessions. Remove or protect anything that's hopelessly attached to your heartstrings. The emotional expense of Rover consuming the last handmade tapestry Great-Grandmother Ethel ever made will be much greater than the few dollars or hours you spend pet-proofing the canine suite. (No matter how grateful your spouse may be to finally be rid of that moth-eaten tapestry.)

If you have a dog or cat that consistently causes problems while you're away, you might consider crate-training him. Dogs may even draw a margin of comfort from being in their crate when they're left alone. But it's important to gradually accustom your pet to being in the crate, or a crate will only worsen the problem. For directions as to exactly how to do this, contact Gwen Bohnenkamp at *perfectpaws.com*. Boredom is the major threat to your pet's behavior. Toys and "acceptable chewies" offer your pet entertainment when you're gone. Be sure to rotate toys and chewies every few days so they're new and exciting to your pet. And put your pet's toys away when you come home. Save them for the lonely times. Keep a favorite toy by the door and toss it to your pet as you go. If you rub it in your palms, he'll be doubly drawn to it by your scent.

If something frightens your animal, he can do a lot of damage alone in your home. Music can help to soothe the anxious pet, and for that matter the lonely, howling pet. It also muffles outside noises like horns and sirens and shrieking

> Boredom is the major threat to your pet's behavior.

kids. A radio playing softly makes a good companion for your dog. Tune in a station with more human chatter than music, as he's more interested in a human voice. A long-playing recording of your voice might serve even better.

Chemical Calming Approaches

There are pheromone sprays for both dogs and cats that duplicate the pheromones released by mother dogs and cats to calm and reassure their young offspring. The cat version is called ComfortZone with Feliway, and the dog version ComfortZone with D.A.P. (dog appeasing pheromone). Both are available in dispensers that release a puff into the air every so often. You can find out more about them at *www.feliway.com*. You can also investigate aromatherapy; many scents have calming properties. An automatic air freshening atomizer of herbal and/or homeopathic remedies may take the edge off for your pet.

As a last resort, there are pet tranquilizers such as Clomicalm, but some of these have unwelcome side effects. They should not be used without consulting your veterinarian and exhausting the avenues of training and soft science first.

Exercise and Obedience Training

Our pets react to boredom in a way we often do—sleep is the primary occupation of the average pet when the master is away. So when you get home, your pet has a store of pent-up energy ready for release the minute you walk in the door.

Exercise your pet in the morning just before you leave, again when you get home, and before he goes to bed. He deserves special care and attention when the family does arrive home. Exercise, walks, and obedience training will help him cope with your daily absences. According to *Dog Fancy*:

> Trained dogs even *look* less bored; perhaps it's because they have something to look forward to at the end of the day. Twenty or thirty minutes a day in a one-on-one

session with you gives your dog quality time to perform all the things he's learned and be praised by you. The security he derives from this will help carry him through the long day without resorting to destructive behavior.

Ideally your pet should be let out at least once during the day to relieve himself. If you can't make it home, then consider a "pet sitter" service or a nearby neighbor willing to take this on. A daily visit with your pet might be a welcome break in the day for a retired or elderly person. Or a petless child might love to take him for a walk after school. Your pet's food and water and toilet needs can be tended and at the same time a little companionship will interrupt an otherwise lonely day.

Professional pet sitters are popping up all over the country. They feed, water, exercise, and even administer medication to pets. They will either come to your home or have you bring your pet to them. The right sitter can alleviate a lot of potential mess for you.

In our latchkey society, imagine the number of pets home alone with children after school. If a pet alone can make a mess, add a kid or two to the recipe and see what cooks up. Kids sharing snacks with Fido, six feet instead of two tracking mud in the back door—the possibilities are endless. Establishing some rules here will help keep cleaning down. And be careful after chastising a child for a co-made mess, that the child doesn't dole out some punishment of his own on the animal when left alone with it.

Some undesirable behavior may be the result of a simple case of hunger. Although adult dogs may need to be fed only once a day, left alone all day with little to do and an empty stomach, the rattan rocking chair might get to looking pretty appetizing. A solution for some cases of destructive chewing is to feed your pet a light meal early in the morning, and take him out twenty or thirty minutes later. Then give him another light meal in the evening when you return.

Treat balls are a great way to keep dogs and cats busy while you are away. Pick up the dry food and put the kibble in the treat ball.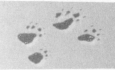

Get Your Pet a Pet

It's often just as easy to care for two pets as one, and another dog or cat can keep your pet entertained and happy while you're gone all day. If your pet is a pup, an older companion is the best idea, as two puppies can get into twice as much trouble. And be sure pet pals are neutered so they don't create a whole litterful of entertainment. Even a bird, well out of reach in a cage, can be a welcome diversion for your dog.

If you have a cat and bring home another one, keep them separated from each other for a few days to a week, then let the new cat come in and meet the old one. Don't make a fuss over the new cat; instead, give your old cat more attention to help reduce any jealousy he might feel. This also applies if you bring home a dog when you have a cat, if you have a dog and get another one, or if you have a dog and bring home a cat.

The following combinations are generally the best recipe for pet peace and harmony: kitten and puppy; two kittens; mature, neutered cat and puppy or kitten; two mature, neutered cats (two females or a male and a female).

Pay Attention to Him

Don't try to discipline your pet when you get home for accidents or damage that occurred while you were gone. It does no good to punish at 5 P.M. for an act that occurred at 10 A.M.—he's forgotten all about it. It will only confuse him and give him negative associations with your homecoming that may cause him to perform other forbidden acts while fretting about it. Nor in this case will it do any good to wait outside until the dog performs an unwanted behavior, then rush in and scold him. Punishment just isn't an effective way to treat separation anxiety. And it'll only compound any guilty feelings you may have about leaving him alone all day.

You can go to great lengths to enrich your pet's life, with toys, pet buddies, etc., but remember that in the end it's *you*, the master, who makes the big difference. As Gwen Bohnenkamp says, "Remember, your pet can't build model airplanes, learn Italian, or shoot pool when you're not home. So when you are, set aside some time to give him undivided attention."

Car (and Plane) Trips with Your Pet

Many people like to bring their dogs and cats on the road with them, preferring companionship and financial savings to the cost of a kennel and the potential for emotional anxiety on the part of pet and owner during the separation. With reptiles, fish, and birds, and for that matter older, ill, or very young cats and dogs, finding a caretaker is the best option because the stress of traveling is especially hard on these types of creatures. Whether in a car, plane, train, or bus, there are precautions everyone should know to ensure a safe and fun trip.

Prep Time

Before you actually leave for the trip, before the bags are packed and the car is loaded, get your pet acquainted with your mode of travel. With planes, buses, and trains, this is more difficult, but you can at least get your pet used to his crate and confinement.

If your dog is smaller, you may want to crate him at first for car travel. **If you want your dog to be loose while you drive, get a doggie seatbelt or travel harness for him.** And get Fido used to being harnessed while he's young, because it's hard to get an older dog to tolerate it. You might want to put an old sheet or blanket over the backseat of your car before you strap in your dog. There are also many types of pet car-seat covers and pet travel beds available.

Most cats feel comfortable and safe in a sturdy, well-ventilated carrier or crate. Put a soft cushion and a T-shirt with your scent on it in there to provide further comfort. Leave the carrier out and open so your cat can explore and smell it before you close the door. Your cat should never be allowed to move around the car while you drive. Cats are small and flexible and can get under the steering wheel, the pedals, and seats—not safe for you or Kitty!

No matter how much your dog loves having his head out the window, don't let him do it. It's dangerous to the dog and to you. Open the windows a crack to let him enjoy the smells and sounds without collecting debris in his eyes and ears.

Once the car is prepared for the pet, just take your dog or cat and sit with him in the car with the engine idling. If he doesn't seem too agitated, try taking a short trip around the block or up the road.

Before you leave for your trip, be sure that your pet has had all necessary shots and that you have the vaccination certificates (check with your veterinarian). This is especially important if you plan on traveling by plane, or if you will be crossing international boundaries. If you've discovered that your dog or cat gets extremely anxious while traveling, you should also ask your veterinarian about tranquilizers.

Just like humans, animals can get motion sickness. Give your dog a light meal a few hours before you leave. Take your cat's food and water away a few hours before you leave as well. Don't give them snacks while you travel, if you can help it. Have food and water on hand, and this goes double for car trips longer than a few hours. Keep the windows cracked for good ventilation. Give your dog a chance to relieve himself right before you go, and make sure you stop along the way so that he can do it again. Cats can go a little longer without having to use their litter, but you should have a small litter box and some kitty litter with you just in case. Remember, the more comfortable your pet is, the more comfortable you are. If your pet has a persistent problem with motion sickness, ask your veterinarian for medicine for it.

Don't forget to call in advance to find out if your pet is welcome wherever you are staying, be it at a hotel, motel, or relatives'. If the hotel or motel doesn't want dogs or cats, you should be able to find another one that does close by. If Aunt May doesn't want "that stinkin' mutt" in her house, well then stay with Aunt Judith!

Most airlines will allow you to bring pets, but they require you to put your pet in a crate. Also, your pet will usually be traveling in the cargo portion of the plane, which can be scary and unpleasant if he is young. Be sure you book a direct flight if you will be bringing your cat or dog. And make sure you call the airline to find out all of its rules and regulations about traveling with pets. Tranquilizers are not usually recommended for pets traveling by air.

The big train and bus companies will not allow animals unless they are service animals such as seeing-eye dogs. It never hurts to ask, though!

Throughout the trip, your pet should wear his collar with proper ID, and make sure you bring some snapshots just in case the worst should happen.

Don't forget to pack the following:

- Leash and collar
- Flea collar
- Favorite toy(s)
- Food and water dishes
- Food and water (some dogs like to chew on ice cubes during long car rides)
- A small carpeted mat with rubber backing
- Any medication the pet is on
- Towels
- Animal bedding

Prepare for Clean-Up

Even with all of your precautions, you're likely to do some clean-up while you're on the road. This will be easy—if you prepare in advance. So make sure you have:

- Scooping equipment and plastic bags to dispose of feces (if your fellow traveler is a dog)
- Paper towels
- A spray bottle of all-purpose cleaner
- A spray bottle of disinfectant
- A spray bottle of odor neutralizer such as X-O
- Your favorite hair removal tool (especially if you're in a hotel; they will charge for extra clean-up)
- Some cleaning cloths, and an old towel to wipe down your pet if he gets muddy

If you leave your dog or cat in the hotel or motel room when you go out somewhere, make sure he or she is confined with food and water, rather than running loose and causing damage.

The cardinal rules when you're on the road or in the air with your pet:

1. **NEVER** leave your pet unattended or unaccounted for.
2. **ALWAYS** clean up after your pet!

Chapter 7

Beyond Barks and Meows:

Caring and Cleaning for the Small Pet Set

Barks and meows might be the most familiar voices in the pet world, but not the only ones by far! There are other four-legged, two-legged—even no-legged—pets that wag a totally different tail and are just as dear to their owners. These critters may not play fetch, but they swim, sing, jump, scurry, and climb like crazy. Plus, they often eat less, take up less space, and make less mess.

They may be little but they require (demand!) care and keeping. When you own one (or more), you own the maintenance, too, and your first order of the day is to make little-pet clean-up as easy as possible.

Many small pets live in cages or aquaria, and this concentrates the care to a confined area, but it needs attention every day to keep your pet healthy. A sick pet is no fun for anyone. Seasoned small pet owners and experts alike say pet ownership here usually has three phases:

1. The excitement and novelty of the new (much like bringing a new baby home)—the thrill of acquisition.

2. The real-world shocker of the keeping—getting a cage or tank and furnishing and cleaning it, providing just the right heat, lights, food, hardware, toys, and time for care.

3. The pet matures—gets older, and sometimes bigger (that cute little 6-inch lizard is now 3 feet long and eats more than your teenage son and his friends).

You need to prepare yourself for these eventualities when you are in the eager childlike stage, *before* you purchase the pet. One good source of surveying the situation and foreseeing the future when a particular pet joins your household is to take counsel from the store. These people breed, feed, and bleed for hundreds of all kinds of creatures *every day.* They can help you find the right reptile, bird, fish, or rodent to fit your situation and environment and live happily in it. **People who own, or have owned, the same type of pet you have in mind can fill you in on both the pleasures and problems of the animal,** and they will usually be objective, because they aren't trying to sell you anything. Books, magazines, and Web sites also abound with information that can fill out your picture of the pet. Try Googling the type of animal you are thinking of getting, and read all of the research, tips, and personal stories associated with it. (And even if you already own this alterna-pet, you should do as much research as possible to know whatever you can about him.)

Then you can decide which bases you are willing to cover—how often you are willing to clean the tank or cage; how comfortable you will feel fiddling with thermostats, rheostats, or hygrometers; how likely you are to visit a pet store twice a week to buy fresh crickets for hungry lizards; or how happy you will be with a nocturnal creature that runs its exercise wheel at night. The bottom line here is: Small pets are precious but dens get dirty. Children forget fast that service to small pets is daily, not occasional.

Buy good hardware made for small pets—cages, aquariums, dishes, cage furnishings—instead of just adapting something you have around the house. Pet supply companies have worked to achieve maximum efficiency and quick care of the various critters, and ensure safety, health, and sanitation. Pet stores, too, have to deal with the realities of pet care daily. Take note of what they do.

Rodents and Other Small Furry Friends

There is a real species span on these furry little fellows ranging from rats, mice, and hamsters, through the gerbil family to rabbits, guinea pigs, chinchillas, hedgehogs, and more.

Housing

There is also a vast array of housing available for these critters, but it boils down to three general types: wire cages, aquariums with screened covers, and (often elaborate) plastic "habitats" complete with tunnels, ramps, and wheels or other exercise devices. Of the three, wire cages are the best for the larger animals, and glass aquaria for the smaller. Plastic habitats are expensive, scratchable, and chewable, and are often hard to clean and poorly ventilated.

Wire cages allow more litter and seeds, etc., to be flipped out, and don't hide odor, but they give the animals more ventilation and exercise opportunities such as climbing the wire. If you use a wire cage, you absolutely need to make sure the mesh is the right size for the animal you have in mind, because rodents are escape artists. You also need to cover part of the wire flooring with pieces of nontoxic unpainted wood, Plexiglas, old clean carpeting, newspaper, or the like to keep the animal from getting sore feet from walking on wire. A sliding tray or drawer beneath a wire cage helps a lot when it's time to clean the cage.

If you're handy, you can make a roomier cage, better than what is commercially available. Just remember that a small animal cage should be as large as possible, secure (from escape or predators), and chew-proof in the areas the animal can get to. Do not use treated lumber anywhere the animal has access too, because it is poisonous.

Bedding

Wood chips or shavings (do not use cedar or pine, both of which contain oils that can irritate your pet's skin and eyes), recycled paper litter (especially the chip style; Care-Fresh is a popular brand), and shredded newspaper (if the newspaper uses nontoxic ink) are all good options. Corncob bedding is not as absorbent and shifts around a lot. For animals that like to burrow, such as gerbils and hamsters, use a thicker layer of bedding.

For animals that may be housed outdoors, you can use hay or straw, as well as any of the litters mentioned earlier.

Most small furry animals also like to have a den, nest, or hiding box, which should have bedding of shredded paper toweling, tissues, or commercial cotton bedding. Bedding in nesting areas, which is usually not fouled, should be changed only about once a month, or the critters may feel insecure.

Litter Pans

Rabbits (and to a lesser extent, guinea pigs) can be trained to use a litter box indoors, although it's not a simple task. Do not let rabbits run loose in a house unsupervised—they can do a lot of damage to wood furniture and even wall coverings, and have a habit of chewing on electric and phone cords. To clean up the "rabbit raisins" a loose rabbit will leave around, use your squeegee and dustpan to pick them up and dispose of them, and then do quick spray-and-wipe of the area with deodorizer/cleaner and a paper towel. If it happens to be a soft surface, first wipe up any visible residue with a paper towel and then treat the area with a spray or two of bacteria/enzyme digester.

Tiny litter boxes or "outhouses" for the inside of a cage are sold for smaller pets, to enable them to use their instinct to put most of their droppings in one place. This is a real aid in keeping the cage clean. Organic litters rather than clay are recommended for any rodent or rabbit litter box.

Food and Water

Heavy ceramic dishes are better for small pets than plastic or metal, which can be chewed or overturned. Water in bowls will be quickly fouled, so the water bottles that hang on the side of the cage are what you want.

The Animal Itself

Small pets such as rodents and their relatives are self-cleaning, but if your pet occasionally gets some dirt on him that he doesn't clean off, brush it off with a soft brush, or wipe with a cloth dampened in lukewarm water. **Rabbits may benefit from brushing during periods of heavy shedding.** Chinchillas like to take dust baths, so provide them with the means, preferably the commercially available sanitized chinchilla dust.

Cleaning

Of all the small creatures you could have as pets, rodents and animals like them are the only ones that really stink in a caged situation. So care and cleaning is not a wait-and-see, it's a smell-and-tell.

Daily

Remove wet, soiled bedding and any accumulated waste in the pet's "potty area" of the cage. Add some fresh litter or bedding if needed; remove stale food. Wash and dry the food bowl and fill with fresh food. Wash the water bottle and refill, even if it's not empty. You can possibly change the water every other day, but don't leave it till it gets stale and mossy.

Weekly

Remove the animal(s) from the cage to another small cage or a secure, ventilated container. Wash and disinfect the cage bottom, dishes, accessories, and toys. Change the bedding; empty the tray if there is one, and clean, disinfect, and replace it. Do not put pets back in until all is good and dry.

Monthly

Wash and disinfect the entire cage. Take care to keep your pets away from any cleaning solutions or sprays that could be poisonous to them and their environment.

Some Rodent-Cleaning Tools and Aids

- A sturdy bottle brush for cleaning the water bottle
- A utility brush (see page 7) for cleaning the cage
- Sprays, such as Cage Shield, to help keep organic messes from sticking to the cage (some people just use Pam cooking spray)
- Quick Clean, an orange-oil based product designed to remove stuck-on debris

We are often in a hurry to "get the job done" so we tend to move fast. No pet likes fast moves or surprises—they will get negative reactions; this is one time to clean slow.

Keeping Small Pets Sweet-Smelling

The main thing to remember about odor and any small pet is that most of the smell is from bacteria. If things are kept clean and fresh so that bacteria have nothing to feed on, odor will not be a problem.

Air fresheners, as nice as they make things smell for a while, are not a substitute for sanitation, and covering one bad smell with a stronger smell (masking) gives a false illusion as to the frequency and quality of cleaning required.

Bacteria/enzyme cleaners can help keep odor down in pet cages and enclosures (remove the pets before using them). There are bacteria/enzyme products specially made for small animal quarters, or you can use any good one. Hard surfaces around small pet cages can be cleaned with a deodorizer/cleaner. Always read label for pet safety and dilution, plus how and where to use it.

See page 12 in Chapter 1 for suggestions on deodorizing the room or area a small pet inhabits.

Reptiles

Lizards, snakes, turtles, and a multitude of other reptiles are more popular than ever—how they bring our prehistoric imagination to life! They may  not make a lot of emotional demands on us, but among the small pets, these need some of the closest care. Temperature, humidity, and lighting need to be "just so"; they eat some fairly exotic things; and cleanliness is a big-time issue here. If their quarters and surroundings are not kept clean, they are prone to bacterial and fungal diseases. And reptiles can carry salmonella and transmit it to humans, unless scrupulous sanitation is observed. Salmonella can be a serious illness, especially in young children, the elderly or immune-compromised, or pregnant women.

The Right Home for the Right Rep

Most reptiles are kept in aquariums or terraria inside, or wire enclosures outside. The first and most important thing when you are thinking about what kind of reptile to get is to research the possibilities. **Different species can call for quite different living conditions,** depending on what their living conditions were in the wild—desert or rain forest, etc. Once you are sure of what type of lizard, snake, turtle, or the like you can handle taking care of, you can research its requirements (via the Internet or your local friendly pet store owner) and set up an environment to meet them. Otherwise, your reptile will not thrive, and may even die.

Floor Coverings and Furnishings

Once you have an enclosure of the right size and type, with the right lighting, temperature, and humidity (books and Web sites will help you here), there comes the question (for indoor reptile housing) of what to put on the floor. The fancy word for this is "substrate," and there is a wide variety of options: newspaper, paper toweling, terrycloth towels, rabbit pellets, and more. Fine gravel, cat litter, corncob litter, wood shavings, and even sand are frowned upon as hard to keep clean and possibly able to cause harm if T. Rex, Jr., accidentally eats some. The best choices here, from both a cleaning and health standpoint, are indoor-outdoor carpeting (there is even a version of this specially made for the purpose by pet suppliers) or the special edible, calcium-rich "sand" sold under names like Cal-Strate, Calci-Sand, and Lizard Litter Calcium Sand. This specialty lizard sand even "clumps" like cat litter, easing waste removal. When indoor-outdoor carpeting becomes soiled, it can be easily removed and cleaned with warm water and then dried and replaced. Reptile owners often keep several pieces on hand so one can be used while the other is being cleaned. There are other litters sold specially for reptile-cage bottoms, and they all are designed to be both sanitary and safe for the animal. (Iguanas and possibly some other lizards can be litter-box trained, if you're feeling ambitious.)

When it comes to furnishings for the reptile home, a lot depends on the type of reptile you are housing (does it like to climb? etc.). But whatever you put in the cage should be either disinfectable or disposable, and be sure to arrange things so that perches and the like are not suspended over food and water, to help avoid fouling. Most reptiles appreciate one or more good hiding places, and at least one rough-surfaced branch or stone to aid skin shedding.

Cleaning

> Whatever you put in the cage should be either disinfectable or disposable.

Although we are into the cleaning aspects, not the diets, of these little creatures, preparation and clean-up of feeding are big items. It takes almost as much effort to feed some reptiles as to make a Caesar salad. Cleaning, chopping, and otherwise preparing fruits, vegetables, clover, eggs, insects, and yes, vitamins and minerals; you make a mess! And old, uneaten food is one of the most common health and cleaning problems with reptiles.

Daily

You need to remove any uneaten food, pet droppings, shed skin, etc., every day. Clean food and water dishes well daily. Water needs to be changed daily, even if it doesn't look dirty, because in the warm, humid environment of a reptile cage, especially, it is a breeding ground for bacteria.

A great small pet tool to own is a quality pair of long tongs. Useful for quick, safe, selective retrieving of dead insects, shed skin, and large droppings, and arranging plants, etc.

Your reptile himself needs to be kept clean, too. If he doesn't have a place to bathe, you need to at least mist him regularly.

Weekly

Once a week, you need to clean and disinfect the entire cage, clean or replace the substrate, and clean and disinfect any cage furnishings, too. Move your reptile to a clean spare small cage while performing this operation, to keep him from being alarmed and to keep him safe from chemicals and their fumes.

First, clean the cage itself and all of the furnishings well, using a brush as needed and a mild solution of dish detergent and water. After the cage is good and clean, disinfect it, following the instructions on page 38. Never use pine cleaner or Lysol disinfectant around reptiles; use Nolvasan. Household bleach can be used, too, in a ratio of 1 part bleach to 16 parts water. Don't put your pet back in until everything is completely dry.

For Safe and Healthy Reptile Ownership

Public health officials, veterinarians, and pet store owners offer the following guidelines to those who own reptiles:

1. Do not permit unsupervised handling of reptiles by children.
2. Keep other pets away from reptile cages.
3. Don't handle reptiles if you have open cuts or sores.
4. Never eat or put anything in your mouth during or right after handling your animals.
5. Never clean cages in the kitchen or anywhere you prepare food for human consumption.

6. Always wash your hands with a disinfectant soap after handling your animals. Washing with water alone will not eliminate salmonella.

7. Do not use kitchen sinks, bathtubs, or shower stalls for cleaning reptiles or their cages unless you thoroughly disinfect afterward with a bleach-containing product.

8. Wear rubber gloves when cleaning reptile cages and disinfect them regularly. Use heavier gloves when handling possible biters.

Birds

It is pretty well agreed upon by owners and sellers of smaller pets that birds are the most demanding in the cleaning department. They can fling as well as they can fly and sing, and they can fan bird fallout farther than Rover can quiver off bath water. A little forethought here can brighten the bird zone.

Cages

When you go to buy a birdcage, you face quite an array—from tiny bamboo pagodas to entire room-size aviaries. How do you choose from all this? With your bird's comfort and safety in mind, of course, but also taking into account how durable a cage is and how well designed it is to take its inhabitant's inevitable messing. In other words, how easy it is to *clean*!

As for size, the larger the better. The bird will be happier, and larger cages are usually easier to clean, and less mess escapes from the cage, too. Avoid fancy, ornate styles—square or rectangular cages are much easier to keep clean (and give the birds more room, too). Large cages should be on casters for ease of cleaning and overall convenience.

For the material of the cage itself, you want a durable, nontoxic finish that will hold up to repeated cleanings. Metal is best, because it withstands bird abuse and vigorous cleaning and disinfection. Avoid painted metal if you can, because birds can chip off the finish and possibly harm themselves in the process, as well as making the cage look ugly.

A tray at the bottom of the cage that slides out for cleaning—preferably a rust-resistant one—will simplify daily maintenance. Some cages also have a grid above the tray, to keep birds from shredding cage liners, walking in their own droppings, and eating soiled or spoiled food from the cage floor.

If the cage doesn't have a clear plastic seed guard around the base, add one of your own, made from 4- to 6-inch-high clear plastic. You can also buy seed-catching "skirts" for bird-cages, and seed guards made of nylon fabric held in place by elastic, from pet catalogs such as Doctors Foster & Smith Just for Birds.

Food dishes and waterers, too, should be designed to help keep things sanitary and placed so that the seed guard can function effectively. Keep food and water dishes away from perches to help prevent soiling.

The Bird Zone

Finally, when choosing where to put the cage, after you've followed all the directions in the bird guide about placement for your pet's health (mental and physical) and safety—avoiding drafts and fumes, too much commotion, etc.—consider placement from the cleaning standpoint, too. **Put the cage in a hard-surface room or area if at all possible,** one without cracks and crevices all over to collect debris. Dust, grit, seed, and other bird fallout can be swept off of hard surfaces quickly and easily. For the walls around the cage, consider vinyl wall covering, plastic laminate, semigloss enamel, or even a sheet or two of clear Plexiglas.

Cage Liners

You want something on the bottom of the cage to absorb droppings. Newspaper, the old standby, is inexpensive, but far better if the ink used on it is nontoxic, such as soy ink. A call to your local paper should clue you in here. Other possibilities include unprinted newsprint paper, inexpensive plain paper commercial liners, cardboard, shredded paper, even old towels that can be tossed in the washer and reused. **The latest and most favored cage litters are ones made from recycled paper** (which is dust-free, clumping, and flushable) and corncobs, such as Kay-Kob. Litters like these do a good job of keeping down odor. Wood shavings or chips are not desirable because they are dusty and can irritate bird airways.

Cage Cleaning

Like reptile cages, bird cages need regular attention to keep our feathered friends happy and healthy in there.

Daily

Replace paper liners and remove soiled parts of other litters. Some people put a small stack of paper liners in the cage at once, so they can just reach in and peel off the top layer each day. Remove uneaten or stale food. Clean dishes, waterers, and frequently used toys in a hot solution of liquid dish detergent and water, or run them through a dishwasher. Rinse and dry well before returning to the cage. Vacuum, dust mop, or sweep the area around the cage.

Weekly

Do this weekly for large birds or twice a month for smaller ones: Remove the bird(s) from the cage to a spare cage preferably in another room. Remove all dishes, toys, and other accessories and clean them well and then disinfect them. Brush off any droppings or other debris you can with a stiff nylon brush and then scrub the whole cage with hot, soapy water. Rinse and dry thoroughly before returning birds to the cage. Clean perches with a wire brush or perch scraper. Natural branches can be put in a 250-degree oven for 15 minutes to sanitize them.

A pressure washer can be used to help clean large cages.

When you're doing your weekly or bimonthly deep cleaning, wash the floor and walls around the cage as well, and disinfect them.

Warning: Avoid using strongly scented cleaners or pine oil disinfectants around birds, and avoid exposing them to strong chemicals of any kind. Birds are super-sensitive to fumes—that's why canaries were once used to detect toxic gases in coal mines.

Tools and Aids for Bird Cleaning

- For cleaning water bottles and tubes, a bottlebrush with a smaller tube brush on the other end (*www.DrsFosterSmith.com*)
- A small wire brush with stainless steel bristles, or a linoleum knife—great for perch cleaning
- To help keep splatters, regurgitated food, droppings, bug residue, etc., from sticking to the cage, a product such as Cage Shield spray, to be sprayed on after cleaning (some people just use Pam cooking spray)
- Disinfectant and bird cleaning wipes to speed the daily clean-up

A variety of droppings cleaners are also available, such as Poop-Off. Many of these are enzyme preparations with brush applicator tops, designed to "clean, disinfect, and deodorize" in one step. Bird droppings contain a great deal of nitrogen, so they are very corrosive; you want to get them off of any surface as soon as possible.

Birds Loose in the House

I'm just going to say a little about this, because it is a BIG subject, especially for a professional cleaner. The worst mess I've ever seen as a pro was a place I'll call "the bird house," where a large parrot roamed at will. The curtains hung in strings and shreds and every wall and floor was plastered with guano.

If you are going to let your bird loose in the house, try to confine the inevitable mess. One room or a couple of rooms with hard-surface flooring and a minimum of (or no) upholstered furnishings, innocent lampshades, delicate draperies, and winsome window trim is a lot better than a house full of targets of opportunity. And remember that birds think windows and mirrors are sky and can knock themselves unconscious (or worse) flying into them.

Wear an old terry beach jacket or thick towel over your shoulder if you're hopelessly addicted to the role of perambulating bird perch. Specialty catalogs offer products like flight suits that include mini disposable diapers to reduce aerial bombardments from "bird loose in the house."

Fish

Fish are more popular than ever today, and with all the color and drama contained in the little world of an aquarium, it's easy to understand why. But as you experienced fish-keepers know, you can't just throw a few fish into a tank or bowl with some rocks and plants and expect all to go well from there. Keeping fish happy and healthy—and the tank good-looking—takes constant monitoring and attention, and cleaning of various kinds is a big part of this.

Cutting Aquarium Maintenance

First let's look at a few things that can help reduce aquarium maintenance.

Larger tanks are usually easier to maintain—as long as you don't overcrowd them. While we're on that subject, you don't want to overcrowd even a smaller tank. We always want to add a few more neat fish, but overcrowded aquariums get fouled fast, and those neat fish may soon be floating on top!

Filters are an important aid. The bigger and better, the cleaner the tank will stay. There are many different kinds, including filters that remove dirt from the water, and ones that break down waste in the water; chemical filters, mechanical filters, and even live filters. There are out-of-tank filters, trickle filters, under-gravel filters, wet-dry filters, and more. Consult your local fish store as to which type would be best for your tank and fish you plan to put in it, and buy the best model you can afford.

> Get the same tools the shops use to keep their fifty aquariums beautiful and functioning.

Tank janitors (a personal favorite, for obvious reasons) are live creatures you can add to a tank to help remove algae and organic debris. For freshwater tanks, these are mostly algae eaters. There are a wide variety of algae eaters from all parts of the world, but they are mostly sucker-mouthed catfish. Be sure to read up on these before you get one, so you can get the right size and type. Some algae eaters can get big and aggressive, and some can start nibbling on other fish when they run out of algae.

Remember, fish need daily maintenance. To lessen the burden of this, spend a few bucks up front and get the same tools the shops use to keep their fifty aquariums beautiful and functioning well. Some other things to remember include the following:

1. Use gravel, not sand, in the bottom of a freshwater tank. Sand will quickly get polluted.

2. Don't leave the tank light on 24/7—this is one of the main causes of algae overgrowth.
3. Don't overfeed the fish! Uneaten food quickly turns into a pollutant.

Cleaning the Tank

Important as it is, cleaning the tank is not something done all at once by removing the fish and replacing the water and gravel. **In an established tank, beneficial bacteria build up in the gravel and elsewhere and help keep the tank clean by breaking down fish waste.** An all-in-one-fell-swoop cleaning would destroy these bacteria, as well as stress the fish. So we have to do our tank cleaning in carefully timed installments, and for the most part while the fish are in place.

Weekly

Unplug any electrical equipment, and first clean the inside of the glass. Use one of the special scrub pads made just for this purpose, such as the Jungle Algae Remover, available in the pet department of Wal-Mart. Use no chemicals or cleaners of any kind with it, and be careful not to get any gravel or the like caught under it or it will scratch. For extra stubborn spots you can use a razor scraper. If your tank is plastic, be sure to use pads or scrapers designed for plastic.

There are also sets of cleaning magnets: one stays in the tank, the other sticks to it through the glass, and when you move the outside unit, the inside unit moves with it, cleaning the glass. Whatever tool you use, work your way from the top of the tank walls to the bottom, and move slowly to avoid panicking the fish.

Use a scrub pad to also clean any dirty or algae-covered tank decorations, and the outside of the filter siphon tube. The inside of the tube can be cleaned with a test-tube brush, also available at Wal-Mart. Here, too, use no detergents or chemicals of any kind.

Clean the outside of the glass with a squeegee (and scrubber if necessary) and aquarium-approved glass cleaners.

About Once a Month

You need to replace 20 percent of the water in a freshwater tank with clean water. When we replace part of the water in a tank, we are doing what rain and flood, tides and currents do in nature.

No matter how good a filter you have, it can't remove all the waste from the water, and dirty water will mean stressed or sick fish. **If your tank is crowded, you may have to make this water exchange twice a month.** In a small fishbowl or unfiltered tank, you need to change about half the water every week. Testers are available to test the water for ammonia or nitrate levels if you want to be more precise. If the water in a tank is cloudy, water replacement is overdue!

For a water change, the tools you need are two large clean buckets (never used for anything else) and a gravel siphon (plus gravel vacuum if possible). Figure out how much water you need to change by dividing the capacity of your tank by five. Siphon out that much water (don't siphon out your fish though!), and then clean as much dirt and debris as you can out of the tank with the siphon. It can help to move the gravel toward the back corners of the tank, so the debris floats toward the front. If you have a gravel vac, vacuum the entire surface of the gravel.

Then make ready the fresh water. Tap water can be used in most parts of the country (check with a local fish fancier if you are not sure) as long as you add water conditioner to it. Conditioner removes chlorine and other harmful chemicals and minerals from water. If you're in doubt about chlorine removal, leave the water in an open bucket overnight. (Some of the chlorine will escape from water left standing.) Make sure the water you are adding is not more than three degrees different in temperature from the water in the tank, and add it slowly, cup by cup.

A tool that can simplify the process of water changing/tank cleaning is the Python No Spill Clean and Fill (*www.pythonproducts.com/nospill.htm*). With this attached to a sink faucet—following the directions that come with it—you can clean and refill a tank in one operation.

When you are making a water change, you should also clean the filter. Unplug the filter first, and if it is a mechanical filter, rinse it in cool water alone; if it is a floss filter, replace only half of the floss (to retain some of the beneficial bacteria, which also reside in the filter). If it is a carbon, ammonia, or ion exchange type, replace it. Some fanciers use some of the dirty tank water they have just siphoned out to rinse the filter, to help avoid destroying the bacteria in the filter.

When You Want to Do a Thorough Cleaning
You can add these operations to the ones described earlier:

1. Wipe/scrub off the aquarium light and use aquarium-approved hard water deposit remover on it if necessary.
2. Scrub algae off rocks and decorations with a new stiff toothbrush.
3. Remove plastic plants and scrub them off (using no cleaner), then rinse well and replace.
4. Decorations or fake plants with stubborn discolorations can be soaked for twenty-five minutes in a 10 percent bleach solution (1 part bleach to 9 parts water), then rinsed very well, dried, and replaced.
5. Disinfect your fish nets and rinse well and dry.
6. Whenever you do an ambitious all-points cleaning of a tank, wait to do any filter cleaning until about two weeks later (to avoid depleting those helpful bacteria too much).

A Few General Rules for "Fish Cleaning"

- Do things a little at a time.
- Use only aquarium-approved chemicals and supplies.
- Save any other tools you use (sponges, buckets, etc.) for this use only.
- Rinse, rinse, rinse!
- Always remember that these are live creatures (complete with nervous systems) in there, so do whatever you are doing as gently and quietly as possible.

Saltwater Tanks

Saltwater aquaria are often thought of as more difficult to care for, but pretty much the same basic cleaning and maintenance operations need to be done for them as for freshwater tanks. The big differences are in timeliness and precision.

You can't wait until you get around to performing your cleaning chores, as many might be guilty of doing with freshwater fish. If you don't change the water or clean the filter of a freshwater tank on time, the fish will get by. They will survive, if not thrive, because freshwater fish in nature must adapt to a variety of changes and often adverse conditions in their surroundings. Saltwater fish, on the other hand, are always immersed in a huge ocean that, despite its waves and currents, is always about the same chemically. **Saltwater fish need unchanging conditions.** If they don't have stability, they will quickly sicken or die.

In a saltwater tank, you need to monitor the water quality closely at all times (there are test kits available for this) and change 25 percent of it every two weeks. You need to condition the water you add here, too, which in this case means adding sea salt and perhaps other minerals as well. And the replacement water needs to be made up twenty-four hours ahead of time.

The filtering of a saltwater tank is extra important, too. For marine tanks, there is even a wider variety of types of filter available, including protein skimmers that remove tank wastes by means of air bubbles, and a single tank may use more than one system. Saltwater tanks make wider use of biological filtering systems—everything from "live rock" and "live mud" to a fascinating assortment of larger live creatures enlisted to help keep the tank clean—including fish, shrimp, crabs, snails, sea urchins, and sea cucumbers. Saltwater tanks that use the best of these biological means of cleaning, if properly maintained, come close to being naturally self-cleaning.

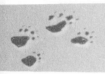 Saltwater tanks will grow more algae than freshwater tanks, and if you don't stay on your toes, the bottom of a marine tank will soon be covered with reddish deposits from bacteria as well.

Exactly how all of the above is done is beyond the scope of this little volume, but this is the "big picture," and if you want to have your own little ocean, you need to find a good book or Web site with all of the details.

Epilogue

Are Pets Worth Cleaning Up After?

Next time you're patting yourself on the back for all you do for your pet, including cleaning up after it, the next time a tiny tendril of doubt creeps in and you're wondering if the pet is worth the mess, remember a couple of things. You've had the same thoughts about your kids a few times, your marriage, your school, your job. For all the money those pets cost, all the worry they can cause, all the trips to the vet and shattered nerves when a car screeches out on the street, those little creatures do more than a little to better our quality of life, and give us a few gifts that nothing can replace.

Although the bottom line of life is to be loved, we humans work hard to have that not happen to us. We become obsessed with ambition and success, and cut off from our fellow humans, or lazy, selfish, and undisciplined (all the very qualities that tend to reduce our chances of loving and being loved). Our parents let us do it, our friends let us do it, our kids let us do it, the government lets us get away with it . . .

But pets won't! If we take from them, we have to give back—with the caress we get some mess, which we can't leave or forget about like we can and do so many things. Pets won't let us be ungrateful.

The next time you get disgusted with the dog dish, a little lethargic about the litter box, stop and think about what we get in return for this price of a little pet cleaning. The facts are proven (in clinical tests, even, if you please). Pets are:

- Good company
- Fun
- An encouragement to exercise
- Good healthy exercise for our emotions, too
- A bit of nature we can enjoy in even the most crowded city
- A nudge toward organizing our schedules and our lives
- Promoters of self-esteem and confidence in us, their owners
- Vivid instruction in the art of caretaking
- An opportunity to observe and adjust to the realities of life and death
- An aid and catalyst in human relationships, even marriage
- Mental and even physical salvation for thousands of people (the blind, hearing impaired, mentally ill, wheelchair bound, etc., as well as all the rest of us)
- Protectors of our property
- Pest exterminators
- An aid in crime prevention and law enforcement

Pets also save us from loneliness and take our minds off our troubles—and for all this they get no regular pay or benefits, bonuses, vacations, just a few morsels of food and a few minutes of care a day. Now that's a deal if I ever heard one!

The chemistry of pets and people has delighted mankind for centuries, and it can't be measured by the cost of flea remedies or eroded by a midnight bark or meow or two. Pets make our lives a lot richer and we owners get a lot for a little cleaning—we get total unquestioning love, absolute loyalty, and a pattern of forgiveness no human has yet perfected. Anything that would do all this for us and a hundred times more, is certainly worth getting out the scrub brush for on occasion.

> Pets are . . . antidote to the mental poisons of an urban environment. If they don't fit in this environment, then neither do we, for we are all animals together.
>
> —*The Handbook of Animal Welfare*

A word of thanks . . .

Everyone who reads a good book stops somewhere and says, "Wow, this author sure knows a lot, how did he ever get all this material together?"

You can bet I didn't sit in a lakeside cabin in Alaska for a few months and suddenly show up, unshaven, with a 200-page polished manuscript solving one of society's big problems—pet mess. I've had lots of real-life experience with the subject, and firsthand knowledge of the need for the book, but I was only the driver of the project. A team of tireless huskies pulled it though:

Carol Cartaino, our lead dog (and top cat), came up with the original idea for the book, drafted much of it, and edited and art directed the book, as well as spearheaded the research on the whole project.

Steve Medellin, pet enthusiast and word processor wizard, was a fine man at the phone when it came to eliciting and recording information from all those other experts out there.

Skip Berry, George Wagner, Tracy Monroe, and **Susan Waddell** helped us ferret out the pet wisdom of the ages (or at least the early twenty-first century).

Tobi Flynn, General Manager of Marsh Creek Press, contributed her considerable information-assimilating and word-crafting skills to the original edition, when they were most needed.

At the beginning of this book I mentioned the many places and organizations that provided information and expertise for the original edition. The following people did a great deal to help us "vet" and update the book for this new edition:

Robert T. Sharp, D.V.M., and **Susie Sharp**, of the Hillsboro Veterinary Hospital

Melissa Schelling, registered veterinary technician

Award-winning cat expert **Dusty Rainbolt**, the author of *Kittens for Dummies* and the product reviewer for *Catnip* magazine

Micky Niego, who is now an animal behavior counselor based in Rockland County, New York, working with family dogs and teaching them the dos and don'ts of cohabiting with humans

Jill A. Richardson, D.V.M., consulting veterinarian in Clinical Toxicology with the ASPCA Animal Poison Control Center, and leader of many nationwide pet safety campaigns

Beth Racine, a freelance researcher (writer, and editor) with the tenacity of a bulldog, who has yet to come up empty-handed on a research assignment

Gary Krebs, **Paula Munier**, and **Bridget Brace** of Adams Media, whose enthusiasm and expertise was a pleasure every step of the way

AND FINALLY, THANK YOU TO THE TWENTY-TWO CATS AT THE COUNTY LINE IN SEAMAN, OHIO, FOR THEIR ENDLESS INSPIRATION AND UNDERSTANDING.

Index

absorbent compound, 19
accidents: cleaning up quickly,
2–3, 108–109; reasons for, 106–
108; tips for cleaning, 119–120;
see also specific types
adhesives, 25
allergies, alleviating, 32–34
anal gland impactions, 201–202
animals, dragged-in, 192–194
aquariums, 222–224, 229–235
area deodorizers, 19–20

bacteria, 30
bacteria/enzyme digesters, 15–16,
111–113, 221
bathing: how-tos, 144–148; need
for, 139–141; places for, 142;
products, 141–144; waterless,
141–142
beds: for pets, 132–135; pets on
human, 137–138
behavior modification tools,
24–27
birds, 225–229
blankets, hair removal from,
131–132
bleach, 40
blood stains, 204
body odor, 21–22
brooms, 7
brushes, 7–8, 18

cages: bird, 225–228; for small
pets, 216–218, 220–221
carpet deodorizers, 20–21
carpeting, 59–61, 63, 110–115
carpet powders, 157
car trips, 211–214
cat litter, 81–85

cats: bathing, 141, 147–148; clipping nails of, 180; jumping by,
164–167, 170–171; scratching by, 175–183; spraying by,
90–97; toilet training, 87–90;
see also litter boxes
chemical deodorizers/cleaners,
13–15
chemical repellants, 26
chewing, 183–188, 194–199
chlorhexidine, 11–12, 41–42
cleaning: simple steps in, 3–4;
tools for, 4–12, 18–19; *see also*
specific spills/surfaces
cleaning solutions: all-purpose, 3,
4; for pets, 4–5; types of, 13–17
clothing, hair removal from,
131–132
conditioners, 143–144
counters, pets on, 166–168
crates: cleaning, 69–70; training
with, 66–69

declawing, 182–183
deodorizers, 12–16, 19–23
destructive behavior, 205–211
digging, 188–189
dips, flea, 154
dirt, tracked in, 171–175
diseases, 28–30, 34–38
disinfectants, 11–12, 38–42
dogs: bathing, 139–147; chewing
by, 183–188; clipping nails
of, 180–181; housetraining,
64–74; jumping by, 166–170;
scratching by, 175, 178–183;
spraying by, 90–97; training, to
eliminate in designated areas,
100–103

drooling, 199–201
dust mops, 7, 128–130
dustpans, 6

electronic repellants, 26–27, 167
elimination: cleanup of, 97–99, 104–105, 116–117; on command, 103–104; in designated areas, 100–103; *see also* feces; urine/urine stains
exercise, 208–209

feces: cleanup of, 97–99, 104–105, 116–117; diseases spread by, 34–35; disposal of, 101–103
feeding areas: placement of, 47–48; spills in, 50
feeding schedules, 54
fish, 229–235, 229–235
flea collars, 154–156
flea combs, 153
fleas, 35, 148–162; products for eliminating, 150–156; treating house for, 156–159; treating yard for, 159–160; ways to discourage, 160–162
flea shampoos, 154
flea traps, 158–159
floors, 30; carpeting, 59–61, 63, 110–115; cleaning hair from, 127–130; hard surface, 57, 115; sealing, 61–63; waxing, 58–59
floor squeegees, 5–6
foggers, 157–158
food dishes, 48–52, 219
foods, specialty, 53–54
food storage, 45–47
food types, 52–54
furnishings, 57–58, 61; pets on, 135–138; removing hair from, 130–131; sealing, 61–63

garbage, 189–192
gates, 71–72
germs, 29

Get Serious! (cleaner), 113–114
grooming, to control shedding, 122–125

hair pickup devices, 126–130
hair removal, 127–132
hard surfaces, 57, 109–110
heat, females in, 202–204
houseplants, chewing, 195–199
houses: designing, with pets in mind, 55–63, 164–166; off-limit areas in, 70–72; tracking dirt/mud in, 171–175; treating for fleas, 156–159
housetraining: cats, 75, 87–90; dogs, 64–74; *see also* litter boxes

insecticides, 150–153

jumping, 164–171

keyboards, hair removal from, 131

lawns, urine stains on, 99–100
litter boxes: cleaning, 85–87; covered, 77–78; diseases spread by, 34, 36; litter for, 81–85; placement of, 79–81; self-cleaning, 78–79; for small pets, 219; types of, 73–79

mats, 10–11, 25–26, 173
mud, tracked in, 171–175

nail caps, 182
nail clipping, 179–180
neutering, 90–92

obedience training, 208–209
odor encapsulators, 12–13
odor neutralizers, 12, 20
odor removers. *See* deodorizers
odors, 2–3
outdoor hazards, 192–195
oxygen cleaners, 16–17, 113–114

paper-training, 65, 73
pens, 72
people, pets jumping on, 168–171
pet allergies, 32–34
pet beds, 132–135
pet deodorizers, 21–22
pet rakes, 8, 127
pets: dragging in animals, 192–194; living area for, 56; rewards of, 236–238; *see also specific types*
pet supplies, storage of, 43–47
plane trips, 211–214
plant chewing, 194–199
plastic scrapers, 6
playpens, 72
powders, flea, 152–153

rabbits, 217–221
repellants, 26–27
reptiles, 221–225
rodents, 217–221

saltwater tanks, 234–235
sanitary measures, 30–32
scooping equipment, 98–99
scrapers, 6
scratching, 175–183
scratching posts, 23, 176–178
scrub brushes, 7–8
sealed surfaces, 61–63
self-feeders, 50–51
separation anxiety, 205–211
shampoos, 143, 154
shedding, 121–122; controlling, 122–125; tools for cleaning up, 126–130
sick pets, 37–38
skunk odor removers, 22–23
small pets, 215–217; birds, 225–229; fish, 229–235; reptiles, 221–225; rodents, 217–221
soil retardants, 62–63
spaying, 90–92
sponges, 7
spot removal brushes, 18

spray bottles, 18
spraying: cleaning up after, 96–97; ways to eliminate, 90–95
sprays, flea, 151–152
squeegees, 5–6
squirt bottles, 24–25
stain removers, 12
stain repellants, 19
storage areas, 43–47

tables, pets on, 166–168
tar, 175
ticks, 35
toilet training, 87–90
tools: behavior modification, 24–27; cleaning, 4–12, 18–19; hair pickup, 126–130; *see also* cleaners
towels, 18
toxoplasmosis, 36
toys, 23–24, 183–184
traveling, 211–214

urine/urine stains: cleaners for, 12–17; cleaning old, 112–114; clean-up of, 109–116; on clothing/fabrics, 116; on lawn, 99–100

vacuums, 8–10, 127–128
vomit, cleanup of, 117–119

walls, 30–32
waste digesters, 102–103
water dishes, 51–52, 219
wood floors, cleaning urine from, 115
worms, 35, 35–36

yard: designating spot in, for elimination, 100–103; treating for fleas, 159–160

zeolite products, 20, 23

About the Author

Don Aslett is an energetic, successful businessman, author, entertainer, and consultant who is called the world's #1 cleaning expert.

Don had a rural background, so his childhood, luckily, was filled with the companionship and responsibility of numerous pets and animals. "Feed your animals before you eat," "Never leave an animal without clean bedding," "Take care of an overheated animal before you worry about your own sunburn or sore feet" were the kinds of rules Don was raised to live by. As a college student, he started to clean for friends and neighbors to earn his way through school. This "college job" operation, Varsity Contractors, Inc., has grown into one of the nation's leading professional cleaning companies, and Don has become a true leader of the industry.

In fifty years of professional cleaning, he and his company have cleaned thousands and thousands of pet households. In the course of writing his many bestselling books on cleaning and making more than 5,000 TV, radio, and other media appearances, he also listened to thousands of questions about cleaning up after pets around the house. He knew this book was needed—and a natural.